Canon EOS 60D

Michael Guncheon

MAGIC LANTERN GUIDES®

Canon
EOS 60D

Michael Guncheon

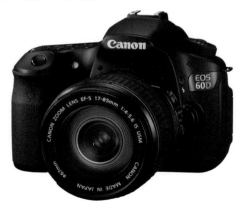

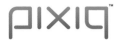

An Imprint of Sterling Publishing Co., Inc.
New York

For more information,
visit our website at www.pixiq.com

Book Design: Michael Robertson
Cover Design: Thom Gaines, Electron Graphics

Library of Congress Cataloging-in-Publication Data

Guncheon, Michael A., 1959-
 Canon EOS 60D / Michael A. Guncheon. -- 1st ed.
   p. cm.
 ISBN 978-1-4547-0134-7
 1. Canon digital cameras--Handbooks, manuals, etc. 2. Photography--Digital techniques--Handbooks,
manuals, etc. 3. Single-lens reflex cameras--Handbooks, manuals, etc. I. Title.

  TR263.C3G956 2011
  771.3'2--dc22

                              2011000341

10 9 8 7 6 5 4 3 2 1

First Edition

Published by Pixiq, An Imprint of
Sterling Publishing Co., Inc.
387 Park Avenue South, New York, N.Y. 10016

Text © 2011, Michael Guncheon
Photography © 2011, Michael Guncheon unless otherwise specified

Distributed in Canada by Sterling Publishing,
c/o Canadian Manda Group, 165 Dufferin Street
Toronto, Ontario, Canada M6K 3H6

Distributed in the United Kingdom by GMC Distribution Services,
Castle Place, 166 High Street, Lewes, East Sussex, England BN7 1XU

Distributed in Australia by Capricorn Link (Australia) Pty Ltd.,
P.O. Box 704, Windsor, NSW 2756 Australia

This book is not sponsored by Canon.

If you have questions or comments about this book, please contact:
Pixiq
C/O Lark Books
67 Broadway
Asheville, NC 28801
(828) 253-0467

Manufactured in Canada

ISBN 13: 978-1-4547-0134-7

For information about custom editions, special sales, premium and corporate purchases, please contact
Sterling Special Sales Department at 800-805-5489 or specialsales@sterlingpub.com.

For information about desk and examination copies available to college and university professors,
requests must be submitted to academic@larkbooks.com. Our complete policy can be found at
www.larkbooks.com.

To learn more about digital photography, go to www.pixiq.com.

Contents

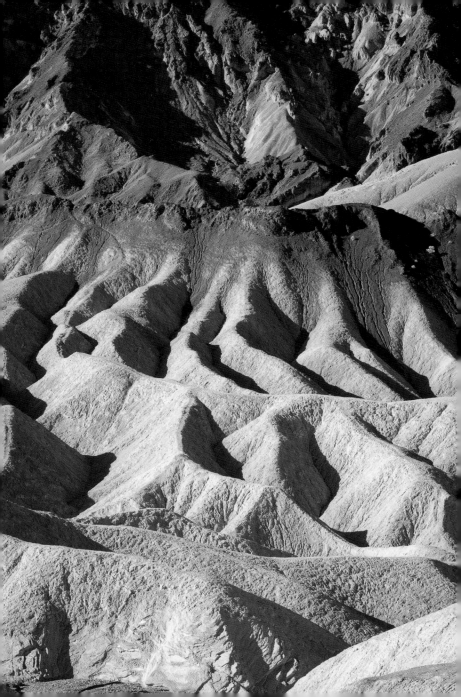

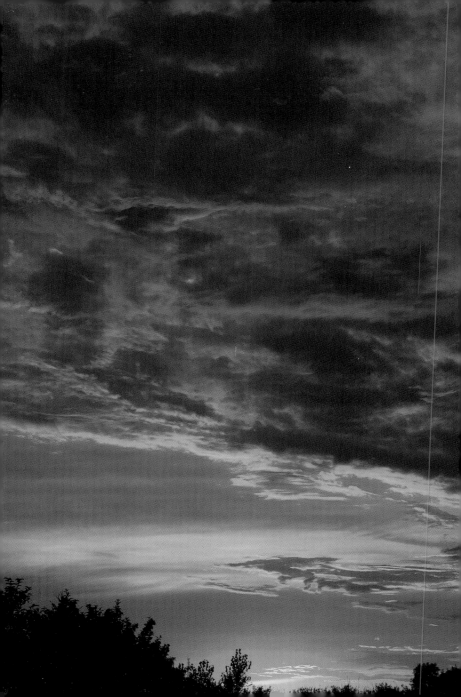

Introducing the Canon EOS 60D

Since the beginning of the digital photography revolution, Canon has kept busy updating their EOS cameras. Those photographers looking for their upgrade from a Digital Rebel and not wanting to move into the 7D price range have long awaited the EOS 60D. Others might think of this camera as a simple upgrade from the 50D, but Canon includes a few 7D features with this camera.

The EOS 60D offers high-definition video recording, quick start-up, and fast memory card writing speeds. Canon completely redesigned the camera's body, enhancing the picture-taking ergonomics. The chassis, built using aluminum, which is both lightweight and rigid, allows the camera to stand up to years of use. The body consists of a specially engineered polycarbonate resin with glass fiber. This again helps create a lightweight yet strong unit. The camera's exterior is ergonomically designed and the controls are positioned for easy use.

The 60D's body measures only 5.69 x 4.17 x 3.09 inches (144.5 x 105.8 x 78.6 mm) and weighs just 23.8 ounces (675 g) without a lens. Yet the 60D offers a newly designed 18-megapixel image sensor and a high degree of technological sophistication at an affordable price. In many ways, it sets the bar for all other DSLRs in this price range.

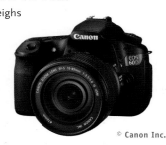

© Canon Inc.

The new sensor incorporates improved circuitry and "gapless" microlenses that increase the sensitivity of the image sensor. A key feature of this new CMOS sensor is low power consumption, enabling you to shoot with Live View on the LCD and record HD video. The 60D can record in 1080p with full HD frame rates.

But digital cameras are not just sensors. Image processing is the key to superb image quality. At the heart of the 60D's image-processing circuitry is the Digital Image Core 4 (DIGIC 4) processor. This special chip is the latest in a long line of Canon-designed processors. Canon has boosted the 60D's continuous shooting speed to 5.3 fps (frames per second) with bursts of up to 58 JPEGs or 16 RAW images when used with an appropriate memory card. The DIGIC 4 processor is not just about shooting speed; it provides fast image processing, improved light sensitivity, and low image noise.

The 60D gets the new iFCL metering system first introduced with the 7D. This new 63-zone dual-layer metering sensor uses color, luminance, and focus information in order to achieve well-balanced exposures. This system is one of the most advanced metering systems in a DSLR.

For optics, Canon has used its EF-S lens mount for this camera. Introduced with the original Digital Rebel (EOS 300D), this mount accepts all standard Canon EF lenses. In addition, it accepts compact EF-S lenses, built specifically for small-format sensors. Note that EF-S lenses can only be used on cameras designed expressly to accept them.

Probably the most significant addition to any Canon EOS camera is the new Vari-angle 3.0-inch Clear View LCD monitor. While Canon has included articulating LCDs in their G-series cameras like the G11 and G12, this is the very first EOS camera with this feature.

OVERVIEW OF FEATURES

The 60D offers a number of exciting and useful features that will help you enjoy a great photographic experience. Before we get into a detailed look at the functions and operations, let's take a quick look at some of the highlights offered in the 60D:

O New Canon-designed and built 18MP, APS-C-sized CMOS sensor

O DIGIC 4 image processor for high-speed, low-noise performance

O New Vari-angle Clear View LCD monitor—a large, bright, and sharp 3-inch (7.7 cm), high-resolution, color, articulating display with dual anti-reflective, water-repellent, scratch-resistant coatings, automatic brightness control and an aspect ratio (3:2) that matches the camera's aspect ratio for stills

O In-camera RAW image processing and aspect ratio conversion

O Creative Auto Mode

O New creative image filters

O In-camera image-rating system (1 to 5)

O New electronic level that can be displayed in the viewfinder or the LCD monitor to assure level horizons

O Shoots 5.3 fps and up to 58 frames consecutively at maximum JPEG resolution (16 frames continuously in RAW)

O Supports SD, SDHC, and SDXC memory cards for up to 2TB (terabytes) of storage

O Includes support for Eye-Fi memory cards for wireless connectivity

O ISO range of 100 – 6400, extendable to 100 – 12800

O Live View mode with Face Detection AF

O Integrated sensor-cleaning system and Dust Delete Data system

O Six preset and three user-defined custom Picture Style settings

O Ability to enhance creativity in scene modes through "ambience" selection and scene-lighting settings

O High-speed focal-plane shutter—up to 1/8000 second—with regular flash sync up to 1/250 second

O 9-point autofocus system with extra-sensitive center AF point

O New multilayer, 63-zone intelligent Focus Color Luminance (iFCL) metering system that is tightly integrated with the AF system to achieve unprecedented metering accuracy

O High-definition video recording with full manual exposure control: 1920 x 1080 resolution at 30, 25, and 24 fps progressive recording; 1280 x 720 at 60 and 50 fps progressive recording, all with audio

O Movie-crop video recording gives 7x magnification

O External microphone input

O Quick Control screen that provides fast access to camera settings without going into menus

O New Quick Control screen access button

O User-activated noise subtraction for long exposures

O High ISO noise reduction

○ Auto Lighting Optimizer for automatic adjustment of scene brightness and contrast

○ Lens peripheral illumination correction for automatic compensation of light fall-off at the corners of the image

○ Exposure compensation system with a range of five stops

○ 20 custom functions

○ Integrated Speedlite Transmitter for remote control of Canon Speedlites

GETTING STARTED IN TEN BASIC STEPS

Here are ten steps that will make it easier to record good photos with your 60D. You will probably modify them with experience.

1. Set [Auto power off] for a reasonable time: The default duration in the ❦˙ (Set-up 1) menu is merely 30 seconds. I guarantee this will frustrate you when the camera has turned itself off just as you are ready to shoot. Perhaps it is more realistic to try [4 min.]. (See page 25.)

2. Adjust the eyepiece: Use the dioptric adjustment knob to the right of the viewfinder to make the focus through your eyepiece as sharp as possible. You can adjust it with a fingertip. (See page 55.)

3. Choose a large file size (RAW or L for JPEG): This determines your image-recording quality. Select the ◻˙ (Shooting 1) menu, then press SET and use ❖, ○ or ◠ to select your desired image size (see page 90). It is usually best to choose one of the high-quality options. You can also shoot with both RAW and JPEG at the same time.

4. Set your preferred shooting mode: Use the Mode dial on the top left shoulder of the camera to select any of the exposure shooting modes (see pages 167-192) or fully automatic modes (see page 168). If using any of the exposure modes, select a Picture Style (see pages 66-69).

5. Choose AF mode: Autofocus (AF) mode is set by pressing the AF button. The LCD monitor then displays several AF mode options. Use ❖, ○ or ◠ to select an AF mode, then press SET. A good place to start is AI Servo AF. The selected mode displays in the camera settings on the LCD. (See page 188.)

6. Select drive mode: First press DRIVE, and then select either Single shooting ◻, High-speed continuous ⊒H, Low-speed continuous ⊒, Self-timer:10sec/Remote control ⏱↺, or Self-timer:2-sec/Remote control self-timer ⏱↺₂. (See pages 183-184.) The LCD indicates the mode the camera is in. Depending on the shooting mode, not all drive modes will be available.

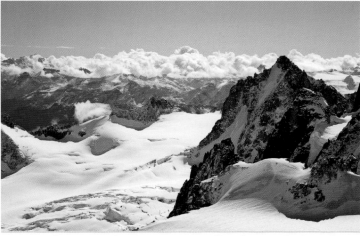

⌃ When you first start shooting with your 60D, you will get better results, faster, if you follow these ten basic steps.

7. Choose metering mode: Metering mode is set by pressing the ⊡ button. Use ☼, ○ or ⌂ to select the metering mode as displayed on the LCD panel. Choose from four different metering modes: evaluative ⊡, partial ⊙, spot ⊡, or center-weighted average ⊏⊐. Press **SET** to accept. ⊡ is a good starting point. (See page 195.)

8. Select white balance: Auto white balance **AWB** is a good place to start because the 60D is designed to generally do well with it. Set white balance via the ⊡⁞ (Shooting 2) menu. Use ☼ or ○ to highlight **[White Balance]** and press **SET**. (See page 75.) The different white balance choices display on the monitor; use ☼ or ○ to select one, then press **SET**. After making your choice, the selected white balance appears in the camera settings display on the LCD.

9. Pick an ISO setting: Though any setting between 100 and 400 works extremely well, you can generally set higher ISO sensitivity (with less noticeable noise) with the 60D than with other digital cameras. (See pages 192-195.) Press the ISO button, located behind the main dial (⌂). The LCD monitor displays a range of ISO speeds. Use ☼, ○ or ⌂ to select one. You can even change ISO without having to take your eyes away from the viewfinder. When you press the ISO button, the information display in the bottom of the viewfinder shows the current ISO setting. Use ⌂ to rotate through the ISO choices.

10. Set a reasonable review time: The default image review time on the LCD monitor is only two seconds. That means that after you take a picture, it will only be displayed on the LCD for two seconds. That's very little time to analyze your photos, so I recommend the eight-second setting, which you can always escape out of by pressing the shutter button. If you are worried about using too much battery power, just turn off the review function altogether. Review time is set in ◻˙. (See page 99.)

CONVENTIONS USED IN THIS BOOK

Note that when the terms "right" and "left" are used to denote placement of buttons and features or to describe camera techniques, it is assumed that the camera is being held in the shooting position, unless otherwise specified.

The 60D has a number of buttons with dual functions and dual labels. For example, the AF point selection button ⊞ is also used as the magnify button ⊕ during image playback. In the interest of clarity, when referring to these dual-purpose controls, I will indicate just the label of the function I am talking about.

Also, keep in mind that the Multi-Controller ❖ and the Quick Control dial ◯ can often be used interchangeably in many menus and settings screens. Use whichever one is more comfortable.

When describing the functionality of the 60D, it is assumed that the camera is being used with genuine Canon accessories, such as Speedlites, lenses, and batteries.

Custom functions are indicated by the Canon nomenclature of C.Fn, followed by the custom function number. The custom function number is made up of a Roman numeral and an Arabic number. For example, C.Fn IV-3.

We are now ready to explore the features, functions, and attributes of the Canon EOS 60D in detail. Before we go any further, let me first acknowledge that this book would be impossible to write without the help of many people. Thank you to Rudy Winston, Chuck Westfall, and Len Musmeci at Canon. I would also like to thank the gang at Pixiq for all of their support, especially Becky Shipkosky, Kara Arndt, Hannah Doyle, Kevin Kopp, Frank Gallaugher, and Marti Saltzman. And finally, a special thanks to my wife Carol, without whom this book would simply be blank pages.

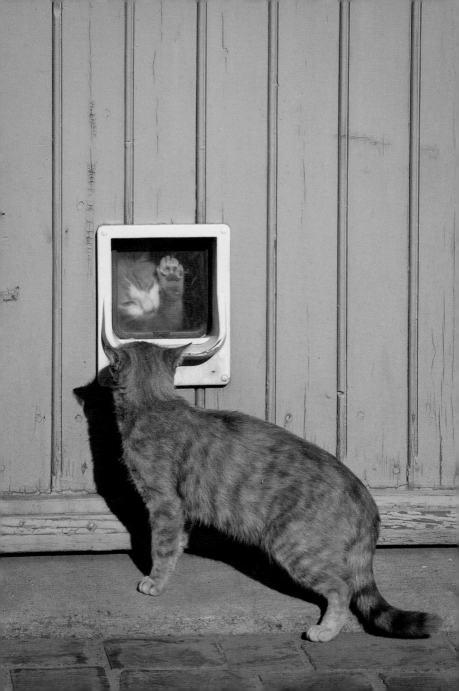

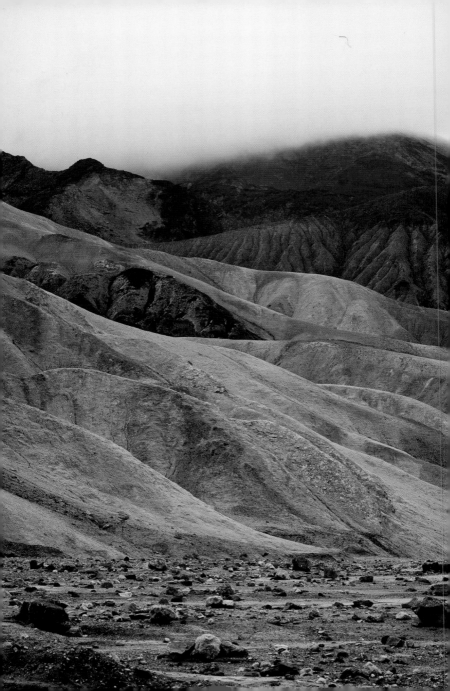

Getting Started

PREPARING THE CAMERA

When you first pick up the EOS 60D it can be a little daunting. But with proper setup, good handling practices, and careful maintenance, this technology can help take your photography to the next level. There are several things you'll want to take care of before you get into the shooting functions and start photographing.

DATE/TIME

Each image file is embedded with the date and time from the camera. The date and time are set by using the Set-up 2 menu ♥. Turn on the camera with the power switch that is beneath the Mode dial on top of the left shoulder. On the back of the camera, press the MENU button and advance to ♥ using the Main dial � or the Multi-Controller ☀. Then use the Quick Control dial ○ or ☀ to select [Date/Time], then press the SET button to enter the adjustment screen. Once there, use ○ or ☀ to step through each parameter on the display. When you are on a setting, press SET to enter its adjustment mode and use ○ or ☀ to adjust the value. Press SET again to accept the setting. Continue using ○ or ☀ and SET to adjust the date, time, and/or to format the date/time display. Once the date and time are correct, use ○ or ☀ to highlight [OK], then press SET again to confirm your selections and exit the adjustment mode.

NOTE: When traveling, keep your camera set to local time. This will help you if you need to figure out when a picture was taken. If the time zone change is a significant one and you don't change to local time, your image's time/date might make you think the picture was taken the day before or after you actually took it.

> It can be very frustrating trying to organize your images if the date and time aren't set correctly.

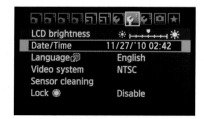

The 60D holds the date and time in its memory even when you remove the LP-E6 battery. If you leave the LP-E6 out of the camera for an extended period of time, the camera may lose this memory. Simply insert a charged LP-E6, and the camera will recharge the date memory system from the battery.

BATTERIES

Canon has included a high-performance battery for the 60D. At 1800mAh in capacity, the lithium ion LP-E6 battery offers much improvement over previous Canon batteries. Milliampere hours (mAh) indicate a battery's capacity to hold a charge. Higher mAh numbers mean longer-lasting batteries.

> The 60D uses the same professional battery system that the 5D Mark II and 7D use.

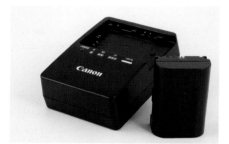

Although the camera is designed for efficient use of battery power, it is important to understand that power consumption is highly dependent on how long features such as flash, autofocus, the LCD, Live View, and movie recording are used. In short, the more the camera is active, the shorter the battery life. Be sure to have backup batteries. And it is always a good idea to shut the camera off if you are not using it.

Canon estimates that at 73°F (23°C), the battery will last approximately 1600 shots when flash is not used (or 1100 shots with 50% flash usage). Lower temperatures reduce the number of shots. For instance, if the temperature is at freezing (32°F / 0°C), the 60D is rated for 1400 shots without flash and 1000 shots with flash.

The enemy of a battery is temperature extremes, particularly heat. Never expose the camera or its accessories to heat or direct sunlight (i.e., don't leave the camera sitting in the car on a hot or a cold day).

Battery life is also different when shooting with Live View since the LCD screen, image sensor, and DIGIC 4 image processor are all on. When you use Live View, the number of shots drops to 350, or 320 shots with 50% flash usage. The approximate length of time you can shoot continuously with Live View is two hours and 20 minutes at 73°F (23°C) with a fully charged battery. When shooting video, the battery lasts approximately two hours at 73°F (23°C).

Extra batteries are always a good first accessory purchase, particularly when traveling. If you own a total of three, one battery can be on the charger, one in the camera, and one in your pocket. For safety, when the battery is not on the charger or in the camera, be sure to use the battery cover that came with the battery. If you don't use the cover, the contacts could short and damage the battery or even cause a fire—not something you want to happen in your pocket!

NOTE: Refer to the menu chapter (page 95) to see how the 60D can use the Set-up 3 menu ♥⁚ to keep track of the charge levels and performance of all of your batteries.

The battery cover can act as a good reminder of whether or not a battery is charged. There is a small rectangular opening that reveals either the blue portion of the battery label or the dark gray portion. I place the cover so the blue portion shows on all of my batteries that are charged and ready to go.

> The rectangular cutout in the battery cover shows blue when the battery is oriented in a specific direction. This is useful if you have multiple batteries; for instance, using the blue to indicate a charged battery. This saves you from inserting the battery into the 60D to check its charge.

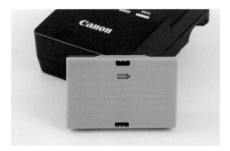

The LP-E6 is rated at 8.4 volts and it takes about 2.5 hours to fully charge on the LC-E6 charger that is included with the camera. Rechargeable batteries lose a bit of charge every day, but this doesn't mean you should leave the battery on the charger all the time. Get in the habit of just charging your battery the day you need it or possibly the day before.

CAUTION: Never operate the 60D with very low battery power (when the battery icon is blinking). If the 60D is writing to the memory card and the battery runs out of power, it could corrupt the directory on the memory card and possibly cause you to lose all the pictures on the card.

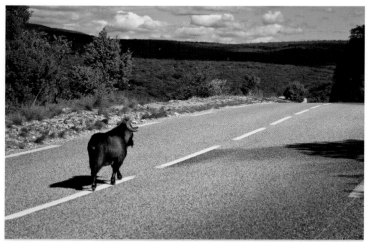

^ Keep a spare, fully-charged battery with you. You don't want to run out of power when something surprising happens.

The charger has a built-in voltage and frequency converter, so it is not necessary to use a transformer when you travel—the charger handles voltages from 100 – 240 and 50 – 60 hertz frequencies. You will, however, need an adapter to change the physical layout of the plug, depending on the country you visit.

An optional battery grip, BG-E9, attaches to the bottom of the camera and can be used with one or two LP-E6 batteries. If two batteries are loaded, power is initially drawn from the battery with the higher voltage. Once the voltage level of the two batteries is the same, power is drawn from both batteries. When attached to the camera, the BG-E9 replaces the 60D's internal battery. The grip also comes with an adapter, which allows six AA-size batteries to be used.

A nice feature of the battery grip is that it duplicates several controls on the camera so that they are just as easily accessed whether the camera is being held vertically or horizontally. The duplicated controls include a shutter button, AE lock button ✱, and the Main dial ⌂.

The AC adapter kit (ACK-E6) is useful for those who need the camera to remain consistently powered up (e.g., for scientific lab work, in-studio use, and lengthy video shooting).

> **NOTE:** There are a couple of limitations if you use AA batteries with the grip. The 60D will not let you perform a manual cleaning of the image sensor, and the battery indicator may not be as accurate.

AUTO POWER OFF

With all this talk of extra batteries it might sound like the 60D is a power hog. It really isn't. Nonetheless, the camera does have options that you can set for optimizing power use. All digital cameras automatically shut off after a period of inactivity to conserve power. The 60D has a selection for **[Auto power off]** in the Set-up 1 menu ♀˙ that can be used to turn off the power after a set duration of idleness.

Although this feature helps to minimize battery use, you may find it frustrating when you try to take a picture and find that the camera has shut itself off. For example, you might be shooting a football game and the action may stay away from you for a couple of minutes. If **[Auto off]** is set to **[1 min.]**, the camera may have shut itself off by the time the players move back toward you. When you try to shoot, nothing happens because the camera is powering back up. You may miss the important shot. For cases like this, try changing the setting to **[4min.]** or **[8 min.]** so the camera stays on when you need it.

> Although it might seem like a simple setting, using a longer power off time can keep you concentrating on things like exposure and compensation.

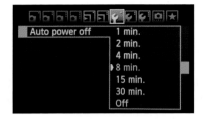

Access the Auto power off function through the camera's menus. Press MENU and advance to 🔧 using 🎛 or ☀, then use ◯ or ☀ to highlight **[Auto power off]**, and press SET. You are given seven different choices, ranging from 1 – 30 minutes (including the **[Off]** option that prevents the camera from ever turning off automatically). Scroll with ◯ or ☀ to highlight the desired duration and press SET to select it.

MEMORY CARDS

The Canon 60D uses Secure Digital (SD) memory cards. You need a card of sizeable capacity to handle the image files of this camera; anything less than 512 MB fills up too quickly (see page 93 for specifics). SD cards are sturdy, durable, and difficult to damage. One thing they don't like is heat; make sure you store them properly.

> Look for the SDHC logo when buying memory cards to assure the best camera/ storage performance.

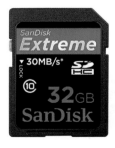

There are three different kinds of SD cards: SD, SD high capacity (SDHC), and the new SD extended capacity (SDXC). The 60D supports all three cards. While the 60D can use any of these, it is important to know the difference when you start downloading your images to the computer. Both SDHC and SDXC cards fit into an SD slot. Other than the distinction in logos printed on the cards, they are impossible to visually distinguish from an SD card. (The regular SD card was developed first; SDHC came later; and the SDXC was introduced in 2009.)

The design difference between SD, SDHC, and SDXC doesn't affect the 60D. However, SDHC cards cannot be used with older SD devices, and SDXC cards may have problems with SDHC devices. By "devices," I mean items such as card readers and printers. If you give an SDHC or SDXC card to someone for printing rather than printing your images yourself, make sure they have the right device for an SDHC or SDXC memory card.

SDHC/SDXC-capable slots, including the one in the 60D, have no problem using regular SD cards. This simple rule applies: SDXC-capable devices can use SDXC, SDHC, and SD cards; SDHC devices can use either SD or SDHC cards; and SD devices can only use SD cards. Remember to look for the SDHC label on all your devices if you plan to use SDHC cards (the same applies for SDXC). If this is your first camera and card reader, I would opt for SDHC or SDXC rather than SD.

NOTE: Be wary of SD cards that are greater than 2GB but that don't have the SDHC icon. They may not be reliable. When you try to use an SD reader to read the memory card, your computer may be unable to read the data.

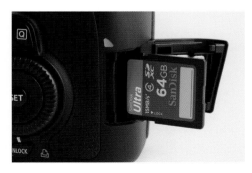

‹ **When recording HD video, note that the file sizes can be quite large. Luckily, memory cards are available in very large sizes.**

Besides a capacity rating, SDHC and SDXC cards also have a speed class that specifies how quickly the card can read and write data. If you are shooting video with your 60D, make sure that the memory card you are using has a speed class of at least 6.

To insert the memory card, open the memory card slot cover on the right side of the camera body. Align the card with the slot, keeping the card label facing toward the back of the camera. Gently push the card into the camera until it clicks into place. To remove the memory card from your camera, press gently on the edge of the memory card to release it from the camera. Carefully grab the edge of the card to remove it.

NOTE: Memory cards are not affected by current airport screening systems.

CAUTION: Before removing the memory card, turn the camera off. Even though the 60D automatically shuts itself off when the memory card door is opened, make sure the access lamp on the back of the camera above the memory card slot cover is not illuminated or flashing. This habit of turning the camera off allows the camera to finish writing to the card. If you should open the card door and remove the card before the camera has written a set of files to it, there is a good possibility you will corrupt the directory or damage the card. You may lose not only the image being recorded, but all of the images on the card.

Formatting your memory card: Before you use a memory card in your camera, it must be formatted specifically for the 60D. To do so, go to ♥˙ and then use ○ or ❀ to highlight **[Format]**. Press **SET** and the Format menu appears on the LCD. It tells you how big the card is and how much of the card is presently filled with data. Use ○ or ❀ to move the choice to **[OK]**, press **SET**, and formatting begins. You will see a screen showing the progress.

CAUTION: Transfer important images to a computer or another downloading device before formatting your memory card. Formatting erases all images and information stored on the card, including protected images.

The format screen also gives the option of performing a low-level format of the card. Low-level formatting rebuilds the card's file structure and flags any memory locations that are unreliable. While low-level formatting takes more time, it is a good idea to do this if you feel the writing speed of the memory card is slowing down or if you are starting to have problems with a card. Press the delete button 🗑 located on the back of the camera in the upper left corner to put a check mark in the **[Low-level format]** box.

It is important to routinely format a memory card to keep its data structure organized. However, never format the card in a computer. A computer uses different file structures than a digital camera and may either make the card unreadable for the camera or may cause problems with your images. So, for trouble-free operation, always format your card rather than just erasing all the images, and always use the camera to do it.

NOTE: My experience is that if memory cards are going to fail, they usually do so early on. Always test a new card by formatting it, taking a lot of pictures and/or video, and then downloading the images/video to a computer. Resist the temptation to buy a new card and pop it, unopened, into your camera bag at the start of a long trip. Open it up and test it to make sure it works properly.

RESETTING CONTROLS

The 60D's menu system and Quick Control screen provide many opportunities to fine-tune and customize its many settings. If at some point you want to reset everything, you can restore the camera to its original default settings by going to the ♈ menu and selecting [Clear all camera settings], then pressing SET. This does not clear out the custom function settings. For that you need to use a similar option in the custom function (C.Fn) menu 🔧.

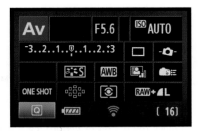

‹ The initial display on the LCD also acts as an interactive camera control. This display is called the Quick Control screen.

NOTE: If the 60D is in one of the Basic Zone modes (page 168), some menus items, including [Clear all camera settings], will not be available.

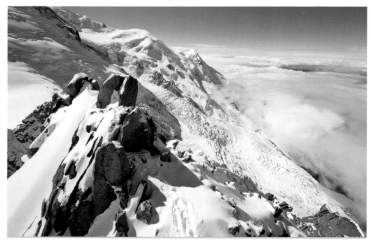

∧ Difficult shooting locations and extreme weather conditions can introduce dust and moisture into the camera. Consider avoiding lens changes in this situation.

CLEANING THE CAMERA

Having a camera with an interchangeable lens can be a double-edged sword. It is nice to have the flexibility to change lenses, but this also introduces dust into the camera. If you use a good technique when you change lenses, and if you keep the camera body clean, you can minimize the amount of dirt or dust that can reach the sensor. A good kit of cleaning materials should include the following: a soft camel hair brush to clean off the camera, an antistatic brush and micro-fiber cloth for cleaning the lens, a lint-free towel or chamois for drying the camera in damp conditions, and a small rubber bulb to blow debris off the lens and the camera.

Always blow and brush debris from the camera before rubbing it with any cloth. For lens cleaning, blow and brush first, then clean with a micro-fiber cloth. If you find the lens has some residue that is hard to remove, you can use lens-cleaning fluid. Be sure it is made for camera lenses. Never apply the fluid directly to the lens, as it can seep behind the lens elements and get inside the body of the lens. Apply with a cotton swab, or just spray it onto your micro-fiber cloth. Rub gently to remove the dirt, and then buff the lens with a dry part of the cloth, which you can wash in the washing machine when it gets dirty.

NOTE: If your lens came with a lens shade, always use it. If your lens didn't come with one, buy a properly sized one. There is no better protection for your lens than a lens shade.

You don't need to be obsessive, but remember that a clean camera and lens help ensure that you don't develop image problems. Dirt and residue on the camera can get inside when you change lenses. If these end up on the sensor, you will have image problems. Dust on the sensor appears as small, dark, out-of-focus spots in the photo (most noticeable in light areas, such as sky).

Your 60D came with a body cap to protect the shutter chamber from dust. Never leave a DSLR for any length of time without a body cap or lens mounted. Lenses should be capped when not in use and rear caps should always be used when the lens is not mounted on a camera. Double check that the caps you use are also free of dust before you use them. If you only own one lens, resist the temptation to take the lens off.

Canon has designed the 60D so that when you change lenses the image sensor is powered down to prevent a dust-attracting static charge from building up. Even so, I recommend that you always turn the camera off before you change lenses. This prevents hitting any wrong buttons or changing menus while holding the camera. It is also a good idea to vacuum your camera bag regularly so that dust and dirt aren't stored with the camera. And finally, watch where you put the lens cap when you take it off your lens. Placing it in a linty pocket is a good way to introduce dust onto your lenses.

AUTOMATIC SENSOR CLEANING

Canon has built a system into the 60D that combats the dust that is inherent with cameras that use removable lenses. This system uses a two-pronged approach: (1) The camera self-cleans to remove dust from the sensor, and (2) it employs a dust detection system using software on your computer to remove dust artifacts from images.

The low-pass filter in front of the sensor is attached to a piezoelectric element that rapidly vibrates at camera power-up and power-down. While self-cleaning at power-up just before taking pictures seems like an obvious time to clean the sensor, why clean it at power-down? Cleaning at power-down prevents dust from sticking to the sensor when the camera sits for long periods of time.

> The self-cleaning function in the 60D is a good first step towards a cleaner sensor. If dust on the sensor persists, follow the instructions for the manual cleaning procedure.

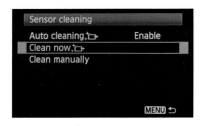

Self-cleaning can be enabled and disabled under ✿. Use ○ or ⊛ to highlight [Sensor cleaning] and press SET. From the Sensor Cleaning screen, select [Auto cleaning⤸] and press SET. From there you can choose to [Enable] or [Disable] the self-cleaning function, then press SET to accept your selection. You can also engage the self-cleaning function immediately by selecting [Clean now ⤸] or start the [Clean manually] procedure (see page 132). The system works best when the camera is sitting on a horizontal surface like a table.

NOTE: In order to prevent overheating, the self-cleaning operation cannot be engaged within three seconds of any other operation. After a brief delay (usually ten seconds) it will be available for use.

There is little reason for not having automatic sensor cleaning always enabled. The power drain and start-up delay that it imposes are very slight.

DUST DELETE DATA

In the event that there is still dust on the sensor, the 60D's Dust Delete Data feature can be used. By photographing an out-of-focus, patternless, solid white object (such as a white sheet of paper), the image sensor is able to detect the shadow cast by dust stuck to the low-pass filter. Coordinates of the dust are embedded into the metadata of each future image. Canon's Digital Photo Professional software (supplied with the 60D) can use this data to automatically remove the dust spots in images.

To store the Dust Delete Data in the 60D:

1. Set up a well-lit white card.
2. Use a lens with a 50mm focal length or greater.
3. Set the lens for manual focus (MF).
4. Set the lens focus to infinity (∞). If the focus scale is not printed on the lens, turn the focus ring clockwise (while viewing the lens from the front of the camera) as far as it will go.
5. In ◻︎ⁱ, select **[Dust Delete Data]** and press **SET**. Highlight **[OK]** and press **SET**.
6. The 60D will execute an auto cleaning cycle and then ask you to press the shutter when ready.
7. Stand about a foot away from the card (20 – 30 cm). Compose the frame so that the white card entirely fills the frame, and then press the shutter. If the camera is not able to capture the data properly, it will ask you to try again. If the camera is new, there may be no dust on the sensor and the process will fail.

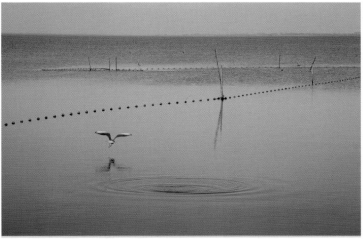

^ With images that have subtle tone changes, dust on the image sensor will be more noticeable.

To use the Dust Delete Data function, use Canon's Digital Photo Professional software to open an image that has the Dust Delete Data embedded in it. In the Adjustment menu, choose Apply Dust Delete Data. The software will attempt to repair the dust spots in the image. You should update the Dust Delete Data from time to time as the amount and location of dust on the sensor will change.

NOTE: If the 60D is in one of the Basic Zone modes (page 168), some menu items, including **[Dust Delete Data]**, will not be available. The Dust Delete Data can only be used by Canon software.

MANUAL SENSOR CLEANING

The 60D allows you to clean the sensor yourself, but there are precautions to be taken. You must do this carefully and gently, indoors, and out of the wind—and at your own risk! Your battery must be fully charged so it doesn't fail during cleaning (or you can use the optional AC adapter). The sensor unit is a precision optical device, so if the gentle cleaning described below doesn't work, you should send the camera to a Canon service center for a thorough cleaning.

To clean the sensor, turn the camera on and go to ❤. Using ○ or ☼, highlight **[Sensor cleaning]** and press **SET**. Use ○ or ☼ in the Sensor cleaning screen and navigate to highlight **[Clean manually]** and press **SET**, then follow the instructions. You'll see options for **[OK]** and **[Cancel]**. Using ○ or ☼, select **[OK]** and press **SET**. The LCD turns off, the mirror locks up, and the shutter opens. Take the lens off. Then, holding the camera face down, use a blower to gently blow any dust or other debris off the bottom of the lens opening first, and then blow off the sensor. Do not use brushes or compressed air because these can damage the sensor's surface. Turn the camera off when done. The mirror and shutter will return to normal. Put the lens back on.

CAUTION: Canon specifically recommends against any cleaning techniques or devices that touch the surface of the imaging sensor. If manual cleaning doesn't work, contact a Canon Service Center for cleaning.

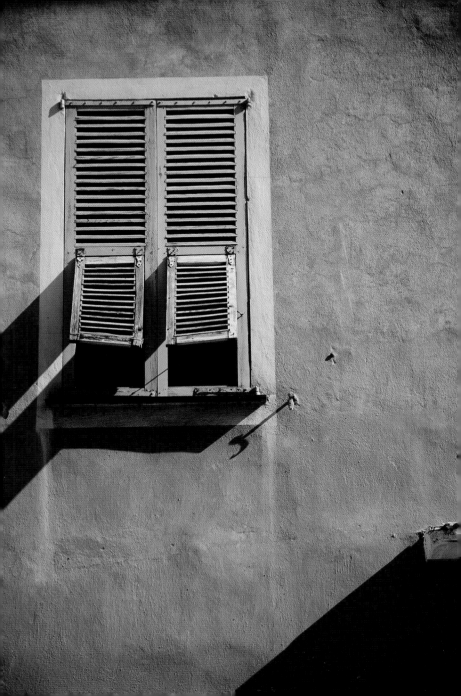

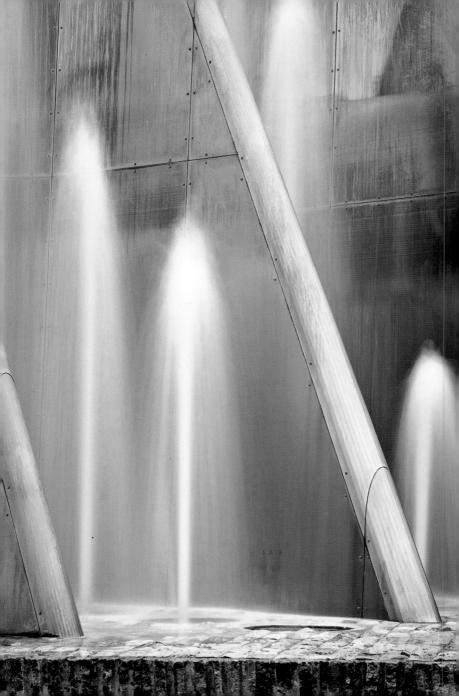

Controls and Functions

The controls on the 60D have been designed using Canon's extensive history of film and digital camera design. It is easy to be overwhelmed by the variety of controls when you first take a look at the 60D. You may find there are some that you do not need or will not use. This book explains all the features on the 60D, and helps you master those that are most important to you. Don't feel guilty if you don't use every option packed into the camera. Learn the basic controls, and then explore any additional features that work for you. You can always delve further into this book and work to develop your 60D techniques and skills at some point in the future. But remember: the best time to learn about a feature is before you need it—you can't "waste film" with digital cameras, so shoot as much as you want, and then erase those images that don't work.

BUTTONS AND DIALS OVERVIEW

When you hold the 60D, it seems as if everywhere your fingers land there is a button or a dial. The 60D is designed so buttons are close to your fingers for quick access to the camera's many features. The following section provides a summary of the controls found on the camera. This overview reveals what the controls do; later chapters explain in more depth how to use them.

The 60D uses icons that are common to all Canon cameras to identify various buttons, dials, and switches found on the camera. Some controls work alone—for instance, press DISP. to change the display on the LCD monitor. Other controls work as half of a pair—for example, sometimes the Main dial 🔄 works in conjunction with buttons that are pressed and released or that are held down while 🔄 is turned.

RESETTING CONTROLS

As you go through this chapter and experiment with all of the controls it is possible to set so many combinations that at some point you may want to reset everything. Before you delve into learning these controls, you can take comfort in knowing that it is easy to restore the camera to its original default settings: go to the 🔧 (Set-up 3) menu, select **[Clear all camera settings]**, use ❖ or ◯ to highlight **[OK]**, and then press SET. This menu option clears all but language, Date / Time, Video System, Copyright Data, Custom Functions, and My Menu settings.

> Don't be afraid of resetting the camera settings if you are confused about how the camera is set up.

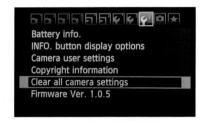

NOTE: If the 60D is in one of the Basic Zone modes (page 168), some menu items, including **[Clear all camera settings]**, will not be available.

MODE DIAL

The Mode dial, located on the top left shoulder of the camera, is used to select the 60D's shooting mode. New to the EOS system is the Mode Dial Lock-Release button. This system prevents the camera from switching to a different shooting mode accidentally. This can happen with other cameras when you carry the camera around your neck using the neck strap. To adjust the Mode dial, first press down the Lock-Release button, and then rotate the dial. It is useful to think of the Mode dial as having three zones: Basic, Creative, and Movie shooting.

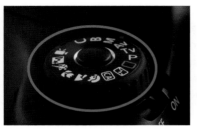

< The new Mode Dial lock prevents the dial from accidentally turning. This is especially useful in situations where the camera is supported only by the strap and is more likely to bump against something.

CONTROLS AND FUNCTIONS

Basic Zone: The Basic Zone on the Mode dial is the automatic section. It contains three fully automatic settings—Full Auto ▢, Flash Off ⚡ and Creative Auto ᴄᴀ—and several scene modes. When set to ▢, the only shooting adjustments you can make are to select a particular image-quality recording (a combination of pixel count, which is resolution; and quality, also known as level of compression) and to determine whether you want to use the Self-Timer. ▢ is a useful mode if you hand the camera to someone else to take a picture. Very few buttons will operate, so they can't accidentally put the camera into the "wrong" mode.

In automatic mode, the camera takes care of all of the exposure, focus, and picture settings. If the scene is dark, the camera automatically flips up the flash and uses it. If the scene is too dark to lock focus before you take the picture, the 60D fires a few bursts of the flash to illuminate the scene enough so that focus can be set.

You should pay attention to the focus points that are illuminated in the viewfinder. They indicate which AF (autofocus) point the camera is using to achieve focus. If the AF point is not located near your subject, then your subject might not be in focus if you take the picture.

When you shoot in ▢ you still have a little control. For example, you can lock focus by pressing the shutter release button halfway, then recompose your shot. This is a very useful technique when you want to place your subject somewhere besides the center of the frame.

Live View shooting is also available when the 60D is in ▢. Press 📷 to turn on Live View shooting. Press 📷 again to turn off Live View shooting. Learn more about Live View shooting with the 60D on pages 209-224.

The second automatic mode, ⚡, is identical to ▢ except, as the icon implies, the flash will not fire. Even if the flash is popped up from another mode, it won't fire. It also won't be used to illuminate a dark scene in order to set focus. This mode is useful in museums or places where you don't want the flash to disturb the scene.

With ⒸⒶ, you can access a few more settings, including Ambience, Picture Styles, and Continuous drive modes. ⒸⒶ also provides two easy-to-use exposure adjustments available through the ⓠ (Quick Control) button: background and exposure. (See pages 168-170.)

The five scene modes (Canon calls this the Image Zone) can be used for specific shooting situations like taking portraits, landscapes, action, or close-up shots, or for shooting at night. Scene modes are covered in more detail on pages 171-173.

Creative Zone: This zone differs from the Basic Zone because these modes only affect exposure settings. (In contrast, the fully automatic selections control such functions as white balance, focus, etc., in addition to the exposure settings.) There are four modes in this section that are common to every SLR, whether a film or digital camera, from Canon or another manufacturer. While the icons or acronyms may be slightly different among the various cameras, they all perform the same duties. The four modes are Program autoexposure (P), Shutter-Priority AE (Tv), Aperture-Priority AE (Av), and Manual exposure (M). In addition, there is Bulb (B) mode, which allows you to keep the shutter open as long as you are pressing the shutter button.

The last item in the Creative Zone is the Camera User setting C. This allows you to customize the 60D so that you can quickly set up the camera to an often-used shooting mode. For example, if you shoot a lot of action shots, you might want to be able to quickly set the camera for optimum shutter speed, drive mode, and focus mode. (See page 168.)

Movie Shooting: This last Mode dial option puts the 60D into Movie Recording mode. (See pages 225-235 for more information.)

SHUTTER BUTTON

The 60D features a soft-touch electromagnetic shutter release. When you partially depress the shutter button, you activate such functions as autoexposure and autofocus. But this camera is fast enough that there is minimal speed advantage in pressing the button halfway before exposure. When you are dealing with moving subjects it does help, however, to start autofocusing early, so the camera and lens then have time to find your subject.

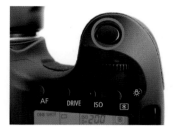

‹ The shutter button requires a gentle touch. Taking a picture involves a gentle squeeze and not a hard tap.

MAIN DIAL

Located behind the shutter button on the top right of the camera, the Main dial (⌂) allows you to use your shooting finger to set exposure as well as other functions. ⌂ works alone when setting shutter speed and aperture in **Tv** and **Av** respectively. For a number of other adjustments, it works in conjunction with buttons that are pressed and released or that are held down while it is turned.

AF *AUTOFOCUS MODE SELECTION*

The 60D has several different methods for achieving focus. The **AF** selection button is located behind ⌂. To select an autofocus mode, make sure your lens is switched to AF and press the camera's **AF** button. Use ☼, ⌂, or ○ to choose from **ONE SHOT**, **AI FOCUS**, and **AI SERVO**. During adjustment, you can view the settings on the LCD panel on the top of the camera, and on the LCD monitor on the back of the camera. (See pages 188-191 for more information about the autofocus modes.)

In Basic Zone modes this button has no function. When the camera is in ▢, ▣, or ▣, AF mode is locked to **AI FOCUS** mode. In ▲, ▲, ♥, or ▣, AF mode is set to **ONE SHOT** mode. When shooting in ✎ mode, the focus mode is automatically set to **AI SERVO**.

DRIVE *DRIVE MODE SETTING*

Drive mode relates to how many pictures are taken once the shutter button is pressed or if the Self-Timer is used. The drive mode is set by first pressing DRIVE, and then using ☼, ⌂, or ○ to select from Single shooting (□), High-speed continuous (⊒H), Low-speed continuous (⊒), 10 sec. Self-Timer / Remote Control (⏱☽), and 2 sec. Self-Timer / Remote Control (⏱☽2). The drive options are more limited while the 60D is in one of Basic Zone shooting modes. During adjustment, you can view the settings on the LCD panel on the top of the camera, and on the LCD monitor on the back of the camera. (See page 183 for more information on drive modes.)

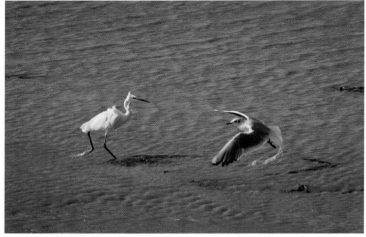

⌃ With large memory cards, continuous drive mode can help you capture the right "moment."

ISO *SPEED SETTING*

The ISO button is located behind ⌂ to the right of DRIVE and it controls how sensitive the 60D is to light. After pressing ISO, use ☼, ⌂, or ○ to adjust ISO speed. The range varies depending on how you have set C.Fn-2 (ISO expansion). Normally, it ranges from 100 – 6400 and also has an Auto mode. With ISO Expansion enabled, the ISO range is 100 – 12800, including Auto. The highest ISO setting in this mode is labeled "H" and represents 12800. During adjustment, you can view the settings on the LCD panel on the top of the camera, on the LCD monitor on the back of the camera, and in the viewfinder.

When the 60D is in any of the Basic Zone modes—□, ⊡, ⒸⒶ, ●, ▲, ♣, ♦, or ◪—the ISO button does not function. The camera will be in Auto ISO and the camera will pick an ISO setting between 100 – 3200.

⊙ METERING MODE SELECTION

The ⊙ button is located behind the Main dial ⌂ and to the right of the ISO button. It controls how the 60D evaluates the light in your scene to achieve the correct exposure. When ⊙ is pressed, use ✳, ⌂, or ○ to select from four different metering modes: Evaluative ⊙, Partial ⊡, Spot ⊡, and Center-Weighted Average ⊡. (See page 195 to learn more about metering in the 60D.)

During adjustment, you can view the settings on the LCD panel on the top of the camera, and on the LCD monitor on the back of the camera. This button does not work when the 60D is in any of the Basic Zone modes—□, ⊡, ⒸⒶ, ●, ▲, ♣, ♦, or ◪.

☀ LCD ILLUMINATION BUTTON

Located to the right of ⊙, this button illuminates the LCD panel on the top of the camera. The LCD panel will stay illuminated for 6 seconds.

⊞/⊕ AUTOFOCUS POINT SELECTION / MAGNIFY BUTTON

The outside button on the back of the camera in the upper right corner is the ⊞/⊕ button. When shooting, press ⊞/⊕ to display the currently selected AF points in the viewfinder, on the LCD monitor on the back of the camera, and on the LCD panel on the top of the camera.

In the Creative Zone modes and Movie Recording mode, you can use a combination of ✳, ⌂, and ○ to select different AF points. Press SET to switch to automatic point selection. All the AF points are illuminated and the 60D will intelligently use AF points based on the scene. Press SET again to select the center AF point. If you use ✳ to select AF points and you tilt ✳ in the same direction twice, the 60D will also switch to automatic AF point selection. When the 60D is in any of the Basic Zone modes, the AF point is selected automatically, and ⊞/⊕ will not function. Learn more about AF on pages188-191.

43

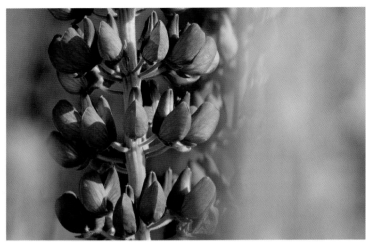

∧ Choosing a specific focus point can help when your subject isn't in the center of the frame.

The ⊞/🔍 button has a different purpose during Live View shooting and Movie Recording. ⊞/🔍 can be used to magnify the focus frame. With the first press of ⊞/🔍, the display magnifies about 5x; a second press magnifies the display about 10x. The third press returns the display to normal view. This is a powerful tool. Even if you normally use the viewfinder for composition, turning on Live View shooting and using this focus-checking method is a great option when you are facing difficult focusing situations.

⊞/🔍 offers yet another function when the 60D is in Playback mode in both the Basic and Creative Zones. During Playback, press ⊞/🔍 to magnify from 1.5 – 10x the original size. To move around the magnified image, use ⁙. Use ▶ to return to an unmagnified display.

NOTE: You cannot magnify the image during Image Review (immediately after image capture). You can only magnify it during Playback.

And finally, during direct camera printing this button crops the image before printing. Press ⊞/🔍 to decrease the trimming frame (more of the image will be cropped) and use ⁙ to move the trimming frame around the image. (Learn more about direct camera printing on pages 300-303.)

This button is duplicated on the optional BG-E9 battery grip to allow for easy access when you hold the camera in a vertical shooting position. (In this case, the corresponding button is in the same relative position as the one intended for horizontal shooting.) The vertical shooting version is only active when the vertical grip's on / off switch is in the on position.

> **NOTE:** This button is one of several on the 60D that have dual functions. The buttons are labeled with white and blue icons. The blue icons represent functions used during Playback, file transfer, or printing. For example, the AF point selection / magnify button can be thought of as two buttons: the AF point selection button ⊞ and the magnify button ⊕.

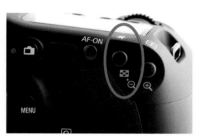

‹ The ✳/⊞·⊕ button wears many hats. It is most commonly used for locking an exposure setting, which is very helpful when shooting in quickly changing light situations, such as clouds moving across bright sunlight.

✳/⊞·⊕ *AE LOCK / FE LOCK / INDEX / REDUCE BUTTON*

To the left of ⊞/⊕ is the multi-purpose ✳/⊞·⊕ button. When you are shooting, press this and the 60D locks the exposure at the current setting. Press ✳/⊞·⊕ again to lock a new exposure setting if you reframe the shot and want to use that exposure value. The viewfinder will display ✳ to indicate that the exposure has been locked.

The exposure that is locked depends on the metering mode. With ⊏⊐ (Center-Weighted Average), ⊡ (Spot), and ⊠ (Partial), the exposure lock uses a meter reading taken from the center AF point. With ⊠ (Evaluative), AE lock is set for the selected AF point, whether selected manually or by the camera. If the lens is in manual focus, the center focus point is used, regardless of metering mode. ✳/⊞·⊕ will not function when the 60D is any of the Basic Zone shooting modes.

When a flash is used—either the built-in flash or an external Speedlite—✳/⊞·⊕ can be used to lock the exposure of the flash, too. Press ✳/✉·❏ and the flash will fire a low-power pre-flash in order to judge exposure. ↳* will display in the viewfinder indicating that flash exposure has been locked. If ↳ is blinking, the flash is not powerful enough to light up the scene. Flash exposure lock is useful to quickly control your flash exposure. You can lock flash exposure while composing your subject closer or farther from the flash to reduce or increase flash output.

During Playback in both the Basic and Creative Zones, press ✳/✉·❏ once to display a grid of four images (index display). Press ✳/✉·❏ again to display a nine-image grid. In both displays, a blue border surrounds the currently selected image. Use ❖ or ○ to move the blue highlight to select a different photo. Use ⬜ to jump through images a screen at a time. Press **SET** and the currently highlighted image will go full screen. Press ⊞/❏ to return to single-image display from the four-image index display; press ⊞/❏ twice to return to single-image display from the nine-image display. Also during Playback, if the image has been magnified by pressing ⊞/❏, use ✳/✉·❏ to reduce the magnification.

✳/✉·❏ is also used during direct camera printing to crop the image before printing. Press ✳/✉·❏ to increase the trimming frame (less of the image will be cropped), and use ❖ or ○ to move the trimming frame around the image.

Again, this button is duplicated on the optional BG-E9 battery grip to allow for easy access while holding the camera in a vertical shooting position. (In this case, the corresponding button is in the same relative position as the one intended for horizontal shooting.) The vertical shooting version is only active when the vertical grip's on / off switch is in the on position.

AF-ON *AF START BUTTON*

On the back of the camera to the left of ✳/✉·❏ is the **AF-ON** button. When the lens is in AF mode, use **AF-ON** or press the shutter release button halfway to start autofocus. When the 60D is set for **ONE SHOT** AF, **AF-ON** or the shutter release button is pressed, and the 60D has achieved focus, the camera beeps and a focus confirmation light ● appears in the lower right section of the viewfinder to indicate that focus lock has been achieved. If the 60D is unable to acquire proper focus lock, the indicator flashes and the camera does not beep.

NOTE: In ONE SHOT you will not be able to take a picture until focus has been confirmed.

Since depressing the shutter release button halfway performs the same function as AF-ON, you might wonder when you would use AF-ON. Because the shutter release also starts the exposure evaluation, there may be instances when you want to lock focus separately from exposure. In this case you would first frame the scene for focus and press AF-ON, then reframe for exposure and press ✳/⊞·🔍 to lock exposure, and lastly, press the shutter to take the picture.

Because the autofocus sensors are located in the viewfinder area, the AF sensors are blocked when the 60D is in Live View shooting or Movie Recording mode. As a result, there are three additional options for autofocus: AFQuick, AFLive, and Face Detection AF ☺ (see page 215). With all three, it is important that you continue to hold down AF-ON until the camera beeps and the autofocus is locked. Depending on which Live View AF mode you are in, the confirmation will be indicated either by the AF point turning green (AFQuick mode), by the Live View AF point turning green (AFLive mode), or by the Face Detection frame turning green (AF ☺ mode).

NOTE: When the 60D is in Movie mode and actually recording video, if you press AF-ON and the AF mode is set for AFQuick, the camera will perform autofocus as if it is set for AFLive.

The AF-ON button is another one that is duplicated on the BG-E9 battery grip to allow for shooting while holding the camera in a vertical shooting position. The vertical shooting version is only active when the vertical grip's on / off switch is in the on position.

📷 LIVE VIEW SHOOTING / MOVIE SHOOTING BUTTON

When the 60D is enabled for Live View shooting in 📷ᵢ, use this button to turn on Live View and display the live image on the LCD. Press the button again to turn off Live View. When the camera is in Movie Recording mode, use 📷 to start and stop video recording.

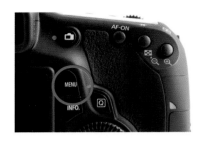

> The menu button takes you to the heart of all the 60D settings.

MENU *BUTTON*

The 60D has several menus for use when capturing and viewing images, as well as for setting up the operation of the camera. This button, located near the top right corner of the LCD monitor, is used to display any of the camera menus on the LCD monitor and to exit menus and submenus.

When the 60D is in a Creative Zone mode, the menu structure consists of 11 menu tabs: four red Shooting menus dealing with image capture; two blue Playback menus to control LCD display options, image transfer, and printing; three yellow Set-up menus; one orange Custom Function menu for advanced camera settings, and a green My Menu that lets you build your own set of options.

When in Movie Recording mode, the menu structure changes. Of the nine menu tabs, there are still four red Shooting menus, but the first two now deal specifically with video settings. There are still two blue Playback menus and three Set-up menus, though the options in some of the menus have been reduced. The My Menu and Custom Function menus are no longer accessible.

Once you have pressed MENU, navigate through the menu tabs by using ☀ or ☀, and use ○ or ☀ to navigate to each menu item. Press **SET**, located in the center of ☀, to select a menu item and view its options. When adjusting settings in the menus, be sure to press **SET** to accept the setting; otherwise, the 60D reverts to the previous setting. (Menus are thoroughly discussed in the chapter entitled The Menu System and Custom Functions, beginning on page 95.)

NOTE: If you are in any of the Basic Zone shooting modes, several menus and many menu items will not be available. If you can't find a menu item as you continue through this book, check to see if the camera is in the Basic Zone.

INFO. *BUTTON*

The main duty of INFO., which is located below MENU, is to cycle through the various display modes on the LCD.

When you are shooting, INFO. cycles through four different displays on the LCD monitor: a shooting functions display, a blank screen, a camera settings display, and the electronic level. You can remove any of the non-blank displays using ♈ (Set-up 3 menu), **[INFO. button display options]**.

Using the LCD monitor, the shooting functions display duplicates information found on the LCD panel (on the top of the camera). This is useful when the 60D is in a position where you are not able to see the top of the camera, but still want to see shooting settings like drive mode, AF mode, or exposure settings.

But the real power of the shooting functions display is when ⌨ is pressed. This turns the display into an interactive quick function menu that allows you to change many of the shooting parameters without having to jump into menus. The camera settings display covers items like Picture Style, Color Space, White Balance Shift or Bracketing, and Rotation Settings, just to name a few.

The electronic level is a new feature in EOS cameras (a two-axis version premiered in the 7D). The 60D's one-axis version allows you to level the camera horizontally. Each hash mark on the level represents 1° of tilt. A horizon line indicates the current tilt amount of the camera. When the camera is not level, the horizon line is red. When the line turns green, the camera is level. You can display the level in the viewfinder and on the LCD panel.

NOTE: The level system only works when shooting with the 60D in the horizontal position.

NOTE: The level appears in the LCD panel based on the setting in **[INFO. button display options]** in the ♈ menu; the one in the viewfinder is based on how the **SET** button is set up in C.Fn IV-2.

When the 60D is used for Image Review or Playback the INFO. button also switches between four displays. Press INFO. repeatedly to cycle through them. The display modes you can cycle through include:

○ Single-image display

○ Single-image display including aperture, Exposure Compensation, shutter speed, current / total number of images captured, image rating (number of stars), protection, Eye-Fi status and folder / file number

○ Shooting information display with histogram and extensive metadata about the image

○ A dual histogram display that shows the RGB and Brightness Histograms, along with pared-down shooting information

When the 60D is in Live View shooting mode, INFO. cycles through five displays: a plain display, exposure display, controls display, histogram, and level. During Movie Shooting mode, the displays are similar, except there is no histogram display. If the camera is set for AF ꞊ autofocus the level feature cannot be displayed.

During direct camera-to-printer printing, press INFO. to change the trimming frame from horizontal to vertical orientation.

⊙ QUICK CONTROL BUTTON

This control engages the Quick Control screen on the LCD monitor, a powerful feature that makes photographing with the 60D quick and easy. Find it on the back of the camera to the right of the LCD. Once the Quick Control screen is displayed, use ❖ to highlight each of the displayed shooting parameters. When a parameter is highlighted, use ○ or ⌒ to change the value that appears on the LCD monitor. The Quick Control screen is explained later in this chapter (see page 58). The number of parameters displayed (and that can be adjusted via the Quick Control screen) will differ depending on what mode the 60D is set for.

> Learn to use the Quick Control screen, accessed by pressing the ⊙ button, and you'll soon become more efficient in changing the shooting settings on the 60D.

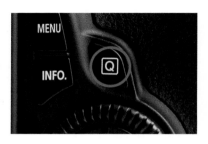

SET *SET BUTTON*

Centered within ⚙ and ⚪, this button is used like a mouse button to "click" or accept menu options presented on the LCD, as well as to confirm settings during other operations. Since **SET** really has no normal function while shooting, it can also be programmed to handle other functions while in shooting mode, using C.Fn IV-2 (see page 149). Possible functions include setting Image Quality, Picture Style, White Balance, and Flash Exposure Compensation, as well as turning on the electronic level display in the viewfinder.

▶ *PLAYBACK BUTTON*

Located near the lower right-hand corner of the LCD screen, the ▶ button puts the camera into Playback mode and displays the last image captured or last image displayed. Press the button again to return to Shooting mode (or press the shutter button). You can also use the ▶ button to exit from magnified playback of images. To play back video, first press ▶, select a movie, then press **SET** to bring up the movie controller. Finally, press **SET** to start Playback.

> **NOTE:** While Image Review and Playback appear the same on the LCD monitor, there are differences. Image Review occurs automatically after you take the picture; Playback occurs only after you press ▶. But probably the biggest difference is that you can't magnify the image during Image Review, only during Playback.

UNLOCK/🖶 *QUICK CONTROL DIAL LOCK-RELEASE /*
DIRECT PRINT BUTTON

Since the Quick Control dial can adjust exposure settings when the 60D is in one of the Creative Zone modes, you might accidentally turn it when you hold the camera up to your eye. You can lock this dial using the **[Lock ⚪]** option in ✿ (Set-up 2 menu). This Lock-Release button can temporarily unlock ⚪ so that you can make adjustments.

> **NOTE:** The lock option only locks the dial during shooting; the dial is still useable in menus and even in the Quick Control screen.

When the 60D is directly connected to a printer, press UNLOCK to quickly print an image.

> **NOTE:** Like ✳/❐·🔍 and ⊞/🔍, this button has two labels. The blue one indicates the function used during Playback.

52

🗑 ERASE BUTTON

Below the power switch is the 🗑 button, used to delete an image or video during either Image Review or Playback. When you press 🗑, you are given the choice to **[Erase]** or **[Cancel]**. Select the appropriate option using ◯ or ✲ and press **SET** to confirm. Protected images can't be erased.

To select multiple images for deletion, first go to the ▣ˉ (Playback 1) menu, select **[Erase images]**, scroll through your images using ◯ or ✲ (or 🔆 to jump through images 10 at a time), then press up on ✲ to choose each image you want to delete. When all images have been selected, press 🗑 to delete the images.

> **HINT:** You can also use 🗑 to lengthen the review time after image capture. If you normally work with a short review time, press 🗑 to keep the just-captured image on the LCD monitor until you press either the shutter release button or 🗑 (again) to cancel the delete function.

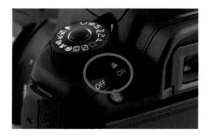

> Since the 60D has an automatic power off feature, you don't always have to worry about shutting off the camera.

POWER SWITCH

The power switch is found on the top left of the camera, below the Mode dial. In the On position, the camera will operate as long as the battery contains a charge and as long as the Auto Power Off setting allows (see page 25).

FLASH BUTTON

Located on the left side of the camera, on the front next to the 60D logo, is the flash button. In the Basic Zone, the 60D will pop up the built-in flash as needed. In the Creative Zone, the flash will never pop up automatically. Use this button to use flash in the Creative Zone.

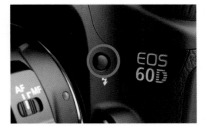

‹ The flash button is nestled into the front of the camera, to avoid popping up the flash accidentally.

DEPTH-OF-FIELD PREVIEW BUTTON

Except for the brief moment when you take a picture, the aperture of a lens is wide open. This ensures that the maximum amount of light reaches the viewfinder so that you can compose and focus your shot. Unfortunately, this also means that you don't know what effect the current aperture will have on the depth of field in the shot you plan to take. (Depth of field is the range—front to back—of your scene that appears in focus.)

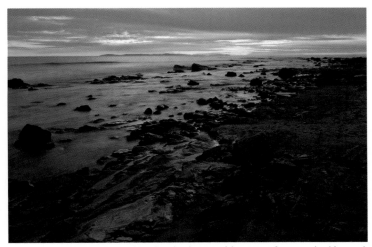

∧ Depth of field is important when shooting images with a strong foreground subject and also a strong background.

In order to help you visualize the depth of field, the 60D has a Depth-of-Field Preview. Located on the front right of the camera near the lens, the Depth-of-Field Preview button stops down the lens to the current aperture setting. Although this darkens the image in the viewfinder, the button can be a good tool to check which elements in the scene will be in focus. If the image in the viewfinder is still too dark, consider switching to Live View.

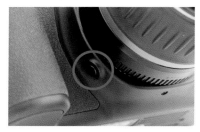

> The Depth-of-Field Preview button is a press-and-hold button.

THE VIEWFINDER

The 60D uses a standard, eye-level, reflex viewfinder with a fixed pentaprism. Images from the lens are reflected to the viewfinder by a quick-return, semi-transparent half-mirror. The mirror lifts for the exposure, then rapidly returns to keep viewing blackout to a very short period. The mirror is also dampened so that its bounce and vibration are essentially eliminated. The viewfinder shows about 96% of the actual image area captured by the sensor, so check the edges of the frame on the LCD after you take the picture for critical evaluation of the composition. The eyepoint is about 22 mm, which is good for people with glasses. (The higher the eyepoint number, the farther your eye can be from the viewfinder and still see the whole image.)

The viewfinder features an interchangeable, precision matte focusing screen. It uses special micro-lenses to make manual focusing easier and to increase viewfinder brightness. The viewfinder provides 0.95x magnification. The camera's nine autofocus (AF) points are superimposed on the focusing screen, and the solid band at the bottom of the screen shows most of the shooting information that you need.

NOTE: See the diagram under the back flap of this book for details of information displayed in the viewfinder.

There are two accessory focusing screens that are available from Canon. The Ef-D screen has additional grid lines that are useful in aligning vertical and horizontal subjects like architectural photography. The Ef-S is a focus screen that allows for more precision when you spend a lot of time manually focusing the 60D. But the Ef-S is really designed for "fast" lenses. By fast, I mean lenses with a maximum aperture of f/2.8 or greater. If you use a slower lens, the viewfinder image won't be as bright as the focus screen that comes with the camera (Ef-A).

There is no eyepiece shutter to block light entering the viewfinder when it is not against the eye (such as when shooting long exposures from a tripod), which affects exposure metering. However, an eyepiece cover, conveniently stored on the camera strap, is provided instead. It is necessary to remove the eyecup to attach the eyepiece cap.

VIEWFINDER ADJUSTMENT

The 60D's viewfinder features a built-in diopter (a supplementary lens that allows for sharper viewing). It is surprising how often this control is overlooked. The diopter helps you get a sharp view of the focusing screen so you can be sure you are getting the correct sharpness as you shoot. For this to work properly, you need to adjust the diopter for your eye. The adjustment knob is just above and slightly to the right of the eyecup. Fine-tune the diopter setting by looking through the viewfinder and tapping the shutter release button to turn on the info display at the bottom. Then rotate the dioptric adjustment knob until the info display appears sharp. You should not look at the subject that the camera is focused on, but at the display on the viewfinder screen. If you prefer, you can also use the AF points superimposed on the viewfinder for this purpose.

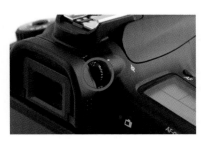

‹ When adjusting the diopter, make sure that you are seeing the difference from one setting to the next. Try "going past" the best setting and then dialing back to get the ideal, and clearest, focus.

While some people can use this adjustment to see through the camera comfortably with or without eyeglasses, I have found that the correction isn't really strong enough for most who wear glasses regularly (like me). But Canon sells accessory dioptric adjustment lenses that give you an additional range of correction. They replace the standard one that comes with the camera, which gives you a range from -3.0 to +1 of diopter correction. There are ten different individual dioptric adjustment lenses that range from -4 to +3.

THE LCD MONITOR

The LCD monitor is probably the one digital camera feature that has most changed how we photograph. Recognizing its importance, Canon has put a 3-inch (7.6 cm), high-resolution articulating LCD screen on the back of the camera. While Canon has featured an articulating screen in the G-Series point-and-shoot cameras, this is the first EOS camera with this feature.

With about 1.04 million dots, this screen has excellent sharpness, making it extremely useful for evaluating images. The LCD monitor features a special coating to reduce smudges, water-repellant and anti-reflective coatings, and an extremely durable scratch-resistant coating.

The LCD can rotate 180° forward and 90° backward. When the LCD is rotated all the way forward so that you can see the display from the front of the camera, the display automatically flips so the image appears with the correct top-to-bottom orientation. If you are shooting with Live View and the LCD is facing forward, such as when capturing a self-portrait, the image will be a mirror image of the scene.

When you first take the 60D out of the box, it comes with the LCD monitor facing the back of the camera — what could be considered a storage position. Typically the 60D is used with the LCD monitor visible. Consider using the storage position to protect the screen when you are finished using the camera or before you place it into a camera bag.

The 60D's LCD monitor can also display a graphic representation of exposure values, called a histogram (see page 205). The ability to see both the recorded picture and an exposure evaluation graph means that under- and overexposures, color challenges, lighting problems, and compositional issues can be dealt with on the spot. Flash photography in particular can be checked, not only for correct exposure, but also for factors such as the effect of lighting ratios when multiple flash units and / or reflectors are used. No Polaroid film test is needed like in the old days. Instead, you can see the actual image that has been captured by the sensor.

While the LCD monitor is sized to display horizontal images, the camera can rotate vertical images in the LCD monitor as well. Some photographers love this feature, others hate it, but you have the choice. The Auto-Rotate function (see page 127) displays vertical images properly without holding the camera in the vertical position—but at a price: The image appears smaller on the LCD. On the other hand, you can keep the image as big as possible by not applying this function, but a vertical picture will appear sideways in the LCD.

You can also magnify an image up to 10x in the monitor by repeatedly pressing ⬛ when in Playback mode. Using the Multi-Controller ⬛, you can scroll through the enlarged photo to inspect it. It is a good practice to check focus using this method.

While the image is magnified in Playback, you can use ⬛ to scroll back and forth through your other images. This way, you can compare details in images without having to re-zoom on each one. Use ⬛·⬛ to reduce magnification of the image. While you can repeatedly press ⬛·⬛ to get back to normal display, the quickest way is to press ⬛. If you press ⬛·⬛ when the image isn't magnified, it brings up an image display of four images with the first press of the button and nine images with the second press. This allows you to jump quickly through your pictures four or nine images at a time. (See page 45 for more on the ⬛·⬛ button.)

But the real power of an articulating LCD monitor is the ability to position the 60D in unusual positions. Instead of taking all your pictures from the same perspective, swivel the LCD so it points up and then get the camera low so you can have a bug's eye view (or at least a small child's view) of the world without having to lie down in the dirt to look through the viewfinder.

Since the LCD is such an essential tool to help evaluate images, it is important to adjust it properly. You can manually set a level of LCD brightness by using the ⬛ (Set-up 2) menu. Use ⬛ or ⬛ to select [LCD brightness] and press SET. The last image displayed on the LCD will be shown along with a grayscale. Use ⬛ or ⬛ to select from seven different levels of brightness. Press SET to accept the setting.

The LCD is not just for displaying images. It is also designed to display shooting information and is always operational when the camera is on. When not used to change menu settings or to play back an image, the LCD displays the current camera settings: exposure, White Balance, drive settings, metering type, focusing type, resolution, and much more. And, of course, in Live View and Movie Shooting, the LCD displays a live image.

To save power, you can also turn off the display manually by using the INFO. button, located on back of the camera to the right of the LCD monitor.

QUICK CONTROL SCREEN

As mentioned above, when the 60D is not in its menu mode, Live View, Movie mode, or playing back an image, it displays the shooting settings on the LCD monitor. This display expands on the information that is shown in the viewfinder. In addition, it also provides quick access to many of the camera's settings. By pressing ⓠ, you can turn this display into an interactive camera-setting menu called the Quick Control screen. Once the Quick Control screen is displayed, use ✺ to highlight any of the displayed shooting parameters. When a parameter is highlighted, use ⌂ or ○ to change the value that appears on the LCD monitor.

> The Quick Control screen is a powerfully interactive screen that offers quick access to some settings that are buried within the menu system.

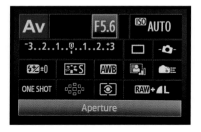

This Quick Control screen offers easy access to some settings that would normally require multiple button presses to change. For example, to set flash exposure compensation, normally you would need to first press MENU, then use ⌂ or ✺ to select ◘˙, use ✺ or ○ to select [Flash control], and press SET to enter the submenu. Then you would use ✺ or ○ to select [Built-in flash func. setting], and press SET to enter the [Flash control] submenu. And once more you would use ✺ or ○ to select [⬊ exp. comp] and press SET. Lastly, you would use ✺ or ○ to set the flash exposure compensation and then press SET.

That is a lot of button presses, particularly when the birthday candles are about to be blown out and you just want to lower the amount of flash in the scene. The steps for making the same change using the Quick Control screen are as follows: Press ⬛, use ✳ to highlight the Flash Exposure Compensation value on the shooting screen, and then use ⛰ or ◯ to change the value. Those birthday candles haven't even begun to drip.

> **NOTE:** When the flash exposure compensation value is zero, the parameter is not displayed on the LCD monitor. It normally is found right above the AF mode setting near the bottom left side of the screen. As soon as you engage the Quick Control screen and move the highlight to the blank area where the Flash Exposure Compensation is found, a +/-0 value will display.

It's true that Flash Exposure Compensation is probably the most extreme example of a shooting setting that is buried in menus, but the quicker you learn how easy the Quick Control menu is to use, the better you'll be at setting the 60D for difficult shooting situations.

Using the Quick Control screen is as simple as highlighting the parameter and using ⛰ or ◯ to change the value. It is not necessary to press **SET** to accept the setting. Just tap the shutter release button to exit and the setting is accepted.

If you want a little more guidance when using the Quick Control screen, press **SET** when a parameter is highlighted. This calls up the normal menu options for that parameter (if there is a menu). For example, use the **SET** button when the ISO value is highlighted to see a list of all the possible ISO speeds.

In ⬛ and 🔲 shooting modes, you can only use the Quick Control screen to change drive modes between Single shooting ⬜ and 10 sec. Self-Timer / Remote Control ⏱�️.

In the other Basic Zone modes, the drive mode options change slightly. More importantly, you have access to two new settings that Canon has introduced to the EOS camera line with the 60D:

Shoot By Ambience: This setting offers nine different options for your image's look. If you are new to DSLR photography, you don't need to get mired in the terminology, just select the type of image you want to shoot. For example, you can select Vivid, a setting that makes your image's colors really pop. This is a two-part adjustment: First, select Vivid, and then select how vivid you want it to be. Experienced DSLR photographers might notice that these settings are basically fine-tuning preset Picture Styles. You can learn more on page 66.

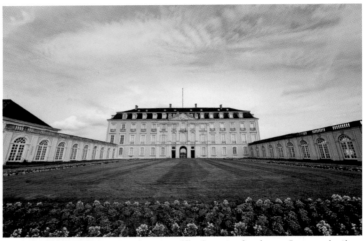

∧ The preset Picture Styles can enhance specific elements of an image. For example, the Vivid preset enhances an image's color.

NOTE: Shoot by Ambience is not available in □ or 🄴 mode.

Shoot By Lighting or Scene Type: Experienced DSLR photographers know about white balance. For those still getting accustomed to DSLR photography, this setting lets you select an intuitive description like Sunset or Shade when you take a photograph. The 60D then adjusts the white balance based on your selection. The 60D is the first EOS camera to give you controls over the white balance while in a Basic Zone mode. (See page 84 for more information.)

NOTE: Shoot by Lighting or Scene Type is not available in □, 🄴, 🄲🄰 or Night Portrait 🄽 mode.

When you shoot in ⒸⒶ, you also have access to continuous shooting ⊒, flash mode control (Auto ⚡ᴬ, Flash On ⚡, and Flash Off ⊘), and a special background adjustment (Background Blur) that allows you to control the focus of your background.

For the first time in an EOS camera, the Quick Control screen is available during Image Playback. When the 60D is in Playback mode, press ⒬ to bring up an overlay of icons on the left side of the LCD monitor. From this menu you can:

○ Protect images
○ Rotate images
○ Rate images (from 0 to 5 stars)
○ Apply creative filters
○ Resize
○ Enable / disable highlight alert
○ Enable / disable AF point display
○ Change the image jump mode

This new playback Quick Control screen has added usefulness to these functions. Previously, a photographer might keep the highlight alert disabled because the flashing indicator might be distracting, and it was too cumbersome to go into the ⊐˙ menu to toggle it off, and then go back and play back the image. Now it is available while viewing the image.

CAMERA SETTINGS SCREEN

When the camera is displaying a menu, you can press INFO. to view a camera settings status screen. You can gain a great deal of information about how the 60D is configured from this one display, rather than diving into various menus. This information includes:

○ Shooting mode assigned to the camera user setting on the Mode dial
○ Current Color Space
○ Current White Balance Shift and Bracketing setting
○ Current numerical color temperature for ◨
○ Red-Eye Reduction enabled status
○ Auto Power Off timer setting
○ Long Exposure Noise Reduction status

○ High ISO Speed Noise Reduction status / level

○ LCD Auto Off Enabled status

○ Number of shots available on memory card at current resolution setting

○ Remaining capacity on the memory card in megabytes (MB) or gigabytes (GB)

○ Date and time

THE SENSOR

Borrowing a new and improved low-pass optical filter technology from the 7D, the 60D employs a Canon-designed image sensor to create great images with low noise. The 18-megapixel (MP) sensor produces RAW files sized at 5184 x 3456 pixels. It can easily be used for quality magazine reproduction across two pages.

Because the 60D's APS-C-sized CMOS sensor (22.3 x 14.9 mm) covers a smaller area than a 35mm film frame, it records a narrower field of view than a 35mm film camera. To help photographers who are used to working with 35mm SLRs visualize this narrower field of view, a "cropping factor" of 1.6 is applied to the lens focal length number. Thus, on the 60D, a 200mm lens has a field of view similar to that of a 320mm lens on a 35mm camera. Remember, the focal length of the lens doesn't change, just the view captured by the 60D's sensor.

This focal length conversion factor is great for telephoto users because a 400mm telephoto lens acts like a 640mm lens on a 35mm camera. However, at the wide-angle end, a lens loses most of its wide-angle capabilities. For example, a 28mm lens acts like a 45mm lens. But since the EOS 60D accepts Canon EF-S lenses (see page 271), which are specially designed for this size image sensor, you can use the Canon 10-22mm zoom if you want to shoot wide-angle pictures. It offers an equivalent 16-35mm focal length.

Though small-format, the sensor in the 60D demonstrates improvements Canon has been making in sensor technology. One 60D feature is that it uses four channels to get data from the sensor to the DIGIC 4 image processor. This allows for a high-speed burst rate of 5.3 frames per second when the camera is set for its greatest resolution.

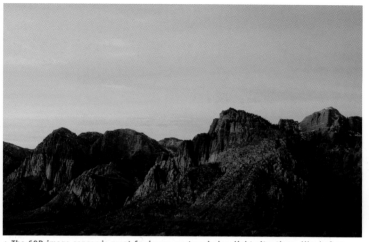

^ The 60D image sensor is great for image capture in low light situations, like before sunrise and after sunset.

Low-noise characteristics are extremely important to advanced amateur and professional photographers who want the highest possible image quality. The 60D gives an extraordinarily clean image with exceptional tonalities, and images can be enlarged with superior results.

In addition, the camera has an improved low-noise, high-speed-output amplifier as well as power-saving circuitry that reduces noise. With such low noise, the sensor offers more range and flexibility in sensitivity settings. ISO settings range from 100 – 6400 (expandable to 12800).

The on-chip RGB primary color filter uses a standard Bayer pattern over the sensor elements. This is an alternating arrangement of colors with 50% green, 25% red, and 25% blue; full color is interpolated from the data. In addition, an infrared-cutoff, low-pass filter is located in front of the sensor. This two-part filter is designed to prevent the false colors and wavy or rippled appearance of surfaces (moiré) that can occur when photographing small, patterned areas with high-resolution digital cameras.

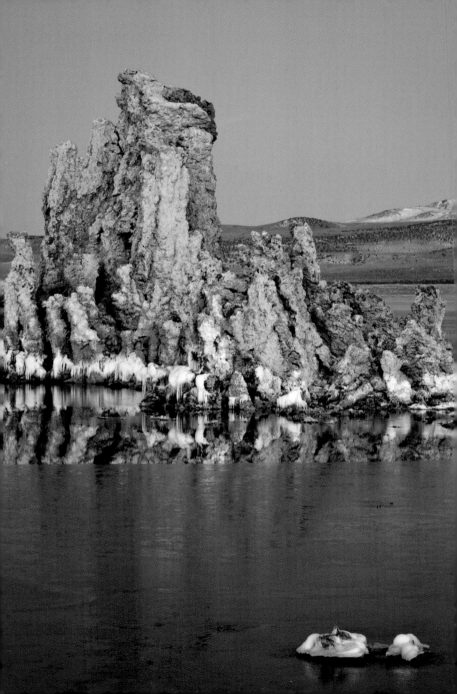

File Processing and Formats

One of the most important aspects of a digital camera is the image processor. A camera can capture all the data available with the image sensor, but without image processing it can't produce great images. Canon has long offered particularly strong in-camera processing capabilities. Like other recent Canon DSLRs, the 60D delivers exceptional JPEG images because it employs Canon's latest version of their high-performance processor, called DIGIC 4.

THE POWER OF DIGIC 4 PROCESSING

The Canon-designed DIGIC 4 processor intelligently translates the image signal as it comes from the sensor, optimizing that signal as it is converted into digital data. In essence, it is like having your own computer expert making the best possible adjustments as the data file is processed. DIGIC 4 works on the image after the shutter is released but before the image is recorded to the memory card, improving color balance, reducing noise, refining tonalities in the brightest areas, and more. In these ways, it has the potential to make JPEG files superior to unprocessed RAW files, reducing the need for RAW processing. (See pages 84-89 for more information about JPEG and RAW files.)

The DIGIC 4 handles data so quickly that it does not impede camera speed. The 60D has a single chip with image data processing that is appreciably faster than earlier units. Color reproduction of highly saturated and bright objects is also considerably improved. Auto White Balance is better, especially at low color temperatures (such as tungsten light). In addition, false colors and noise, which have always been a challenge of digital photography, have been reduced (something that RAW files cannot offer). The ability to resolve detail in highlights is stronger, as well.

DIGIC 4 also enhances the 60D's ability to write image data to the memory card in both JPEG and RAW, enabling the camera to utilize the benefits offered by high-speed memory cards. It is important to understand that this does not affect how quickly the camera can take pictures. Rather, it affects how fast it can transfer images from its buffer (special temporary memory in the camera) to the card. It won't make a difference in the number of shots per second, but it will improve the quantity of images that can be taken in succession. Even at maximum resolution, the camera has a burst duration of 58 JPEG or 16 RAW frames, or 3 RAW + Large/Fine JPEGs.

During the Continuous Shooting drive mode, each image is placed into a buffer before it is recorded to the memory card. The faster the memory card is, the faster the buffer is emptied, allowing more images to be taken in sequence. If the buffer becomes full, buSY appears in the viewfinder and the camera stops shooting until the card-writing can catch up.

Since RAW files need to be processed before they can be printed or shared, the 60D offers photographers the ability to process images in camera. This allows you to capture an image with the maximum amount of image data, and then adjust picture processing parameters after the fact. Simple adjustments like White Balance and brightness can be made along with more advanced tweaks like chromatic aberration and distortion correction. (See page 86.)

PICTURE STYLES

In addition to the optimizing technology of DIGIC 4, the 60D possesses options that you can choose to control how the camera performs added image processing. These are Picture Styles, which can be especially helpful if you print image files directly from the camera without using a computer program to process them. Some photographers compare Picture Styles to shooting with a particular film. They are applied permanently to JPEG files. If you use RAW files, the Picture Style can be changed during computer processing using Canon's Digital Photo Professional software.

Display Picture Styles via ◻⁺, **[Picture Style]**. Press **SET** and use ◯ or ⁙ to select the Picture Style you wish to use. You must press **SET** to accept the setting. (If you leave this menu without pressing **SET**, the 60D will revert to the previous setting.) You can also access Picture Styles via the Quick Control screen: press the Quick Control button ⊡ (located to the right of the LCD monitor), then use ⁙ to highlight the Picture Style parameter. Use ⌂ or ◯ to select the Picture Style. It is not necessary to press **SET** in the Quick Control screen to accept the setting; the change is immediate.

There are six preset Picture Styles and three user-defined styles:

STANDARD

Appropriately named, this is the default style for the ◻, ▦ , ⟦CA⟧, ⚘ , ⚞ , and ◪ shooting modes. During in-camera processing, color saturation is enhanced and a moderate amount of sharpening is applied to the image. offers a vivid and crisp image with a normal amount of contrast.

PORTRAIT

places an emphasis on pleasing skin tones. While the contrast is the same as , skin tones have a slightly warmer look. Sharpening is reduced in order to produce a pleasing, soft texture for the subject's skin. When you shoot with the 60D set for ⚘, this Picture Style is used.

LANDSCAPE

With , saturation is increased with an emphasis on blues and greens. The image is sharpened even more than mode in order to display details. Don't be afraid to use this during cloudy days to help bring out more color. If you are using ⛰, then this Picture Style is already in use.

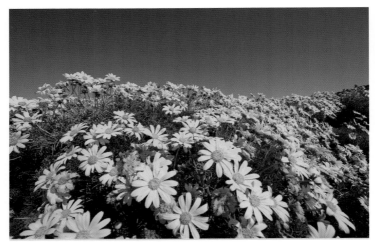

⌃ The 60D's in-camera processing can enhance your images as soon as you take a shot, especially if you understand the Picture Style settings and how each setting affects an image.

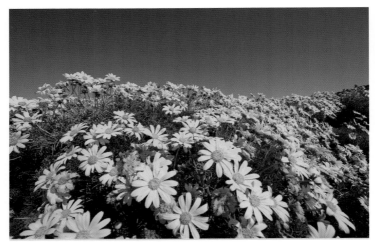 *NEUTRAL*

If you plan to process the image on your computer, either through Canon's Digital Photo Professional software or another image-processing program, this may be the mode to choose. There is virtually no sharpening. Color saturation is lower than other modes, and contrast is lower, too. Since other Picture Styles increase saturation, may be a good style to choose when you shoot in bright or high-contrast situations. Picture details may be more prevalent with this setting. Don't rule it out for candid portraits that may occur in bright lighting situations.

FAITHFUL

This is the choice when you need to accurately capture the colors in a scene. Saturation is low and almost no sharpening is applied to the image. Contrast is also toned down. Accurate color reproduction is achieved when the scene is lit with 5200K lighting (K stands for Kelvin; see page 78 for explanation). Otherwise, you might think of this setting as similar to , except that the color tone is a bit warmer. Like , this mode is designed with further image processing via computer in mind.

⬚ MONOCHROME

This allows you to record black-and-white images to the memory card and to automatically view the image in black and white on the LCD. Sharpness is the same as ⬚ mode, and contrast is enhanced. As with the other Picture Styles, ⬚ permanently changes JPEG files—you can't get the color back. Another option is to shoot in color and then convert images to black and white in an image-processing program—and do so with more control.

PICTURE STYLE PROCESSING

With all of the Picture Styles (except ⬚), you can control the degree of processing applied to four aspects of an image:

O **[◐ Sharpness]:** Refers to the amount of sharpening that is applied to the image file by the camera.

O **[◑ Contrast]:** Increases or decreases the contrast of the scene that is captured by the camera.

O **[⬚ Saturation]:** Influences color richness or intensity.

O **[◐ Color tone]:** When rendering skin tones, this selection helps designate the degree of red or of yellow. However, note that it also affects other colors.

With ⬚, the ⬚ and ◐ settings are replaced with **[◐ Filter effect]** and **[⊘ Toning effect]**. The parameters for ◐ offer four tonal effects that mimic what a variety of colored filters do to black-and-white film. A fifth setting, **[N:None]**, means that no ◐ is applied. Each ◐ color choice makes the colors similar to your selection look lighter, while the colors opposite your selection on the color wheel record darker. Aside from **[N:None]**, the several ⬚ ◐ choices are:

O **[Ye:Yellow]:** This is a modest effect that darkens skies slightly and gives what many black-and-white aficionados consider the most natural-looking grayscale image.

O **[Or:Orange]:** This is next in intensity. It does what red does, only to a lesser degree. It is better explained if you understand the use of red (see next description).

O [R:Red]: This is dramatic. It lightens anything that is red, such as flowers or ruddy skin tones, while darkening blues and greens. Skies turn quite striking, and sunlit scenes gain in contrast (the sunny areas are warm-toned and the shadows are cool-toned, so the warms get lighter and the cools get darker).

O [G:Green]: This makes Caucasian skin tones look more natural, and foliage gets bright and lively in tone.

Of course, if you aren't sure what these filters will do, you can take the picture and see the effect immediately on the LCD monitor.

The other ⌧ parameter, ⊘, adds color to the black-and-white image so it looks like a toned black-and-white print. Your choices include: [N:None], [S:Sepia], [B:Blue], [P:Purple], and [G:Green]. Sepia and blue are the tones we are most accustomed to seeing in such prints.

MODIFYING PICTURE STYLES

Picture Styles can be modified to suit your needs. Once the Picture Styles are listed on the LCD monitor (either via ⌧ or ◙), highlight the style you want to adjust and press INFO., located to the right of the LCD. A series of adjustment sliders will be displayed. Highlight the parameter you want to adjust using ○ or ☼, and press SET. Then, use ○ or ☼ to adjust the parameter. A white pointer shows the current setting, while the gray pointer shows the default setting for that Style. You must press SET to accept the setting. If you leave this menu screen without pressing SET, the adjustment is cancelled.

At the bottom of the screen is a [Default set.] option you can highlight to reset the parameters that you have altered. Parameter numbers displayed in blue indicate a setting that has been changed from the default values. Use MENU (toward the upper right corner of the LCD monitor) to return to the Picture Style menu.

The adjustment slider for ◐ Sharpness is set up differently than the other sliders. Sharpness is generally required at some point when recording digital images. It overcomes, among other things, the use of a low-pass filter in front of the image sensor (to reduce moiré problems caused by the image sensor's pixel grid). The low-pass filter (mounted in front of the image sensor in all digital cameras) introduces a small amount of image blur, so image sharpening compensates for this blur. The ◐ adjustment slider's setting indicates the amount of sharpness already applied to the style. A setting of zero means that almost no sharpening has been applied to the image. You'll notice that the ◑ parameter's default setting is the only one that changes from Picture Style to Picture Style.

USER-DEFINED PICTURE STYLES

The 60D allows you to use a particular Picture Style as a base setting and then modify it to meet your own photographic needs. This allows you to create and register a different set of parameters that you can apply to image files while keeping the preset Picture Styles. You do this under the options for **[User Def. 1]**, **[User Def. 2]**, and **[User Def. 3]**. While specific situations may affect where you place your control points for these flexible options, here are some suggestions to consider:

Create a Hazy or Cloudy Day Setting: Make one of the user-defined sets capture more contrast and color on days when contrast and color are weak. Increase the scales for ◑ Contrast and ♣ Saturation by one or two points (experiment to see what you like when you open the files on your computer or use the camera for direct printing). You can also increase the red setting (adjust the scale to the left) of ◐ Color tone.

Create a Portrait Setting: Make a setting that enhances flesh tones. Start with 🖼️ as your base, then reduce ◑ by one point while increasing ♣ by one point (this is quite subjective; some photographers may prefer less saturation), while also warming the flesh tones (by moving ◐ toward the red—or left—side) by one point.

You can also download custom Picture Styles from Canon's Picture Style website at http://web.canon.jp/imaging/picturestyle/index.html. These custom styles can be uploaded into any of the 60D's three user-defined styles by using the USB connection to the camera. (You'll need Canon's EOS Utility software, included with the camera.) You can also create your own custom Picture Styles using the Picture Style Editor software that comes with the camera. The custom styles can also be used with Canon's Digital Photo Professional software to change styles after capture in RAW images.

NOTE: Downloaded and custom Picture Styles can only be loaded into the user-defined styles and will be deleted if you reset all camera settings using **[Clear all camera settings]** in ♥ᵢ.

SHOOT BY AMBIENCE

A feature introduced with the 60D is Shoot by Ambience. Typically, when an EOS camera is in a Basic Zone mode, you aren't able to control image processing with Picture Styles. With the 60D, Canon has changed this by introducing some control via Shoot by Ambience.

When the camera is in any of the Basic Zone modes (except ☐ or ☒), you can adjust the image processing. There are nine options. You select the setting via the Quick Control screen. Press ⓠ then use ✷ to select the **[Shoot by Ambience]** parameter (the top most setting displayed on the LCD monitor). Once highlighted, you can use ☷ or ○ to select the setting you want to use. If you want to see all the options, press SET and then use ○ or ✷ to scroll through all the selections.

Each option can be further adjusted by pressing ✷ in the down direction on the Quick Control screen to highlight the effect setting, then using ☷ or ○ to make the adjustment. Typically this change controls the strength of the effect. The Shoot by Ambience options are:

[Standard]: This is the setting normally used on EOS cameras. It is not a specific setting used for all scenes. Instead, it makes adjustments depending on the scene. For example, in ☎ mode, colors will be more saturated, and in ♋, skin tones will be softer. There is no additional strength adjustment for this setting.

[Vivid]: If you want colors that pop more than standard, use this setting. You can adjust the strength of this effect. The strength setting can be set for **[Low]**, **[Standard]**, or **[Strong]**.

[Soft]: Try this setting for portraits, as there is less sharpening. Exposure Compensation is adjusted to slightly brighten the image. The strength setting can be set for **[Low]**, **[Standard]**, or **[Strong]**. The Exposure Compensation is +1/3, +2/3, and +1, respectively.

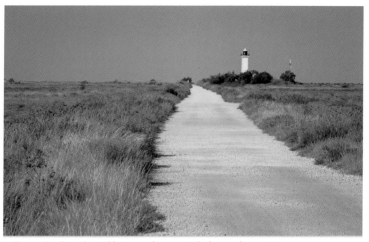
∧ Choose the Shoot by Ambience setting to match the mood you want to create.

[Warm]: Unlike Soft, sharpness is normal but color tones are adjusted for a warmer image. Exposure Compensation is also used to make the image brighter. The strength setting can be set for [Low], [Standard], or [Strong]. Exposure Compensation is changed with each strength setting: +1/3, +2/3, and +1, respectively.

[Intense]: In this case the image is slightly darker as the Exposure Compensation is set for -2/3. The idea is to increase contrast for a more dramatic look. The strength setting can be set for [Low], [Standard], or [Strong]. The strength setting doesn't change the Exposure Compensation setting—it is always -2/3.

[Cool]: The image is less bright as Exposure Compensation is set for -2/3 and colors appear more bluish. The strength setting can be set for [Low], [Standard], or [Strong].

[Brighter]: This is similar to adjusting Exposure Compensation in the plus direction when shooting in any of the Creative Zone modes. The strength setting can be set for [Low], [Medium], or [High]. These settings represent Exposure Compensation settings of +2/3, +1 1/3, and +2, respectively.

[Darker]: The opposite of Brighter in that it is like Exposure Compensation that is adjusted in the - direction. The strength setting can be set for [Low], [Medium], or [High]. These settings represent Exposure Compensation settings of -2/3, -1 1/3, and -2, respectively.

[Monochrome]: This allows you to make a black-and-white image. Rather than a strength setting, you can tint the photo sepia or blue. Exposure Compensation is not used.

Use Live View shooting to check the setting while viewing the image on the LCD monitor. If you are going to use Shoot by Ambience and Shoot by Lighting or Scene Type (see page 59), adjust Shoot by Lighting or Scene Type first.

COLOR SPACE

The 60D has a color space setting in the ◻️⁻ menu. A color space is the range of colors, or gamut, that a device can produce. Cameras have color spaces, monitors have color spaces, and printers have color spaces. (While not technically accurate, you can think of different color spaces as different sized boxes of crayons.)

The two choices for [Color space] on the 60D are [sRGB] and [Adobe RGB]. sRGB is the default setting for the camera and is used as the color space for all of the Basic Zone modes, including ◻️ and ⒸⒶ. It is also the color space for most computer monitors. If you are capturing images for the web, sRGB will work fine. Adobe RGB, as the name implies, was developed by Adobe to help create images for print output. Even so, this larger color space (think bigger box of crayons) contains more colors than can be produced by most of today's printers.

Choosing between sRGB and Adobe RGB is not as complicated as determining a choice between JPEG and RAW. Adobe RGB doesn't take up more room on the card or require special RAW processing software. But you do need to check that your image-processing program can handle Adobe RGB—most do.

There are many times when it is difficult to see the difference between the two color spaces. Try an experiment with some test shots in both. You won't see the difference on the LCD, so print them out and then see if you can tell the difference.

NOTE: When you use Adobe RGB, image file names begin with "_MG" rather than "IMG".

WHITE BALANCE

White Balance (WB) is an important digital camera control. It addresses a problem that has plagued film photographers for ages: how to prevent the different color temperatures of various light sources from producing unwanted color casts in your photos.

WB settings fall within certain color-temperature values, corresponding to a measurement of how cool (blue) or warm (red) the light source in the scene is. The measurement is in degrees Kelvin, abbreviated as K. Unlike air temperature, a higher K number represents a cooler light source – for example, shade with its bluish color. Conversely, a lower color temperature represents a warmer light source, such as a rising sun with its reddish hue.

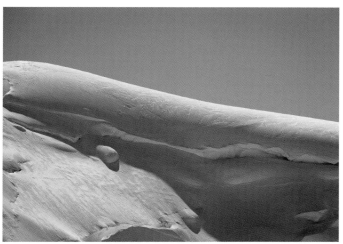

⌃ Setting the right white balance is important for accurately capturing a scene, but it can also be used creatively to change the tone of an image.

You can set White Balance either through the Quick Control screen or via the menus. To set White Balance via the menu system, select ◻️⁝ and highlight **[White balance]**, then press **SET**. Use ◯ or ⁝ to select the White Balance setting, then press **SET** to accept it. A faster method is via the

Quick Control screen. Press ⊙ and use ✷ to highlight the White Balance parameter. While the parameter is highlighted, use ◯ or ⌂ to change the setting. If you want to display a list of White Balance choices on the Quick Control screen, when the WB parameter has been selected, press **SET**. Next, use ⌂ or ✷ to choose the WB setting you want and press **SET**. The display of shooting settings on the LCD monitor shows an icon of the WB setting that you selected.

While color adjustments can be made in the computer after shooting, especially when recording RAW, there is a definite benefit to setting WB properly from the start. The 60D helps you do this with an improved Auto White Balance AWB setting that makes colors more accurate and natural than earlier DSLRs. In addition, improved algorithms and the DIGIC 4 processor make AWB more stable as you shoot a scene from different angles and focal lengths (which is always a challenge when using this setting). Further, White Balance in general has been improved to make color reproduction more accurate, especially under low light.

Although AWB gives excellent results in a number of situations, many photographers find they prefer the control offered by presets and custom WB ⌂ settings. With AWB, ⌂, six separate White Balance presets, and a manual color temperature setting, plus WB compensation and bracketing, the 60D possesses an outstanding ability to carefully control color balance. It is well worth the effort to learn how to use the different White Balance functions so you can get the best color with the most efficient workflow in all situations (including RAW). This is especially important in strongly colored scenes, such as at sunrise or sunset, which can fool AWB.

In Basic Zone shooting modes ☐, ☷, ☐, and ◪, White Balance is set for AWB and cannot be changed. In the other Basic Zone modes you can adjust the White Balance using the new Shoot by Lighting or Scene Type feature. (See page 84.)

In the Creative Zone shooting modes, you can apply the preset White Balance settings (see 77). These are not difficult to learn, so using them should become part of the normal photography decision-making process. However, in order to capture the truest color in all conditions, the more involved but more accurate custom WB ⌂ setting is a valuable tool to understand (see pages 79-80).

WHITE BALANCE PRESETS

The following is a list of the White Balance presets available on the 60D. These are effective in adjusting the color within the image to the color temperature of several specific lighting conditions.

AWB Auto (color temperature range of approximately 3000K – 7000K): This setting examines the scene for you, interprets the light it sees (in the range denoted above) using the DIGIC 4 processor (even with RAW), compares the conditions to what Canon's engineers have determined works for such readings, and sets a White Balance to make colors look neutral (i.e., whites appear pure, without color casts, and skin tones appear normal).

AWB can be a useful setting when you move quickly from one type of light to another, or whenever you hope to get neutral colors and need to shoot fast. Even if it isn't the perfect setting for all conditions, it often gets you close enough so that only a small adjustment is needed later using your image-processing software. If you have time, however, it is often better to choose from the White Balance settings listed below, as colors are more consistent from picture to picture. While AWB is well designed, it can only interpret how it "thinks" a scene should look. If the camera sees your wide-angle and telephoto shots of the same subject differently in terms of colors, it readjusts for each shot, often resulting in inconsistent color from shot to shot.

☀ Daylight (~5200K): This setting adjusts the camera to make colors appear natural when you shoot in sunlit situations between about 10 A.M. and 4 P.M. (depending on the time of year). At other times, when the sun is lower in the sky and has more red light, the scenes photographed using this setting appear warmer than normally seen with our eyes. This setting makes indoor scenes under incandescent lights look very warm.

🏠 Shade (~7000K): Shadowed subjects under blue skies can end up quite bluish in tone, so this setting warms the light to make colors look natural, without any blue color cast. (At least that's the ideal—individual situations affect how the setting performs.) The 🏠 setting is a good one to use any time you want to warm up a scene (especially when people are included), but you have to experiment to see how you like this creative use of the setting.

☁ **Cloudy (~6000K):** Even though the symbol for this setting is a cloud, think of it as the Cloudy/Twilight/Sunset setting. It warms up cloudy scenes as if you had a warming filter, making sunlight appear warm, but not quite to the degree as the 🏠 setting. You may prefer ☁ to 🏠 when shooting people, since the effect is not as strong. Both settings actually work well for sunrise and sunset, giving the warm colors that we expect to see in such photographs. However, ☁ offers a slightly weaker effect. You really have to experiment a bit when using these settings for creative effect. Make the final comparisons on the computer.

☀ **Tungsten light (~3200K):** This is designed to give natural results with quartz lights. It also reduces the strong orange color that is typical when photographing lamp-lit indoor scenes with daylight-balanced settings. Since this control adds a cool tone to other conditions, it can also be used creatively (to make a snow scene appear bluer, for example).

🔆 **White fluorescent light (~4000K):** Though the AWB setting often works well with fluorescents, the 🔆 setting is more precise and predictable. Fluorescent lights usually appear green in photographs, so this setting adds magenta to neutralize that effect. (Since fluorescents can be extremely variable, and since the 60D has only one fluorescent choice, you may find that precise color can only be achieved with the ↘ setting.) You can also use this setting creatively any time you wish to add a warm pinkish tone to your photo (such as during sunrise or sunset).

⚡ **Flash (~6000K):** Light from flash tends to be a little colder than daylight, so this warms it up. According to Canon tech folks, this setting is essentially the same as ☁ (the Kelvin temperature is the same); it is simply labeled differently to make it easy to remember and use. I find both ⚡ and ☁ to be good, all-around settings that give an attractive warm tone to outdoor scenes. The color temperature of this setting will be dependent on the flash being used. Most modern Canon flash units will transmit color temperature information to the camera in order to set the best White Balance adjustment.

K **Color temperature (~2000K – 10,000K):** Think of this as a manual White Balance setting. With this setting, you can directly set the color temperature to a numeric value in degrees Kelvin. To use K via the

Quick Control screen, press ⌕ and use ✲ to highlight the White Balance setting. Press **SET** to bring up the White Balance screen. Use ○ or ✲ to select ◼️ and then use ◒ to select the color temperature value. Press **SET** or lightly tap the shutter release button to accept the setting and exit.

This setting can be useful if you use a color temperature meter or know the color temperature of the illumination source. Unfortunately, most photographers don't. Alternatively, you can use Live View and "dial in" the White Balance using ◼️ while watching the LCD monitor as you adjust the color temperature value. To "dial in" White Balance during Live View shooting, press ⌕ and use ✲ to select the White Balance parameter then press **SET**. The list of WB choices overlays the Live View screen on the LCD monitor. Next, use ○ or ✲ to choose ◼️, then use ◒ to adjust the color temperature setting while you watch the image on the LCD monitor. This method also works for movie mode.

HINT: Even if you aren't using Live View for shooting or using ◼️, you can use the above method to evaluate different White Balance presets for your scene.

◻️ **Custom (~2000K – 10,000K):** A very important tool for the digital photographer, ◻️ is a setting that even many seasoned shooters often don't fully understand. It is a precise and adaptable way to get accurate or creative White Balance. It has no set White Balance K temperature, but is set based on a specific neutral tone from the light in the scene to be photographed. However, it deals with a significantly wider range than AWB (between approximately 2000K – 10,000K). That can be very useful.

The ◻️ setting lets you use either a white (or gray) target on which the camera sets White Balance. First, take a picture of a white or gray card that is in the same light as your subject. It does not have to be in focus, but it should fill the image area. (Avoid placing the card on or near a highly reflective colored surface.) Be sure the exposure is set to make this object gray to light gray in tone, and not dark (underexposed) or washed out white (overexposed).

HINT: I like to use a card or paper with small black print on it, rather than a plain white card. This way, if I can see the type, I haven't overexposed the image.

Next, go to ▣ and highlight [Custom White Balance], then press SET. The last shot you took (the one for White Balance) should be displayed in the LCD monitor. If not, use ○ or ✸ to choose the image you shot of the white or gray object.

When you have the target image displayed in the LCD monitor, press SET. A dialog box asks you if you want to use the White Balance information from the current image to set ◣◢. Highlight [OK], press SET, and ◣◢ is set to measure the color temperature of the light in that stored shot. If the 60D isn't set for Auto White Balance, ◣◢, a note appears, "Set WB to ◣◢," as a reminder. This reminds you that there is one more step to this process: You must choose the ◣◢ setting for White Balance. To take that final step, press SET again to acknowledge the reminder, then highlight [White balance] and press SET. Use ○ or ✸ to select ◣◢ and press SET to accept the setting.

You can save a series of White Balance reference images on your memory card ahead of time that you can flip through. This is useful if you need to switch between different lighting conditions but don't have the time to set up a card to capture the image. The procedure just described produces neutral colors in some very difficult lighting conditions. However, if the color of the lighting is mixed (for example, the subject is lit on one side by a window and on the other by incandescent lights), you will only get neutral colors for the light that the white card was in. Also, when you shoot in reduced spectrum lights, such as sodium vapor, you may not get a neutral white under any White Balance setting.

You can also use ◣◢ to create special color for a scene. In this case, you set the White Balance on a color that is not white or gray. You can use a pale blue card, for example, to generate a nice amber color tint for your image. If you balance on the blue, the camera adjusts this color to neutral, which in essence removes blue, so the scene has an amber cast. Different strengths of blue provide varied results. You can use any color you want for white balancing—the camera works to remove (or reduce) that color, which means the opposite color becomes stronger. (For example, using a pale magenta increases the green response.)

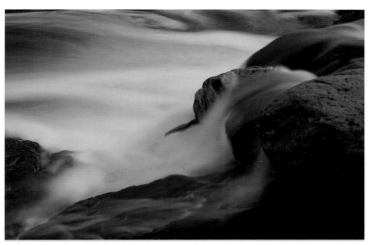

∧ The White Balance correction feature is a useful tool for more than just for correcting a White Balance reading—you can also use it to add creative effects to attain a certain mood or feeling in an image.

WHITE BALANCE CORRECTION

The 60D goes beyond the capabilities of many cameras in offering control over White Balance: There is actually a White Balance correction feature built into the camera. You might think of this as Exposure Compensation for White Balance. It is like having a set of color-balancing filters in four colors (blue, amber, green, and magenta) and in varied strengths. Photographers accustomed to using color-conversion or color-correction filters will find this feature quite helpful in getting just the right color.

The setting is not difficult to manage. First, go to ◻⁑, highlight **[WB Shift/BKT]** and press **SET**. A menu screen appears with a graph that has a horizontal axis from blue to amber (left to right), and a vertical axis from green to magenta (top to bottom). You move a selection point within that graph using ⁑. You must press **SET** before you leave this setting to lock in the value.

As you change the position of the selection point on the graph, an alphanumeric display titled "**Shift**" on the right of the screen shows a letter for the color (B, A, G, or M) and a number for the setting. For example, a White Balance shift of three steps toward blue and four to green displays B3 and G4.

For photographers used to color-balancing filters, each increment of color adjustment equals 5 MIREDS of a color-temperature changing filter. (A MIRED is a measuring unit for the strength of a color temperature conversion filter.) Remember to set the correction back to zero when conditions change. The LCD monitor and the viewfinder information display show ⚏ when White Balance correction is engaged.

WHITE BALANCE AUTO BRACKETING

When you run into a difficult lighting situation and want to be sure of the best possible White Balance settings, another option is White Balance Auto Bracketing. This function operates a bit differently than autoexposure bracketing (see page 200). With the latter, three separate exposures are taken of a scene; with White Balance Auto Bracketing, you take just one exposure and the camera processes it to give you three different white balance options.

NOTE: Using White Balance Bracketing delays the recording of images to the memory card. In other words, the burst mode of the camera is reduced and the number of shots in a row is one-third the normal number. Pay attention to the access lamp on the back of the 60D (just above the card slot cover) to gauge when the camera has finished recording the extra images.

White Balance Auto Bracketing allows up to +/- 3 steps (again, each step is equal to 5 MIREDS of a color-correction filter) and is based on whatever White Balance mode you have currently selected. You can bracket from blue to amber, or from green to magenta. Keep in mind that even at the strongest settings, the color changes are fairly subtle. The White Balance icon on the LCD monitor will blink, letting you know that White Balance Auto Bracketing is set.

NOTE: White Balance Bracketing records an original image at the currently selected White Balance setting, then internally creates an additional set of (1) a bluer (cooler) image and a more amber (warmer) image, or (2) a more magenta and a greener image (useful in fluorescent lighting). Unlike exposure bracketing, you only need to take one shot—and you don't have to set the drive setting to ⚏. So don't expect to hear the shutter release more than once.

To access White Balance Auto Bracketing, go to ◻ᶦ and select **[WB Shift/BKT]**, then press SET. The graph screen with the horizontal (blue/amber) and vertical (green/magenta) axes appears on the LCD monitor. Rotate ◯ to adjust the bracketing amount: to the right (clockwise) to set for blue/amber bracketing, then back to zero and to the left (counter clockwise) for green/magenta. (You can't bracket in both directions.) You can also shift your setting from the center point of the graph by using ⬚. Remember to press SET to accept your settings.

The obvious use of this feature is to deal with tricky lighting conditions. However, it has other uses as well. You may want to add a warm touch to a portrait but are not sure how strong you want it. You could set the White Balance to 🌥, for example, then use WB auto bracketing to get the tone you're looking for. (The bracketing gives you the standard 🌥 white-balanced shot, plus versions warmer and cooler than that.) Or, you may run into a situation where the light changes from one part of the image to another. Here, you can shoot the bracket, then combine the White Balance versions using an image-processing program. (Take the nicely white-balanced parts of one bracketed photograph and combine them with a different bracketed shot that has good White Balance in the areas that were lacking in the first photo.)

RAW AND WHITE BALANCE

The RAW file format allows you to change White Balance after the shot either in camera or using your computer and RAW-processing software. As a result, some photographers have come to believe that when they are recording in the RAW format it is not important to select an appropriate White Balance at the time the photo is taken. While it is true that AWB and RAW give excellent results in many situations, this approach can cause consistency and workflow challenges.

White Balance choice is important because when you bring RAW files into software for processing and enhancement, the files open with the settings that you chose during initial image capture. Sure, you can edit those settings in the computer, but why not make your initial RAW image better by merely tweaking the White Balance with minor revisions at the image-processing stage rather than starting with an image that requires major correction? Of course there will be times that getting a good White Balance setting is difficult, and this is when the RAW software White Balance correction can be a big help.

SHOOT BY LIGHTING OR SCENE TYPE

This is a new feature to EOS cameras. Typically when a Canon EOS SLR is in a Basic Zone shooting mode, the camera selects the White Balance. More specifically, the White Balance is set for ⒶⓌⒷ. When the 60D is in 🌹, 🌄, 🌷, or 🏊 you can adjust White Balance using the Shoot by Lighting or Scene Type function. To set it, press ⒬ and use ✥ to highlight the **[Shoot by Lighting or Scene Type]** parameter, which is immediately above the drive mode parameter. Then use ✥ or ⌨ to choose the White Balance setting.

The choices are a little more user-friendly and use words like "sunset" as opposed to icons. In addition, Canon limits some of the choices in certain modes that might not make sense. For example, in 🌄 mode it is assumed that you are shooting outside. The last time I checked they weren't lighting the Grand Canyon with tungsten or fluorescent lights, so you'll notice that those two White Balance options are not available. Also there are no options for 🄺 or 🏖. If you are unsure which setting to use, turn on Live View and evaluate the image as you make changes.

NOTE: If you are using Shoot by Ambience together with Shoot by Lighting or Scene Type, it is important to get the White Balance set right first. So for best results, set Shoot by Lighting or Scene Type first and then adjust Shoot by Ambience.

FILE FORMATS

JPEG OR RAW

The 60D records images as either JPEG or RAW files. There has been a mistaken notion that JPEG is a file format for amateur photographers, while RAW is a format for professionals. This is really not the case. Pros use JPEG and some amateurs use RAW. (Technically, JPEG is a compression scheme and not a format, but the term is commonly used to denote a format, and that is how we will use it.)

There is no question that RAW offers some distinct benefits for the photographer who needs them, including the ability to make greater changes to the image file before the image degrades from over-processing. The 60D's RAW format (called CR2 and originally developed by Canon for the EOS-1D Mark II) includes revised processing improvements, making it more flexible and versatile for photographers than previous versions. It can also handle more metadata and is able to store processing parameters for future use.

However, RAW is not for everyone. It requires more work and more time to process than other formats. For the photographer who likes to work quickly and wants to spend less time at the computer, JPEG may offer clear advantages.

It is important to understand how the sensor processes an image. It sees a certain range of tones coming to it from the lens. Too much light (overexposed), and the detail washes out; too little light (underexposed), and the picture is dark. This is analog (continuous) information, and it must be converted to digital, which is true for any file format, including RAW and JPEG. The complete digital data is based on 14 bits of color information, which is changed to 8-bit color data for JPEG, or is placed virtually unchanged into a 16-bit file for RAW. (The fact that RAW files contain 14-bit color information is a little confusing since this information is put into a file that is actually a 16-bit format.) This occurs for each of three different color channels used by the 60D: red, green, and blue. Remember that the DIGIC 4 processor applies changes to JPEG files, while RAW files have very little processing applied by the camera.

Both 8-bit and 16-bit files have the same range from pure white to pure black because that range is influenced only by the capability of the sensor. If the sensor cannot capture detail in areas that are too bright or too dark, then a RAW file cannot deliver that detail any better than a JPEG file. But it is true that RAW allows greater control over an image than JPEG, primarily because it starts with more data, so there are more "steps" of information between the white and black extremes of the sensor's sensitivity range. These steps are especially evident in the darkest and lightest areas of the photo. So it appears the RAW file has more exposure latitude and that greater adjustment to the image is possible before banding or color tearing becomes noticeable.

JPEG format compresses (or reduces) the size of the image file, allowing more pictures to fit on a memory card. The JPEG algorithms carefully look for redundant data in the file (such as a large area of a single color) and remove it, while keeping instructions on how to reconstruct the file. JPEG is therefore referred to as a "lossy" format because, technically, data is lost. The computer rebuilds the lost data quite well as long as the amount of compression is low.

It is essential to note that both RAW and JPEG files can give excellent results. Photographers who shoot both (who use the ⟨RAW⟩+◢L quality setting) take advantage of the flexibility of RAW files to deal with tough exposure situations, and the convenience of JPEG files when they need fast and easy handling of images.

Which format will work best for you? Your own personal way of shooting and working should dictate that decision. If your shooting situation causes you to deal with problem lighting and colors, for example, RAW gives you a lot of flexibility in controlling both. If you can carefully control your exposures and keep images consistent, JPEG is more efficient.

IN-CAMERA PROCESSING OF RAW FILES

For the first time in an EOS camera the big decision of whether or not to shoot RAW has been made a little easier. Prior to the 60D, one of the major limitations of shooting RAW was that you really couldn't share the images and you couldn't take your memory card to a photo kiosk for printing. Now the 60D allows you to process your RAW images right in the camera. The processing is similar to how the camera normally processes the data from the image sensor and turns it into a JPEG file. You have control of many of the parameters that the DIGIC 4 processor uses when shooting JPEG.

To process a RAW image, enter the ⟨▣⟩ menu and use ◯ or ✸ to highlight **[RAW image processing]** and press **SET**. The 60D will display only RAW files for processing. First use ◯ or ✸ to scroll to the image you want to convert from RAW to JPEG. (Use ⟨⌂⟩ to jump through many images at a time.) Then press **SET** to select the image for processing. Use ✸ to select the parameter you want to adjust and press **SET**. Use either ◯, ⟨⌂⟩, or ✸ to change the parameter and press **SET** to exit that parameter's adjustment screen.

HINT: Once you have selected the image to process, you can make quick changes (for example, from one Picture Style to another) by merely selecting the parameter with ✸ and then, without pressing **SET** using ◯ to change the parameter.

> **NOTE:** There will be some delay when changing parameters. The effect of the change will not appear immediately on the LCD monitor. Make sure you wait to see the effect of the change before making additional adjustments.

> **HINT:** If you want to reset all your adjustments and start over, press INFO..

Once you have made all of your processing adjustments, select the ⬚ Save Image icon and press **SET**. Just like with any RAW image processing software on a computer, you don't actually write over the RAW file, you just process the image and create a new file. There are 10 parameters that you can adjust.

Brightness: You can make the image brighter. The adjustment is made in 1/3-stop increments up to +/- 1 stop. While you can make the image brighter, you should not use this adjustment as an excuse not to set a proper exposure for your scenes.

White Balance: This is the way to change the White Balance setting after the fact. You can choose from all the White Balance presets and color temperature ⬚. Custom White Balance is not available. The first setting listed on the left of the screen is the White Balance mode that was used when you took the picture. This allows you to return to the initial setting if you don't like any of the others. ⬚ is useful in that you can "dial-in" the White Balance you want by viewing the image as you turn ⬚.

Picture Style: All of the Pictures Styles, including custom Picture Styles, may be applied to the image. Use ⬚ or ⬚ to select the Picture Style. You can further modify the Picture Style once it is selected. Use ◯ or ⬚ to scroll the highlight down to the Picture Style parameters (⬚, ⬚, ⬚, etc.). Once the parameter is highlighted, use ⬚ to adjust. Press **SET** to accept the setting and return to the RAW processing menu. (See page 66 to review Picture Style settings.) Just like with the White Balance parameter above, the first setting listed on the left of the screen is the Picture Style that was used when you took the picture. This allows you to return to the initial setting.

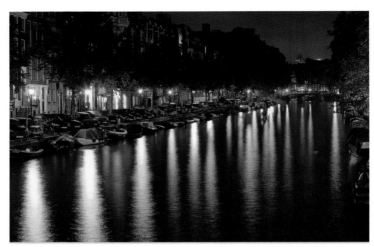

^ If there is an image that you really want to share before you get back to the computer, the in-camera RAW processing makes that a possibility.

Auto Lighting Optimizer: You can apply the auto lighting optimizer to correct dark or low-contrast images, or to turn it off if it was on.

High ISO speed noise reduction: You can apply noise reduction when you capture with a high ISO speed setting. It is difficult to see any noise on the LCD monitor because it is so small, so when you adjust this parameter you should magnify the image using ⊕. If you set noise reduction to the strongest setting, the 60D won't show you the effect on the image until you magnify it.

Image-recording quality: Here is where you decide which size JPEG to create and also how compressed the file should be.

Color space: If you know what color space you want to end up with, you can change it here. The LCD monitor doesn't use the wider Adobe RGB color space, so don't expect to see a real difference when you compare sRGB and Adobe RGB images on the LCD monitor.

Peripheral illumination correction: You can use the lens correction information stored in the 60D to adjust for changes in exposure near the edges of the image due to minor lens imperfections. As with noise reduction, in order to see the change you will need to magnify the image. The lens data must be registered with the camera in order for this function to work. (See page 99 to learn more about peripheral illumination corrections.)

Distortion correction: If the lens mounted on the 60D is recognized by the camera, this function can be used to correct minor distortions near the outer parts of the image. In order to make this correction, the DIGIC 4 chip will slightly crop the image. Distortion correction is also available in the DPP software, but without the need to crop your image. As with peripheral illumination correction, the 60D needs to know which lens you were using and the lens must be in its correction database.

Chromatic aberration correction: Chromatic aberration is when the lens in not able to focus all the wavelengths of light at the same point. In other words, the red, green, and blue do not converge on the same point. You'll notice this artifact at the outer areas of the image in high-contrast objects. It is seen as color fringing on the edges of the objects. This correction is very slight and will only be visible if the image is magnified. It will involve some cropping of the image. Just like distortion correction, the lens must be recognized by the 60D.

The in-camera processing feature in the 60D is not a replacement for Canon's Digital Photo Professional (DPP) or third-party RAW processing software. Those solutions will usually produce better results. For example, DPP will perform distortion correction with less cropping of the image.

EXTERNAL PROCESSING OF RAW FILES

In addition to the fact that it holds 14 bits of data, the RAW file offers some other advantages over JPEG. Because RAW more directly captures what the sensor sees, stronger correction can be applied to it (compared to JPEG images) before problems appear. This can be particularly helpful when there are difficulties with exposure or color balance.

Canon supplies dedicated software programs with the 60D called ZoomBrowser EX (Windows) or ImageBrowser (Mac), along with Digital Photo Professional. All these programs are specifically designed for the 60D's CR2 (RAW) files and allow you to open and smartly process them.

You can also choose third-party processing programs, such as Phase One's Capture One, Adobe's Lightroom, or others, which make converting from RAW files easier. These independent software programs can be expensive, although some manufacturers offer less expensive solutions.

One disadvantage to using third-party programs is that they may not support Canon's Dust Delete Data system (see page 32) to automatically remove dust artifacts in your images. Also, Picture Styles may not be supported in software other than Canon's.

Whatever method you choose to gain access to RAW files in your computer, you have excellent control over the images in terms of exposure and color of light. The RAW file contains special metadata (shooting information stored by the camera) that has the exposure settings you selected at the time of shooting. This is used by the RAW conversion program when it opens an image. You can make modifications to the exposure without causing too much harm to the image. (However, you can't compensate for really bad exposure in the first place.) White Balance settings can also be changed. If you use Canon's software, you can even change Picture Styles after the fact.

IMAGE SIZE AND QUALITY

The 60D offers a total of nine choices for image-recording quality, consisting of combinations of different file formats, resolutions (number of pixels), and compression rates. But let's be straight about this: Most photographers will shoot the maximum image size using RAW or the highest-quality JPEG setting. There is little point in shooting smaller image sizes except for specialized purposes. After all, the camera's high resolution is what you paid for!

All settings for recording quality are selected in ◻' under **[Quality]**, or by using the Quick Control screen and highlighting the current file-recording setting. Press **SET** and two rows of settings will appear.

The top row, which is adjusted via ⌣, contains the three different RAW settings, RAW, M RAW (medium-size RAW files), and S RAW (small-size RAW files). Use the dash found in the first position (–) when you don't want to record any RAW files.

The bottom row shows the three JPEG file sizes along with the two JPEG compression options (◢ L, ◢ L, ◢ M, ◢ M, ◢ S, and ◢ S) and two additional small file sizes S2 and S3 for a total of eight different options,

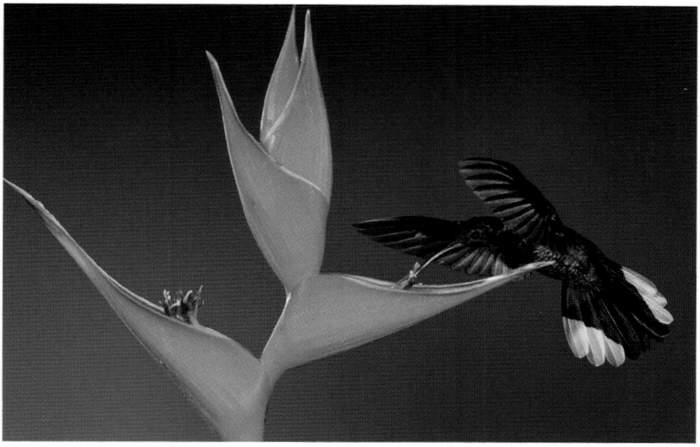

^ Large memory cards are relatively inexpensive so the choice of image size is usually pretty easy. It is a good practice to record the largest image size possible, unless you are limited by storage space.

plus off (the hyphen). Make your selections with ◯ or ✲. The symbols depict the level of compression; the letter stands for the resolution size of the image file (large, medium, and small). Less compression (higher quality) is indicated by the smoother curve on the icon, while more compression (lower quality) is indicated by the stair-step look to the curve.

New to the 60D are the two smaller JPEG settings. S2 is designed for displaying images on a photo frame and S3 is sized for emailing. Keep in mind that these files are very small and would not be useful for printing. If you want to use this feature, consider shooting RAW and then processing the image in-camera or shooting RAW+ S2 or RAW+ S3.

HINT: The blue setting in each row indicates the current setting.

Once you have made your selection on both rows, press **SET** to accept the setting and return to ◘˙. The chart on page 93 shows how these different settings affect the number of megapixels used and the image size.

The smaller RAW files are a rather new development in digital photography. As image sensors contain more and more pixels, the file sizes are getting bigger and bigger. Often photographers don't need all the resolution the image sensor can provide, but they still like the advantages of shooting and processing RAW files. Canon has answered that call by introducing these smaller RAW files.

The most useful settings are ◢ L (the largest image size for JPEG—18 megapixels (MP)—resulting in an approximate file size of 6.4MB) and [RAW] (always 18MPs; since it is uncompressed, no compression symbol is displayed; it results in an approximate file size of 24.5MB).

> **NOTE:** Near the top of the **[Quality]** menu is a status line that shows the current selection, the size of the image file in megapixels, the dimensions of the image file in pixels, and the number of images that will fit in the currently available space on the memory card (at the current image-recording quality).

The 60D can record both RAW and JPEG simultaneously. This option can be useful for photographers who want added flexibility. It records images using the same name prefix, but the different formats are designated by their extensions: .JPG for JPEG and .CR2 for RAW. You can then use the JPEG file (which takes advantage of the DIGIC 4 processor) for printing at a photo kiosk or sending to a friend via email. And you still have the RAW file for use when you need its added processing power.

If you find yourself frequently switching between quality settings, you can set Custom Function IV-2 (see pages 149-150) to change the functionality of **SET**. When this function is used, you won't have to press MENU to call up the display and then navigate to **[Quality]**. You simply press **SET** and the Quality menu appears on the LCD monitor. Then it is just a matter of selecting the desired item using 🖾 or ⬚, pressing **SET** to accept the setting, and then you can start shooting at the new setting.

When you shoot [RAW] + ◢ L the RAW file initially appears in your RAW conversion software with the same processing details as the JPEG file (including White Balance, color matrix, and exposure), all of which can be altered in the RAW software. Though RAW is adaptable, it is not magic. You are still limited by the original exposure, as well as by the tonal and color capabilities of the sensor. Using RAW is not an excuse to become sloppy in your shooting simply because it gives you more options to control the look of your images. If you do not capture the best possible file, your results will be less than the camera is capable of producing.

Each recording-quality choice influences how many photos can fit on a memory card. With the increasing sizes of memory cards this has become less of an issue, but since the 60D can also shoot video on the same card it is useful to consider memory card space. It is impossible to precisely estimate how many JPEG images fit on a card because this compression technology is variable. You can change the compression as needed (resulting in varied file sizes), but remember that JPEG compresses each file differently depending on what is in the photo and how much data is redundant. For example, a photo with a lot of detail does not compress as much as an image with a large area of solid color.

That said, the chart below gives you an idea of how large these files are and how many images may fit on a 4GB memory card. The figures are based on actual numbers produced by the camera using such a card. (JPEG values are always approximate.) Also, the camera uses some space on the card for its own purposes and for file management, so you do not have access to the entire 4GB capacity for image files.

You can immediately see one advantage that JPEG has over RAW in how a memory card is used. Even if you use the highest-quality JPEG file at the full 18MPs, you can store nearly four times the number of photos compared to what you can store when you shoot RAW.

IMAGE SIZE AND CARD CAPACITY WITH A 4GB MEMORY CARD

QUALITY	MEGAPIXELS	FILE SIZE (MB)	POSSIBLE SHOTS	MAX BURST
RAW + ◢L	Approx 17.9 + 17.9	24.5 + 6.4	100	7
M RAW + ◢L	Approx 10.1 + 17.9	16.7 + 6.4	140	7
S RAW + ◢L	Approx 4.5 + 17.9	11.1 + 6.4	180	7
RAW	Approx 17.9	24.5	130	16
M RAW	Approx 10.1	16.7	190	19
S RAW	Approx 4.5	11.1	300	24
◢L	Approx 17.9	6.4	490	58
◣L	Approx 17.9	3.2	990	300
◢M	Approx 8.0	3.4	940	260
◣M	Approx 8.0	1.7	1930	1930
◢S1	Approx 4.5	2.2	1500	1500
◣S1	Approx 4.5	1.1	3100	3100
S2	Approx 2.5	1.3	2580	2580
S3	Approx 0.35	0.3	10780	10780

All quantities are approximate, based on the photographic subject, brand, and type of memory card, ISO speed, and other possible factors.

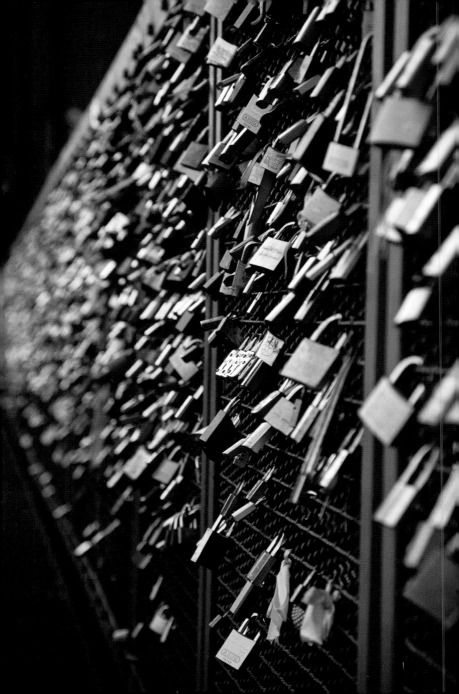

The Menu System and Custom Functions

The 60D's menu system, which can be viewed via the LCD monitor on the back of the camera, is your key to controlling the camera. DSLR menus are an indispensable way to manage a great number of settings found in these sophisticated cameras. Still, in some cameras, menus are more of a "necessary evil" because they are not easy to navigate. Canon, however, has put a great deal of thought into the design of the 60D's menus so that they can be used easily and efficiently.

USING THE MENUS

Understanding the menu system is necessary in order to get the most from your camera. To gain access to the 60D's menus, press the MENU button, located on the back of the camera near the top-right corner of the LCD monitor. The camera's eleven menus are grouped into five categories. The intuitively named menu groups, in order of appearance, are the Shooting, Playback, Set-up, Custom Functions, and My Menu menus. There is a sixth menu category called Movie Shooting mode, but it only appears when the camera is set for ᠁ via the Mode dial.

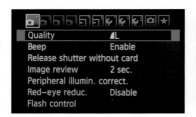
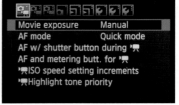

∧ The menu tabs and menu contents—particularly the first four—differ depending on if the 60D is in still or movie recording mode.

NOTE: The first time the camera is used, pressing MENU takes you to the Shooting 1 ◻ menu. After that, pressing MENU takes you to the last menu you selected, even if you have just powered the camera on.

After pressing MENU to display the menu tabs, you can scroll left or right from one menu to another in a couple of different ways: (1) use the Main dial ◌, located on the top of the camera just behind the shutter button; or (2) use the Multi-Controller ◌ (pressing right or left), found on the back of the camera to the right of the LCD monitor. To highlight menu items, scroll up or down by turning ◌ or by pressing up and down on ◌. The menus loop back on themselves; in other words, if you are at the bottom of a menu and keep scrolling down, you will go back up to the first menu item. Press the SET button, located in the middle of ◌/◌, to select and apply the item you want. Additionally, some items have further submenu options to choose from, which require you to again scroll and make selections using ◌/◌ and SET. To back out of a menu, press MENU.

NOTE: If the 60D is set for any of the Basic Zone shooting modes, some menus and menu items will not be available.

Comprised of four red-coded menus, the shooting menu category is reserved for controls that affect the functionality of the 60D when shooting stills. As you first start taking pictures with your 60D, the shooting menus will be those most used. They help control how the camera captures images, but they also give access to controlling how the camera operates when it takes a picture (e.g., whether it makes a sound during certain operations and how long images are displayed on the LCD monitor). And as you start using the flash, you'll find the available flash control to be indispensable.

QUALITY

There are several choices for file recording in the 60D. When the **[Quality]** menu item is selected, there are two main options available: The one for RAW files is controlled by 🖾, and the one for JPEG is controlled by pressing left and right on ❖. When you shoot RAW files, you can choose from three different resolutions:

- ○ **[−]**: None. Use if you want to shoot JPEG only.
- ○ **[RAW]**: highest possible pixel count (~17.9MP) and file size (~24.5MB)
- ○ **[M RAW]**: Medium RAW (~10.1MP; ~16.7MB)
- ○ **[S RAW]**: Small RAW (~4.5MP; ~11.1MB)

When shooting JPEG, you select both the quality (higher or lower amount of file compression), and the pixel count or resolution (large, medium, or small).

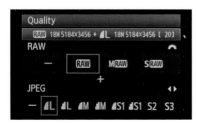

‹ Since the 60D offers a wide range of image recording resolution/ quality options, it is necessary to choose both a RAW and JPEG setting.

o **[–]**: None. Use if you want to shoot only RAW.

o **[◢ L]**: (default) highest possible pixel count (~17.9MP) with low compression; file size is ~6.4MB

o **[◢ L]**: high resolution (~17.9MP) with high compression; file size is ~3.2MB

o **[◢ M]**: Medium resolution (~8.0MP) with low compression; file size is ~3.4MB.

o **[◢ M]**: Medium resolution (~ 8.0MP) with high compression; file size is ~1.7MB.

o **[◢S1]**: Low resolution (~4.5MP) with low compression; file size is ~2.2MB.

o **[◢S1]**: Low resolution (~4.5MP) with high compression; file size is ~1.1MB.

o **[S2]**: Resolution for picture frame (~2.5MP); file size is ~1.3MB.

o **[S3]**: Resolution for email or web use (~0.35MP); file size is ~0.3MB (300KB).

As indicated, choose ◢ L (least compressed and largest size) to apply the maximum JPEG file quality and size. For the least resolution and maximum compression, choose S3, which gives you the smallest file size.

You can also choose to shoot RAW and JPEG formats simultaneously. Make your choice for each format from the options described above by turning the appropriate dial, then confirm with SET. If you select [–] for both RAW and JPEG, the camera will record every photo as ◢ L.

BEEP

Use this for those times when you want to be a bit more discreet in your picture taking. This function controls the audible signal heard during focusing and when the Self-Timer is used. There are two options:

o **[Enable]**: (Default) Sound is audible.

o **[Disable]**: No sound when focus locks or when Self-Timer is used.

RELEASE SHUTTER WITHOUT CARD

When you first go through the 60D and all of its features and functions, you may just want to experiment with the camera's controls, without necessarily taking any pictures. So, if you want to, you can simply leave the memory card out of the camera, and set this option to **[Enable]**. Just don't forget to change it back when you're ready to take some pictures!

○ **[Enable]**: (Default) This setting allows you to "take a picture" without a memory card in the 60D. The 60D shows you the image in Review, but since it is not recorded anywhere, the image disappears when the Review period is over.

○ **[Disable]**: This setting will not allow you to fire the shutter when there is no memory card in the camera. This is generally the setting to use once you get through that initial learning period. There is probably nothing more frustrating than taking a picture and not realizing that you don't have a memory card installed in the camera.

IMAGE REVIEW

This option controls how long the image stays on the LCD monitor immediately after you take the picture. I typically set this to eight seconds (it really doesn't use that much more battery power than a shorter duration).

○ **[Off]**: The image will not be displayed after recording. I use this when I don't want my subjects, most often children, to keep running to the camera to see the image. I find that checking the LCD monitor breaks the mood and stops subjects from doing whatever they were doing when I decided to photograph them.

○ **[2 sec.]**: (Default) For me, this is too short to properly evaluate the image.

○ **[4 sec.]**

○ **[8 sec.]**: This is the display duration that I prefer.

○ **[Hold]**: The image will display until you press another camera button or until the Auto Power Off function takes effect.

PERIPHERAL ILLUMINATION CORRECTION

Canon introduced this feature into their professional cameras a few years back, and now they have brought it into other models. Peripheral illumination correction refers to the fact that all lenses have some light fall-off at the edges of their optics. This appears as subtle (and sometimes not so subtle) vignetting (darkening of the image near its edges and corners). Since Canon builds their own lenses, they know how

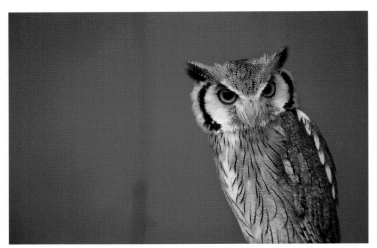

^ Subtle vignetting can help direct the viewer's eye toward the subject of the image, such as in the above image; however, too much vignetting can be distracting. Canon's peripheral illumination correction helps to minimize the latter.

much fall-off each lens model has. When you attach a lens to the 60D, the lens communicates with the camera and registers the lens model that is attached.

○ **[Enable]**: (Default) The 60D adjusts the image to reduce the vignetting. If you are using a third-party lens or an older Canon lens, this feature will be disabled.

○ **[Disable]**: No correction will occur even if the data is available to do so.

NOTE: You can select which lenses get correction via the EOS Utility software that came with the camera. See page 297.

RED-EYE REDUCTION

Red-eye is caused when the light from the built-in or camera-mounted flash reflects off the back of your subject's eyes (retinas). The 60D can emit a strong light from the front of the camera near the shutter button. This causes people's irises to narrow, which reduces the amount of flash light that enters and reflects back from their eyes. See page 249 to learn more.

○ **[Disable]**: No light is emitted from the front of the camera.

○ **[Enable]**: (Default) This causes the Red-Eye Reduction lamp on the front of the camera to illuminate and shine into your subject's eyes, reducing red-eye.

NOTE: This menu item is not available when the 60D is in Movie mode.

FLASH CONTROL

This feature not only provides control for the built-in flash, it also offers extensive control of the EX series II Canon Speedlites. For years, photographers who don't use external flashes on a daily basis have been frustrated because it is hard to remember how to adjust various settings on a Speedlite. The **[Flash control]** menu item has helped to simplify things.

NOTE: This item is not available for use with any of the Basic Zone shooting modes or in Movie Recording mode.

Besides allowing access to external Speedlite functions (Speedlite control is model-dependent), this menu item offers options that allow you to disable flash firing, set built-in flash functions, control external Speedlite Custom Function settings, and clear external Speedlite Custom Functions. Learn more about this advanced and powerful menu item in the flash chapter (see page 237).

The options in this menu are not available for any of the Basic Zone shooting modes. Instead, this menu is replaced by a limited Live View shooting menu, but is still labeled as ◘ᵢ Shooting 2 Menu.

> Several items in this menu are accessible using the Quick Control screen, but in Live View mode this is the only way to access many of these settings.

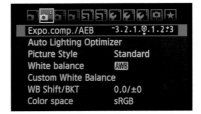

THE MENU SYSTEM AND CUSTOM FUNCTIONS

102

EXPOSURE COMPENSATION / AUTOEXPOSURE BRACKETING

Exposure Compensation is a way to override the exposure that the 60D automatically sets when you are shooting in P, Tv, and Av modes. When the **[Expo.comp./AEB]** option is selected, press SET. A scale from -5 to +5 is displayed on the LCD monitor (0 is the default). Press right or left on ❖ and you can set the exposure to be brighter (+) or darker (–); press SET to apply the exposure adjustment. The compensation value will be displayed on the scale in the viewfinder and on the LCD monitor.

NOTE: Exposure Compensation is not reset when you power off the camera. Make sure you keep an eye on the scale to double-check that Exposure Compensation is not set for a previous shot.

NOTE: The viewfinder scale only goes from -3 to +3. Exposure Compensation settings beyond -3 or +3 will be indicated with an arrow.

HINT: You can also set Exposure Compensation without going into a menu with the ◙ button. See page 199.

The 60D can also automatically bracket your exposure. Bracketing involves taking one picture with normal exposure, then one image that is underexposed (from normal) and one that is overexposed. If the camera is set for Continuous drive mode (⬛ or ⬛H; see page 183), the three shots are taken with one shutter button press. Otherwise, the shutter release button needs to be pressed three times. Until all three shots are captured, the bracketing icon ⬛ will blink on the LCD panel on top of the camera and ✳ will blink in both the viewfinder and the LCD monitor.

To set the 60D for AEB, rotate ⬛ to select the amount of Bracketing, then press **SET** to accept the setting. Unlike Exposure Compensation, Exposure Bracketing is turned off when you power off the camera.

While bracketing was an invaluable tool for shooting with film, its original purpose isn't quite as important now that digital cameras include the histogram display and allow for Image Review on the LCD monitor. But, a new digital photography technique—high dynamic range (HDR) photography—has brought Bracketing (and Auto Bracketing, in particular) to the forefront. HDR handles difficult exposure situations by merging several identically-composed images that have been recorded at different exposure settings. This is usually done with special software in the computer during post-processing. Using a tripod while shooting is also helpful. (To learn more about HDR imaging, check out *Complete Guide to High Dynamic Range Digital Photography*, by Ferrell McCollough.)

NOTE: The Quick Control screen is a quick way to access both Exposure Compensation and AEB. Once you learn how to use that screen, you'll rarely go back to using this menu item.

AUTO LIGHTING OPTIMIZER

This recent introduction to EOS cameras is an exposure correction mode that makes use of the power and design of the DIGIC 4 image-processing chip in the 60D. By evaluating the image after capture, the camera can help brighten underexposed scenes while still maintaining image details. This setting only affects JPEG images, but you can also apply this correction during RAW processing when you use Canon's software.

- **[Disable]**: This option for brightness correction is disabled.
- **[Low]**: A slight amount of correction is applied.
- **[Standard]**: (Default) This is a good starting point if you want to experiment with the Auto Lighting Optimizer control.
- **[Strong]**: The highest amount of correction is applied.

NOTE: When the 60D is in one of the Basic Zone shooting modes, Standard is automatically set.

NOTE: If Highlight Tone Priority is enabled in C.Fn II-3, then this option will be disabled.

PICTURE STYLE

Much like choosing from assorted film stocks to make images appear differently, the 60D allows you to customize the look of your images via the [Picture Style] menu selections. There are nine presets that you can use or modify, with [⊞⊞ Standard] as the default. Additionally, there are three user-defined Picture Styles that allow you to create your own look. Canon also includes software for creating custom Picture Styles on your computer, and you can visit http://web.canon.jp/imaging/picturestyle/ to download additional Picture Styles. (Learn more about Picture Styles on pages 66-72.)

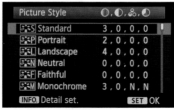

∧ At a glance you can quickly see if the Picture Styles have been modified or are set to their default setting.

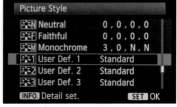

∧ User-defined Picture Styles can be either downloaded or created in the Picture Style editor software that comes with the 60D.

NOTE: In Basic Zone shooting modes, the Picture Style is automatically set. For most modes, it is set for ⊞⊞. In Portrait (🙎), the Picture Style is set for ⊞⊞ and in Lanscape (🏔), it is set for ⊞⊞. Although you cannot change a Basic Zone mode's Picture Style, you can fine-tune it. See Shoot by Ambience on page 72 for more details.

WHITE BALANCE

You can choose one of the nine White Balance (WB) presets here. When you shoot JPEG, the White Balance setting is used to create the recorded JPEG image. When you shoot RAW, the White Balance setting is just a piece of data (metadata) recorded in the RAW file header. It can be changed when processing RAW images on your computer. Even though you can change RAW White Balance later, I recommend that you get it right in the first place—when you shoot the image. It is still used to create the image displayed on the LCD that you use for evaluating your photo. The default WB setting is ⬛ⓦ (Auto). Learn more about White Balance on pages 75-84.

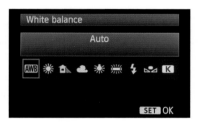

‹ Auto White Balance can work in many situations, but it is often fooled and your images might take on color casts. Try to use the given presets instead.

NOTE: When the 60D is in one of the Basic Zone shooting modes, ⬛ⓦ is automatically set. You can change White Balance via the Shoot by Lighting or Scene Type mode. See page 84 for more details.

CUSTOM WHITE BALANCE

If you use a custom White Balance ▨▨ setting, you'll need to tell the 60D which image to use as a basis for White Balance (see page 79). Once you have captured an image, select this menu item, scroll to the image you want to use as a reference and press **SET**. By storing several different White Balance reference images ahead of time, you can quickly set new custom White Balances as you move from location to location.

WHITE BALANCE SHIFT / BRACKET

Just like Exposure Compensation and Bracketing, you can adjust how the 60D does White Balance by accessing the **[WB Shift/BKT]** menu item. Learn more about this tool on page 81.

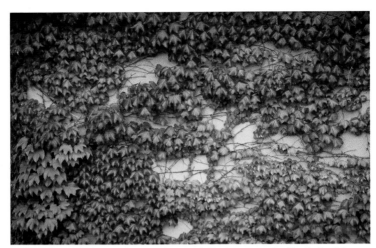

∧ If you shoot JPEG images that you plan on printing later, pay attention to the Color Space setting in the ◻ⁱ menu.

COLOR SPACE

This setting is for JPEG images. When setting Color Space, you decide what palette (range) of colors you want the 60D to use when it creates images. Somewhat like choosing between a box of 64 crayons or 128 crayons, choosing a color space can be important, depending on how you will use your images.

- ○ **[sRGB]**: (Default) This choice is the smaller color space and is typically the one used by inkjet printers.
- ○ **[Adobe RGB]**: This is a wider gamut of colors, but images may look duller on computer displays or in inkjet prints than sRGB color space.

When shooting in the RAW file format, color space is selected on the computer during image processing. When the camera is set for Adobe RGB, file names will begin with an underscore: _MG_0201 vs. IMG_0201. During Basic Zone shooting, Color Space is automatically set for sRGB. When you shoot video, Color Space is set automatically to the HD video color space.

◻️ *SHOOTING 3 MENU*

You won't spend much time in this menu on a daily basis, as it only has two menu options. But one very important setting in this menu is the ISO Auto. If you want to control how much noise is in your images, you'll want to get acquainted with that setting.

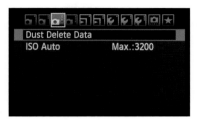

‹ Canon has placed these functions in a separate menu in order to keep lesser used functions separate.

NOTE: This menu is not available for any of the Basic Zone shooting modes.

DUST DELETE DATA

Canon's Digital Photo Professional software can be used to automatically eliminate persistent dust that may have accumulated on the 60D's sensor. This menu option shows you the date and time of the last Dust Delete Data capture, and it also takes you through the process of capturing the Dust Delete Data reference file. Learn more about dealing with dust beginning on page 32.

ISO AUTO

In addition to having the 60D automatically control the shutter speed or the aperture, you can have it control the ISO speed—the sensitivity of the camera. Since image noise increases as you increase the ISO speed, you may want to limit the maximum speed that the 60D uses when ISO is set for AUTO. That is the purpose of the options in this menu selection.

- ○ **[Max.: 400]**
- ○ **[Max.: 800]**
- ○ **[Max.: 1600]**
- ○ **[Max.: 3200]**
- ○ **[Max.: 6400]**

You should try various ISO speed settings on the 60D and then look at the images on a computer or print them—it is difficult to evaluate noise on the small LCD image. Look at the images and decide how much noise you are willing to accept. There is no one "right" setting. Once you know the ISO setting you can live with, you can set the ISO Auto maximum level.

> Usually, shooting in low light situations will require that you use higher ISO speed settings, especially if you are not using a tripod.

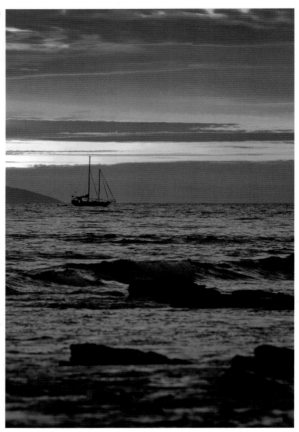

◘▮ SHOOTING 4 MENU

This menu contains settings for operating the 60D in Live View shooting mode.

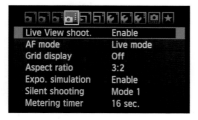

< This menu only deals with Live View shooting functions, but these settings are shared with Movie shooting.

LIVE VIEW SHOOTING

Arguably the most important innovation in digital SLRs since the histogram, Live View allows you to see on the LCD monitor what the image sensor is seeing. Normally, you would keep this option enabled. But if you find yourself accidentally hitting the button or if you hand over your camera to someone else to take a picture, you might want to disable this feature.

- ○ **[Enable]**: (Default) The camera allows Live View shooting.
- ○ **[Disable]**: You are not able to use Live View.

NOTE: When the 60D is in one of the Basic Zone shooting modes, this item is available in the ◘▮ Shooting 2 menu.

AF MODE

During Live View shooting, the autofocus (AF) sensor is blocked by the reflex mirror. This selection offers alternative AF modes.

- ○ **[Live mode]**: (Default) Uses the images coming from the image sensor to measure contrasting edges in order to determine proper focus. This method of focusing is slower and not as accurate as Quick mode.
- ○ **[⎍ Live mode]**: This focus mode detects faces in a scene where people are photographed and sets focus to ensure the people are in focus.

○ **[Quick mode]**: This selection temporarily flips the reflex mirror down and uses the normal AF sensor for setting focus. While it sounds as if flipping the mirror down and then back up would be slow, it is actually the fastest method of achieving autofocus in Live View.

> The AF mode can also be set via the Live View Quick Control screen.

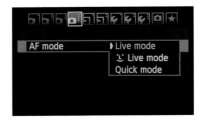

NOTE: When the 60D is in one of the Basic Zone shooting modes, this item is available in ◘▪ Shooting 2 menu.

GRID DISPLAY

This option is useful for image composition, helping you to accurately place your subject off center, giving you a more interesting photograph. A grid displayed on the LCD can also help with leveling a horizon or making sure a building looks straight.

○ **[Off]**: (Default) No grids are displayed.
○ **[Grid 1]**: A rule-of-thirds grid overlays the Live View display.
○ **[Grid 2]**: An architectural grid displays.

> Try experimenting with Grid 1 in order to practice keeping scenes level, as well as utilizing the "Rule of Thirds" composition techniques.

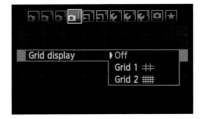

NOTE: When the 60D is in one of the Basic Zone shooting modes, this item is available in ◘▪ Shooting 2 menu.

ASPECT RATIO

The normal aspect ratio of the image sensor in the 60D is 3:2. This means any print created from a file will be 3 units wide by 2 units tall. An uncropped enlargement might be 12 x 8 inches (30.5 x 20.3 cm) or 21 x 14 inches (53.3 x 35.6 cm). When you shoot JPEG, this feature crops your images to the selected aspect ratio. This cannot be undone. When you shoot RAW, the aspect ratio is just metadata (just like White Balance) and can be changed after the fact. Aspect ratio lines will appear on the LCD monitor to indicate the current setting when a Live View image is displayed. Aspect Ratio is only available when using Live View shooting.

- ○ **[3:2]**: (Default) This is the normal aspect ratio when you don't use Live View.
- ○ **[4:3]**: Standard-definition television also uses this aspect ratio.
- ○ **[16:9]**: This widescreen aspect ratio is the same that is used for high-definition television.
- ○ **[1:1]**: A square aspect ratio where the width equals the height.

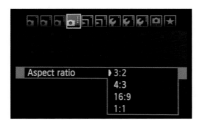

‹ The aspect ratio selection feature is only available during Live View shooting and can help you frame your subject if shooting for non-standard aspect ratios.

NOTE: When the 60D is in one of the Basic Zone shooting modes, this option is not available.

EXPOSURE SIMULATION

This feature is specific to Live View shooting. When this feature is enabled, the 60D tries to simulate on the LCD monitor what the final captured image will look like. There might be instances, such as low-light shooting, when you want to be able to see more detail in the image for focusing or judging composition. When exposure simulation is disabled, the 60D tries to present a bright image on the LCD monitor, even if your actual exposure setting will produce an under- or overexposed photo.

○ **[Enable]**: (Default) The brightness in the LCD is close to what you can expect to see in the recorded image.

○ **[Disable]**: The image presented on the LCD monitor is bright, even if your actual exposure setting will produce an under- or overexposed photo.

If this option is normally set to **[Disable]**, you can always use the Depth-of-Field Preview button (located on the front of the camera, on the right of the lens mount) to quickly see a preview of the exposure on the LCD. When Exposure Simulation is set to **[Enable]** and the LCD monitor is set for one of Live View's more comprehensive displays, the [Exp.SIM] icon is displayed at the lower right of the LCD monitor. If the 60D is not able to simulate the exposure (e.g., when the camera is set for an extremely overexposed shot), the icon blinks. If the camera is not set for Exposure Simulation (**[Disable]** is selected), [●DISP] is displayed instead.

NOTE: When the 60D is in one of the Basic Zone shooting modes this option is not available.

SILENT SHOOTING

Though there is less sound when taking a picture in Live View because the reflex mirror is already in the up position, there is still some noise as the shutter is opened, closed, and reset for the next exposure. You can use the following options to lessen the camera's noise even further.

○ **[Mode 1]:** (Default) This resets the shutter right after the picture is taken, but the noise it makes is quieter than normal.

○ **[Mode 2]:** The reset happens only after you take your finger off the shutter release. There will be no reset sound as long as you keep the shutter depressed.

○ **[Disable]:** The shutter operates normally. This option should be used when you shoot with tilt-shift lenses or close-up tubes. This is required to ensure that exposures are accurate. This option must also be selected when using a third-party flash, or else it will not fire. When you use the built-in flash or a Canon Speedlite, the 60D will not perform the Silent Shooting function.

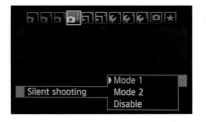

< Mode 1, the default setting, is pretty quiet, but if you want full control over when the shutter is reset, use Mode 2.

NOTE: When the 60D is in one of the Basic Zone shooting modes this option is not available.

METERING TIMER

By default, the metering system stays engaged for 16 seconds when you tap the shutter release button. Use this option if you want the meter to shut off earlier or stay on longer. The range is 4 seconds – 30 minutes. If you use Exposure Lock (✳), the metering timer setting also affects how long the exposure setting will stay locked, since the lock is released when the meter turns off.

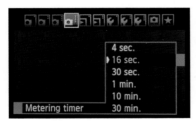

< Just like setting the image review time (see page 99), the metering time should be set long enough so that the camera doesn't shut down and reset exposure before you can take the shot.

NOTE: When the 60D is in one of the Basic Zone shooting modes, this option is not available.

⤒ *PLAYBACK 1 MENU*

This blue-coded menu is the first of two Playback menus that affect how you view images on the LCD monitor.

> Several new features have been added to the 60D's ⤒ menu.

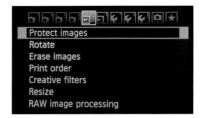

PROTECT IMAGES

This is a useful tool to prevent images from being erased. Although protecting images prevents them from being erased, formatting a memory card ignores protection and deletes all data from the card. This menu item affects movies too.

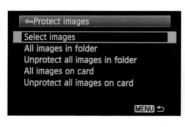

^ There are several different ways of choosing which images to protect.

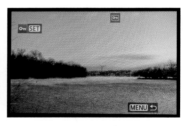

^ A key icon is displayed on any image that has been protected.

○ **[Select images]**: To protect individual images, choose this option and press **SET**. An image displays on the LCD monitor with a key symbol next to the word SET at the top left of the photo. Go through your photos one by one using ○ or ✳ (or use ✑ to jump). Push **SET** for every image you want to protect (press again to unprotect). A small ⊡ appears in the information bar at the top of the LCD monitor. Press MENU to exit.

○ **[All images in folder]**: You can protect all of the images in a particular folder. When selected, press **SET** and a list of all the folders on the memory card, together with a thumbnail of the first and last images in the currently selected folder, will be displayed. Use ○ or ⁘ to select the folder and press **SET**. Highlight **[OK]** and press **SET**.

○ **[Unprotect all images in folder]**: Use this option to remove protection from images in a particular folder. The operation is the same as above.

○ **[All images on card]**: If you want to protect all of your images, use this function. This is also useful if you want to protect most of your images. Rather than going through each folder and selectively protecting images, you can protect them all and then unprotect just the few that don't need protecting.

○ **[Unprotect all images on card]**: This feature will unprotect all images. The operation is the same as above.

CAUTION: Protecting an image does not prevent it from being deleted when you format the memory card.

HINT: If you use an Eye-Fi memory card, protecting your images takes on more significance. You can set up your Eye-Fi card to upload / download only those images that have been protected. (Learn more about Eye-Fi cards on page 130.)

ROTATE

The 60D has a built-in sensor that can tell if you are holding the camera in a horizontal or vertical orientation. When a feature called **[Auto rotate]** in the ❡˙ (Set-up 1) menu is turned on, the orientation data is embedded in the image file and the image displays correctly on the camera's LCD or on your computer (see page 127). If **[Auto rotate]** is turned off and you want to rotate your image, use **[Rotate]** instead. When selected, the last image displayed is presented. Press **SET** to rotate the image clockwise, press **SET** again to rotate it counterclockwise. Press **SET** again to return to the original orientation. Use ○ or ⁘ to scroll through (or use ⌒ to jump) to other images you wish to rotate. Press MENU to exit after rotating the desired image files.

ERASE IMAGES

The great thing about digital cameras is that you can delete images that you don't like, which frees up room on your memory card. Even though this menu item refers to images, it performs this function on movies too.

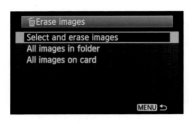 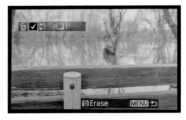

∧ If you have to delete a number of images, using the Erase Images function will lessen the number of button presses.

○ **[Select and erase images]**: To erase individual images, choose this option and press **SET**. Use ○ or ❋ to scroll through your images (or use 🗇 to jump). Press up on ❋ whenever you want to delete an image (press down on ❋ to uncheck). A checkmark is placed next to a 🗑 icon in the upper left corner of the display. The total count of how many images you have selected for deletion will also be indicated. Once you have selected the images to delete, press 🗑 to erase the images. You'll be asked to confirm the erasure. Although this feature seems similar to erasing images while in Image Playback mode, it allows you to select multiple images and you only have to confirm the deletion once. (During Playback, you have to press 🗑 and confirm for each image.)

○ **[All images in folder]**: Select this menu item if you want to erase images in a particular folder. When selected, press **SET** and a list of all the folders on the memory card, together with a thumbnail of the first and last image in the currently selected folder, will be displayed. Use ○ or ❋ to select the folder and press **SET**. Highlight **[OK]** to confirm that you want to erase all of the images and press **SET**. Only those files not protected will be deleted. This function does not delete the folder.

○ **[All images on card]**: This will erase all the images on the card. Why would you erase all the images on the card instead of formatting the card? Because formatting the card erases images that are protected (see Protect images menu item, detailed on page 114); using the **[All images on card]** selection leaves protected images alone. Like deleting all images in a folder, this function does not delete folders, just the files within them.

> **NOTE:** Once a file is erased, it is gone for good. Make sure you no longer want an image or video before making the decision to erase it.

PRINT ORDER

You can specify the images to print when you bring your memory card to a photo retailer, or when you connect the 60D directly to a PictBridge-capable printer. Learn more in the Output chapter (see pages 285-308).

CREATIVE FILTERS

Newly introduced to Canon EOS cameras with the 60D, Creative Filters allow you to apply effects to images and create new JPEG files. You can only apply filters to RAW (but not M RAW and S RAW) and JPEG files. You can't apply Creative Filters to movies. Applying a Creative Filter does not affect the original image, but creates a new JPEG. Each filter allows you to adjust one parameter of the effect. There a four filters that you can choose from:

Grainy B/W: Don't confuse this with the Monochrome Picture Style. Instead, Grainy B/W results in a heavily treated image. Grain is added and contrast increased to create a gritty image. You can use this filter for interesting treatments of nighttime shooting. You can adjust the contrast to Low, Standard, or Strong.

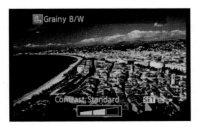

< You can use Creative Filters to experiment with different looks. You might not use the exact look that the creative filter creates, but it might give you an idea of an effect to try in your image-editing software.

Soft focus: This is similar to adding a diffusing filter on the front of the lens. You can adjust the contrast to Low, Standard, or Strong. This could be useful to soften skin tones on portraits. Be aware that it applies the effect to the entire image, not just skin tones.

Toy camera effect: With this filter, you can turn your 60D into a poorly constructed toy camera. This filter adds a strong vignette to the image, darkening the corners and reducing the contrast slightly. It can also add a color cast to the image. You can adjust the color cast of this effect to Cool, Standard, or Warm.

> This effect can give an old '50s-style look to images.

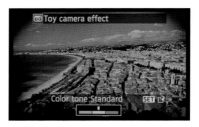

Miniature effect: A very popular effect these days is to shoot a scene with a special lens called a tilt-shift lens. This lens allows you to change the focus plane of the image. The overall effect makes the scene look like a diorama or a miniature of a scene. While Canon does sell several tilt-shift lenses for EOS cameras including the 60D, the lenses are expensive and are limited in use for general photography. But the effect has become so popular that many people are approximating the look by selectively blurring sections of an image.

This Creative Filter blurs the whole image except what appears in a rectangular strip overlaid on the image. Use ○/✳ to position the strip of the scene that will be in focus. Press MENU to flip between a horizontal or vertical orientation of the in-focus section. Typically you would use horizontal for images captured when holding the 60D in a horizontal orientation and vertical for vertical images.

> A popular technique in photography is the miniature effect created by using a special lens called a tilt-shift lens. It can make a real scene look like a miniature scene—almost like you were looking at a tiny dollhouse.

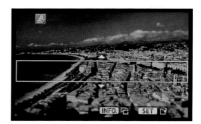

When you adjust any of these Creative Filter parameters, it takes some time to process the image. Be patient, because you won't see the image update with the effect immediately.

RESIZE

When the 60D is set for its highest resolution, it can produce very large files. There may be times when the file sizes are too big. Sometimes you may want to quickly resize an image to email it to someone, for example. At one time, you had to use a computer to resize a file; now you can do it in-camera.

To resize an image, choose **[Resize]** and press **SET**. The camera will display the last image captured. The 60D will allow you to resize all types of JPEG images except S3 size. It will not allow you to resize RAW images. (Use the RAW image processing option detailed in the next menu selection to resize RAW files.) If all of the images on the card are incompatible (RAW or S3 JPEGs), then the camera will display a message saying there are no compatible images to resize.

Scroll through to the image you want to resize using ○ or ❖ (or use ⌕ to jump). Push **SET** to select the image to resize. You can then use ○ or ❖ to choose from **[M]**, **[S1]**, **[S2]**, or **[S3]** for a new image size. Then press **SET**, then highlight **[OK]** and press **SET** again to create a new file at the selected size.

> **NOTE:** If a file has already been resized or you have selected a file to resize that is already at M, S1, S2 or S3 size, then that option will not be available.

RAW IMAGE PROCESSING

Since RAW images need to be processed before they can be used, until now, Canon EOS users had to download images to a computer and process them before they could share them. New with the 60D is the ability to capture a RAW file and process the file in the camera to create a JPEG image.

> **NOTE:** In-camera RAW processing is only possible when you shoot with RAW setting. If you shoot with M RAW or S RAW you will have to use DPP or another RAW processing software on a computer.

To process a RAW image, choose this option and press **SET**. The camera will display the last RAW image captured. JPEG images are already processed so they will not display. If all of the images on the card are JPEGs, then the camera will display a message saying there are no compatible images to process. Use ○ or ✳ (or use ◌ to jump) to scroll through to the image you want to process. Push **SET** to select the image. There are 10 processing parameters that you can adjust:

Brightness: You can make the image brighter. The adjustment is made in 1/3-stop increments up to +/- 1 stop. While you can make the image brighter, you should not use this adjustment as an excuse not to set a proper exposure for your scenes because no amount of adjustment after the fact can take the place of a good initial exposure.

White Balance: Use this adjustment to change the White Balance setting after the fact. You can choose from all the White Balance presets plus Color temperature **K**. Custom White Balance is not available. The first setting listed on the left of the screen is the White Balance mode that was used when you took the picture. This allows you to return to the initial setting if you don't like any of the others. **K** is useful in that you can just dial in the white balance you want by viewing the image as you turn ◌.

Picture Style: All of the Pictures Styles, including Custom Picture Styles, are available to apply to the image. Use ◌ or ✳ to select the Picture Style. You can further modify the Picture Style once it is selected. Use ○ or ✳ to scroll the highlight down to the Picture Style parameters (Sharpness, Contrast, Saturation, etc.). Once the parameter is highlighted, use ✳ to adjust. Press **SET** to accept the setting and return to the RAW processing menu (see page 66 to review Picture Style settings). Just as with White Balance above, the first setting listed on the left of the screen is the Picture Style that was used when you took the picture. This allows you to return to the initial setting.

Auto Lighting Optimizer: To apply correction for dark or low-contrast images, you can apply the Auto Lighting Optimizer, or turn it off if it was on when the picture was taken.

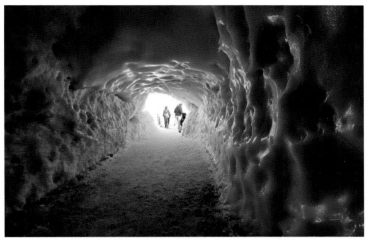

^ Capturing images as RAW files has many benefits. In the case of a high-contrast image with a wide range from light to dark, you can use the 60D's internal RAW image processing to correct the RAW file and achieve a better-looking exposure.

High ISO Speed Noise Reduction: You can apply noise reduction in images captured with a high ISO speed setting. It is difficult to see any noise on the LCD monitor because it is so small, so when adjusting this parameter you should magnify the image using 🔍. If you set Noise Reduction to the strongest setting, the 60D won't show you the effect on the image until you magnify it.

Image-Recording Quality: Here is where you decide which size JPEG to create as well as how compressed the file should be.

Color Space: If you know what color space you want to end up with, you can change it here. The LCD monitor doesn't use the wider Adobe RGB color space, so don't expect to see a real difference when you compare sRGB and Adobe RGB images on the LCD monitor.

Peripheral Illumination Correction: You can use the lens correction information stored in the 60D to adjust for changes in exposure near the edges of the image due to minor lens imperfections. As with Noise Reduction, in order to see the change, you will need to magnify the image. The lens data must be registered with the camera in order for this function to work. (See page 99 to learn more about Peripheral Illumination Corrections.)

Distortion Correction: If the lens mounted on the 60D is recognized by the camera, this function can be used to correct minor distortions near the outer parts of the image. In order to make this correction, the DIGIC 4 chip will slightly crop the image. Distortion correction is also available in the DPP software, but without the need for cropping. As with Peripheral Illumination Correction, the 60D needs to know which lens you were using and the lens must be in its correction database.

Chromatic Aberration Correction: Chromatic aberration is when the lens is not able to focus all the wavelengths of light at the same point. In other words, the red, green, and blue do not converge on the same point. You'll notice this artifact, referred to as color fringing, at the outer areas of the image in high-contrast objects. This correction is very slight and will only be visible if the image is magnified. It will involve some cropping of the image. Just like Distortion Correction, the lens must be known by the 60D.

Once you have made all of your processing adjustments, select [🄲] and press SET. Just like with any RAW image processing software on a computer, you don't actually write over the RAW file, you just process the image and create a new file.

HINT: If you want to reset all of your adjustments and start over, press INFO.

NOTE: If the 60D is in one of the Basic Zone shooting modes, the [RAW image processing] option is not available.

HIGHLIGHT ALERT

This is an important tool for evaluating exposure on the LCD monitor, second only to the histogram. Overexposed areas of an image can extend beyond the dynamic range of the sensor and become pure white in the image (clipped), with no detail.

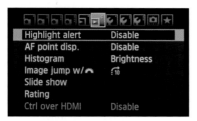

‹ Initially, Highlight alert can be distracting, but once you are accustomed to it, it can be a great feature to help you judge your exposure.

○ **[Disable]**: (Default) No blinking areas will display on the LCD monitor during Image Review or Playback.

○ **[Enable]**: This will cause overexposed areas to blink on the LCD monitor during Image Review or Playback. While there may be times when overexposing parts of the image is okay, this feature shows you just how much is overexposed.

AUTOFOCUS POINT DISPLAY

This option identifies the AF point(s) used to set focus when the image is displayed on the LCD monitor. When the 60D is set for automatic AF point selection, you can quickly determine which AF point it used to set focus for each image. Sometimes this display can be distracting, for instance when you are trying to evaluate other aspects of the image.

○ **[Enable]**: The Playback image shows red AF point overlays to indicate the AF points that were active when the image was captured.

○ **[Disable]**: (Default) No overlays display on AF points.

HISTOGRAM

The 60D offers two types of histograms for evaluating image exposures. Use this menu selection to choose which will be displayed during Playback.

○ **[Brightness]**: (Default) Shows the overall distribution of tones in the image.

○ **[RGB]**: Shows the tonal distribution within each color channel.

NOTE: The histogram display is based on a JPEG image. If you are shooting only RAW, the histogram will still be based on a JPEG file display. There is much more to learn about using histograms on pages 205-206.

IMAGE JUMP W /

When you are in Playback mode, you scroll through images one at a time using ○ or ❁. By using 🗘 instead, you can navigate more quickly by jumping past multiple images. The **[Image jump w/ 🗘]** feature sets the number of pictures that you are jumping past at a time. You can also jump by date, folder, movies, still photos, or image rating. This is useful if you shoot both stills and movies and want to see just the movies that are scattered about in the image folder. Your options are:

○ **[1 image]**
○ **[10 images]** (Default)
○ **[100 images]**
○ **[date]**
○ **[folder]**
○ **[movies only]**
○ **[stills only]**
○ **[image rating]** Use 🗘 to select the minimum star rating.

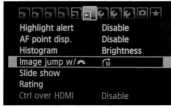

＾ When the 60D is in Playback mode, the Mode dial will let you jump through images quickly.

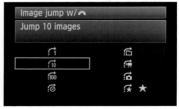

＾ There are several options for how you can navigate through the images on your memory card.

The image rating option is a new one, introduced with the 60D (see page 126). You can give an image a rating of from 0 to 5 stars. If you want to just scroll through your best images, you can jump via the star rating. In other words, if you set the jump for 3 stars, it will show you images that are rated 3 stars and above.

SLIDE SHOW

This option automatically creates a slide show on the LCD monitor of the images that have been recorded on your memory card. Using the **[Set up]** submenu, you can set the length of time each image is displayed (from 1 to 20 seconds). The slideshow can be set to repeat, you can choose from three transition effects, and you can also choose to filter the files you include in your slideshow:

O **[All images]**: Includes all still photos and movies.

O **[Date]**: Select a specific date for stills and movies. Press INFO. to select the date.

O **[Folder]**: Select a specific folder to use for the slide show. Press INFO. to select the folder from a list of folders.

O **[Movies]**: All movies, and only movies, will be played back.

O **[Stills]**: All stills, and only the stills, will be displayed.

O **[Rating]**: Select a minimum rating (number of stars) for images to be displayed.

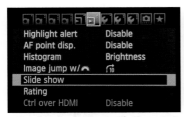 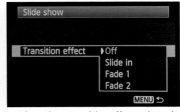

∧ The slide show option in ▣ allows you to select from three transition effects, shown in the menu selection above.

RATING

The 60D is the first Canon EOS camera to offer this feature. If you take a lot of pictures, you'll often have to spend of lot of time sorting through images to determine which are your best shots. Since memory cards hold more and more images and there is no longer a processing cost like we had with film, it is not uncommon to end up with hundreds of images to sort through. Rating images is a great way to mark them so that you can easily look at just your best shots. Typically, this sorting process is done on the computer. With the 60D, you can now do it right in the camera.

To rate an image, highlight the [Rating] selection and press SET. An image displays on the LCD monitor with a star symbol at the top left along with the rating of the current image. Press up on ☀ to increase the rating from OFF to 5 stars. Press down on ☀ to decrease the rating. Across the top of the display will be a count of how many images are rated at 1 star, 2 stars, 3 stars, and so on. Go through your photos one by one using ◯ or ☀ (or use ◲ to jump) and push up or down on ☀ to adjust the rating for each image. Press MENU to exit.

NOTE: The rating will carry over to the software that comes with the 60D. It is also supported in some operating systems and image-editing applications.

CONTROL OVER HDMI

HDMI is a way of connecting your 60D to a digital TV. Some sets use the HDMI CEC (Consumer Electronics Control), which will allow you to control the playback of the 60D via the television's remote.

○ [Disable]: Control of playback is through the 60D.
○ [Enable]: When enabled, use the left and right arrow buttons of your TV's remote to control playback of images.

☝°SET-UP 1 MENU

Color-coded yellow, this is the first of three Set-up menus, each of which presents selections to control overall camera operation.

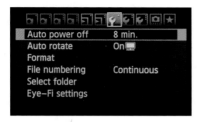

Auto power off   8 min.
Auto rotate   On🖵
Format
File numbering   Continuous
Select folder
Eye–Fi settings

‹ The 60D battery has great capacity, so a longer Auto Power Off setting will not use much energy. But if you are shooting in cold weather or don't have ready access to a battery charger, you should use the shorter times.

AUTO POWER OFF

The 60D shuts itself off after a period of idleness in order to save battery power. The **[Auto power off]** setting offers six options, ranging from 1 minute to 30 minutes, plus an **[Off]** setting (i.e., the camera will not power off). Even when you select **[Off]**—which you might elect to do, for example, if you shoot in a studio with the optional AC adapter—the LCD monitor will still turn off after 30 minutes of inactivity.

AUTO ROTATE

The 60D has a positional sensor that can determine if you are holding the camera vertically or horizontally. This information is embedded in the image's file header so that, when the image is displayed, it is oriented properly.

○ **[On🗖🖵]**: (Default) Images shot with the 60D in a vertical position are rotated to display correctly on the camera's LCD monitor and on your computer monitor.

○ **[On🖵]**: The vertical image is only rotated on the computer's display. I like this option because the image is larger on the 60D's LCD monitor when it is not rotated, allowing me to evaluate it more easily. And, since I am usually still holding the camera vertically, I don't have to physically rotate the camera back to a horizontal shooting position to view the image.

○ **[Off]**: The image is not rotated on the LCD monitor or the computer screen. Even if you later set this option to **[On ☐ 🖵]** or **[On 🖵]**, images previously shot will not have embedded orientation data. If you want to rotate the image in-camera at that point, you must use **[Rotate]** in ⊡ˈ (see page 115).

NOTE: Automatic image rotation on your computer depends on the software you use to view your images.

FORMAT

SD cards need to be formatted for use in the 60D. Format any card the first time it is used in your 60D, as well as on a semi-regular basis after that so the card will continue to function at its best. The **[Format]** menu item performs this function. It is also a quick (though slightly risky) way to determine how much space (in GBs) has been used on your memory card, as that information is displayed on the formatting screen right before you confirm that you want to format. Formatting should always be done in the camera rather than on the computer. Learn more about when to format on pages 28-29.

> The Format option will show you how much free space you have on the memory card.

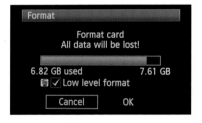

CAUTION: There is no "undo" for formatting. Formatting ignores any file protection settings, and all data will be erased. While you might be able to use a recovery service or software in an attempt to retrieve your data, there is no guarantee, and recovery services are very expensive. If you do run into a situation where you need to retrieve data, make sure that you don't attempt to write any new file information to the memory card in the interim.

The 60D stores image and movie files in folders. Within each folder, the filenames must be unique. The [File numbering] menu item determines how the 60D will assign subsequent filenames.

○ **[Continuous]**: (Default) File numbers increase by increments of one, no matter what memory card is inserted in the camera. If there is a conflict between a new file and an existing file (i.e., if you use a card with files already on it), the new file picks up the number sequence after the last file in the folder. To avoid confusion, use freshly formatted cards or create new folders.

○ **[Auto reset]**: This option resets the file name to start at 0001 each time you insert a memory card in the camera. Once again, if there is a conflict with existing files on the inserted memory card, the numbering picks up after the last image in the folder. As stated above, use freshly formatted cards or create new folders to avoid confusion.

○ **[Manual reset]**: This allows you to control when to reset the file numbering. When you select this option, a new folder is created and the file numbering is reset to 0001. This is useful when you are photographing in different locations and want to group your images by location.

When you decide how to set your file numbering, consider how you will deal with the images once they are on your computer. I try to avoid the possibility of duplicate file names, and I use folders on my computer to group my images, so I prefer to use the **[Continuous]** option. If you want to organize your images into folders before moving them to your computer—for example, you might want to organize by day or location— you'll want to select **[Manual reset]** to create a new folder.

> **NOTE:** When the camera reaches folder 999 and image 9999, even if there is sufficient space on the card, the 60D will not be able to record another picture until you replace the memory card.

SELECT FOLDER

This menu item displays a list of the folders on the memory card so that you can select which one you want to record to. It also has an option that allows you to create a new folder.

O **[Create folder]**: Folder names start at 100CANON and increase by increments of one (e.g., 101CANON, 102CANON, etc.).

Creating folders is a great way to organize your images before you download to your computer. When you travel, you might create a folder at the beginning of the day, or at each location where you are photographing. You also might use folders to separate your images from your movies.

You can also use your computer to create a folder-numbering scheme on the memory card. Start with a DCIM folder at the top level. Within that folder, create folders using a naming scheme of 100AAAAA. The first three digits must be numbers only, between 100 and 999, and must be unique. There cannot be two folders that start with the same three digits, even if the last five characters are different. The five following characters can be upper- or lower-case letters from A to Z, numbers, or an underscore. Do not use special characters or spaces.

NOTE: If you use custom folders, you must first format the memory card in the 60D. Do not use the computer to format the card.

EYE-FI SETTINGS

The 60D supports the use of Eye-Fi cards for wireless image-transmission. These specially designed SD memory cards have a tiny embedded wireless radio and will transmit images via wireless hotspots to your computer. Learn more about Eye-Fi on page 288.

O **[Eye-Fi trans.]**: This selection allows you to enable and disable wireless transmission of images.
O **[Connection info.]**: Brings up a status screen giving you detailed information about the Eye-Fi card, including the currently connected Wi-Fi network name, connection status, and the Eye-Fi card firmware version.

NOTE: This menu selection is only displayed when you use an Eye-Fi card.

LCD BRIGHTNESS

This menu item allows you to set the LCD monitor's brightness level. Use ○ or ※ to choose among seven levels of brightness.

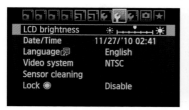

∧ Make sure to adjust the LCD brightness depending on the viewing conditions.

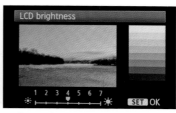

∧ When setting the LCD brightness, the last image played back will be displayed along with a gray scale so that you can set the LCD brightness.

DATE / TIME

Use this option to adjust the date and time that is recorded with images. You should check this setting when you travel so that you are able to keep track of when you took pictures. Date and time information is retained in the camera even when you change batteries. See page 21 for details on setting the date and time.

LANGUAGE 🗩

The 60D is able to display menus and information in 25 different languages. If you accidentally change the language and can't read the new language to set it back, just look for the comic-strip-word-bubble icon 🗩 in the menu. No matter which language the camera is set for, selecting this icon will take you back to the main list of languages.

VIDEO SYSTEM

Countries in North America (and a few other countries) use a system called NTSC for analog television; a system called PAL is used outside of North America. When you connect the camera using the A/V terminal (not HDMI), you need to match the 60D's video setting to the video monitor system. Don't worry if you are not sure which to use. You can't harm anything by using the wrong setting; the television just won't display the 60D's images.

NOTE: The **[Video system]** option is also used to access video frame rates. With NTSC, the frame rate selection will include 30 and 60 frames per second (fps). When set for PAL, the frame rates will include 25 and 50 fps.

SENSOR CLEANING

The 60D is equipped with an Auto Cleaning System that vibrates part of the sensor assembly to shake off any accumulated dust.

- ○ **[Auto cleaning ⌂]:** (Default) This option engages the cleaning function when the camera powers on and off. You should normally leave this option on. Probably the only time you would turn it off is when you are using the **[Dust Delete Data]** function and are shooting a series of shots (without moving the camera), so you don't want to keep shooting reference frames for the detection system.
- ○ **[Clean now ⌂]:** Start the Auto Cleaning function immediately.
- ○ **[Clean manually]:** This option to manually clean the sensor should only be used with care. See pages 30-32 to learn more about sensor cleaning. This menu option is not available in the Basic Zone modes.

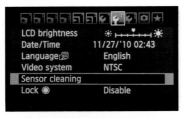

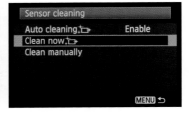

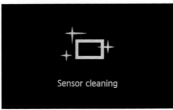

You should always have the Auto cleaning turned on. If you start noticing dust spots on your images, use the [Clean now] function to activate a cleaning cycle.

LOCK ○

The Quick Control dial is used to dial in Exposure Compensation or set other exposure parameters when the 60D is not in one of the Basic Zone modes. It is possible that you might accidentally rotate this control when handling the camera. By engaging the lock function you can prevent this from happening.

- ○ **[Disable]**: The Quick Control dial will operate normally.
- ○ **[Enable]**: When the lock is enabled, it is first necessary to press the UNLOCK button immediately below ○ before you can use the Quick Control dial to adjust exposure compensation, or aperture (when the Mode dial is set for **M** or **B**). The control is only unlocked for 4 seconds when shooting stills.

NOTE: The lock system does not apply when you use ○ to make menu selections.

♥: *SET-UP 3 MENU*

BATTERY INFO.

This menu item brings up a display that presents valuable information about the battery in your camera. Among other data, this screen will tell you:

1. The remaining battery level as a percentage.
2. The number of pictures taken since the battery was last charged. (The shutter count is reset when the battery is recharged.)
3. How well the battery is recharging.

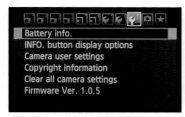

^ The battery info function allows you to keep track of battery performance.

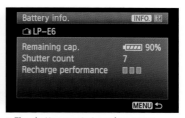

^ The shutter count stores how many pictures were taken with the installed battery since it was last charged.

Press INFO. while viewing the **[Battery info.]** screen to register up to six batteries so you can keep track of performance and charge level. This feature only works with genuine Canon batteries (LP-E6).

> The 60D can keep track of up to six different batteries.

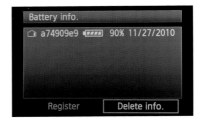

INFO. *BUTTON DISPLAY OPTIONS*

INFO. cycles through various displays on the LCD monitor (see page 49). Use ○ to highlight a desired option and press **SET** to select it with a √ and add it to the cycle.

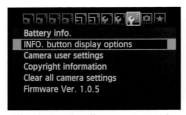

⌃ The menu option allows you to control which display option appears each time you press the INFO button.

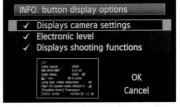

⌃ If you find yourself not using one of the display options, you can turn it off.

○ **[Displays camera settings]**

○ **[Electronic level]:** This option will display a level on the LCD screen to help keep the camera perfectly level.

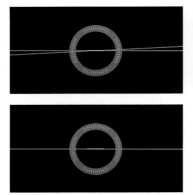

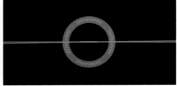

The level display can help you to keep the horizons level in your shots.

○ **[Displays shooting functions]:** This is invaluable when you are shooting. It displays almost all the parameters: exposure settings, file-recording mode, metering, White Balance, and battery level. More importantly, it gives you access to (and follows the same layout as) the Quick Control screen.

After the last checked option displays, another press of INFO. blanks the screen completely.

CAMERA USER SETTINGS

There is a customizable setting on the Mode dial—C. This allows you to customize the 60D for your shooting style. For example, you may want a setting for taking portraits of people where the depth of field is narrow (large aperture) so that the background is more out-of-focus. Use this menu option once you have customized the camera.

○ **[Register settings]**: First set up your camera for the custom mode you would like to register. For example, choose the drive mode, AF mode, metering mode, shooting mode, etc. Once the camera is set up the way you want, highlight this option and press **SET**. The settings will be stored and can be immediately recalled by rotating the Mode dial to C.

○ **[Clear settings]**: Select to make the camera user settings revert to default.

The breadth of camera settings that can be stored is quite comprehensive. Even though the settings have been stored, when you switch to C mode on the Mode dial, you can still adjust any of the stored settings. However, those adjustments will not be stored when you turn off the camera.

COPYRIGHT INFORMATION

The 60D can embed your name and other copyright information in every image captured by the camera. Entering the data can be a bit tedious using the camera controls. A better option is to use Canon's EOS Utility software that comes with the 60D. See page 298 for more information.

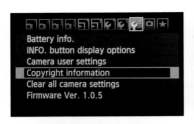

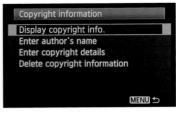

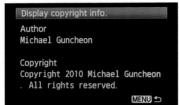

While there is more to copyrighting your images than just setting the copyright information on your camera, it doesn't hurt to enter this information so that people are aware of who created the photograph. This information is written into the metadata of the image.

○ **[Display copyright info.]**: Use this to display the information that will be embedded in each file.

○ **[Enter author's name]**: Use this to enter your name. Even if you don't want to deal with copyrighting your images, it is still a good idea to identify yourself as the photographer.

○ **[Enter copyright details]**: This is where you would enter information about the rights reserved for your image.

○ **[Delete copyright information]**: Resetting the camera via the **[Clear settings]** option will not reset the copyright information. This option is the only way to erase copyright data via camera controls. (It can also be deleted via the Canon EOS Utility software.)

CLEAR SETTINGS

This is a useful tool when you are first trying out your camera. You may activate so many features and options that you'll become a bit overwhelmed! This menu selection allows you to quickly and easily return to the camera's default settings.

○ **[Clear all camera settings]**: While the option says "all," it does not reset the Custom Functions, Camera User settings, Date / Time, Language, Video System, Copyright Information, or My Menu items.

FIRMWARE VERSION

Cameras run on software, and firmware is the portion of the software that can be updated. This option displays the current firmware version. Check the Canon support site on a regular basis to see if the firmware version has been updated. Once a new firmware update is available, follow the procedure that comes with the update. It usually requires that you copy the update to a memory card, insert it into the camera, and select **[Firmware Ver.]** to start the update process. Afterwards, confirm the version number to make sure the update installed correctly. Always follow the instructions exactly or you may end up with an unusable 60D.

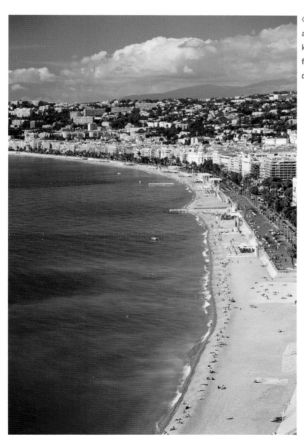

‹ Life is a beach as long as you keep your 60D's firmware up to date.

138

In addition to allowing choices about exposure mode, metering, drive, Picture Style, and so forth, the 60D also permits you to further customize and personalize the camera settings to fit your method of, and approach to, photography. This is done through the Custom Functions menu 🔧. Some photographers never use these settings, while others use them all the time. The camera won't take better photos by itself when you change these settings, but using the Custom Functions may make it easier for you to take better pictures with the camera.

NOTE: Custom Functions can only be used in the Creative Zone shooting modes.

The 60D has 20 different built-in Custom Functions (though they are not available in the Basic Zone shooting modes). Canon organizes them into four groups: C.Fn I: Exposure, C.Fn II: Image, C.Fn III: Autofocus/ Drive, and C.Fn IV: Operation/Others.

Custom Functions are found in the 🔧 menu. There is also an option to reset all the Custom Functions to their default value. Once in the 🔧 menu, navigate to the desired Custom Functions group—I through IV— using ○/✷ and press **SET**. Use ○/✷ to select the Custom Function you want to adjust and again press **SET**. Use ○/✷ to select a new option and press **SET** to accept. The new setting will be displayed in blue. The setting number will appear below the function number in the lower left of the LCD monitor. Press MENU once if you want to select another function in the same group. To exit 🔧, press MENU repeatedly or lightly tap the shutter release button.

The current function number will be displayed in the upper right corner of the LCD monitor when you are navigating through a particular set of custom function options, while all of the function numbers and their current settings are displayed at the bottom of the LCD monitor. Settings displayed in blue indicate that the particular Custom Function is not set for its default.

NOTE: The first option within each Custom Function is the default setting for the camera.

C.FN I: EXPOSURE

With this group of functions you can customize how the 60D controls exposure. You will likely find the function most used in this group to be ISO expansion, which allows you to increase the 60D's already impressive sensitivity.

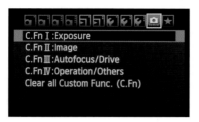

‹ The Custom Functions are divided into four operational groups.

C.Fn I-1 Exposure Level Increments: Incremental steps for shutter speed, aperture, Exposure Compensation, and Autoexposure Bracketing (AEB) can be set here.

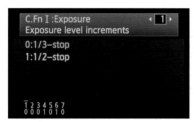

‹ If you want finer control over your exposure settings, use the default 1/3-stop; but, if you want a greater exposure difference when bracketing your exposure, use 1/2-stop.

When this option is changed, you'll see a difference in the exposure scale displayed in the viewfinder and LCD monitor. When in 1/2-stop, there is only one mark between full stops instead of two.

C.Fn I-2 ISO Speed Setting Increments: Like exposure level increments, you can change the ISO speed increment.

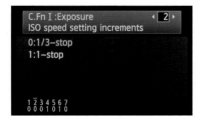

‹ As with many custom functions, there is no "right" setting. If you want to have more dramatic changes when adjusting ISO speed, use 1-stop.

With the default settings, the ISO speeds will be: 100, 125, 160, 200, 250, 320, 400, etc. With the 1-stop setting the ISO series will be: 100, 200, 400, etc.

C.Fn I-3 ISO Expansion: You can extend the ISO speed range into the expanded ISO values using this Custom Function.

○ 0: **[Off]**: The normal ISO range of the camera will be used (100 – 6400).
○ 1: **[On]**: An expanded ISO range is made available (100 – 12800).

> If you use ISO Expansion, make sure that you evaluate the image on a computer display (or by printing the image) in order to see the actual amount of noise, and whether that noise is acceptable.

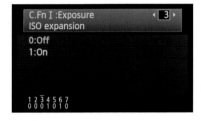

NOTE: ISO 12800 is represented by "H."

C.Fn I-4 Bracketing Auto Cancel: This function allows the camera to cancel Bracketing—both Exposure Bracketing and White Balance Bracketing—when you turn the camera power off, when camera settings are cleared, when the flash (built-in or accessory) is ready, when the camera is set to Movie mode, or when bulb exposure (**B**) is selected.

> If you do a lot of bracketing, such as with HDR photography, consider switching from the default setting.

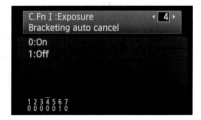

NOTE: If C.Fn I-4 is set to **[Off]** and a flash is used, the bracketing will not be executed, but the amount set for bracketing will be remembered.

C.Fn I-5 Bracketing Sequence: You can change the order of the bracketed shots with this function—with both Exposure Bracketing and White Balance Bracketing. Either the first shot or the middle shot is normal exposure. When using White Balance Bracketing, the + represents amber and green, the – represents blue and magenta.

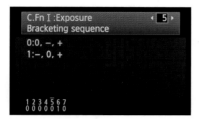

‹ Using the second option will change the picture taking order of the bracketed shots. The resulting files will be displayed on the computer in a sequence that makes a little more sense.

Since High Dynamic Range (HDR) photography is becoming more popular, this Custom Function might be used more often. HDR is a technique where you combine, via software, multiple exposures of the same image in order to create an image with a wider dynamic range (range from dark to light) than the camera's image sensor can capture.

This setting doesn't affect HDR, but it can help you quickly see, in a series of thumbnails, which scenes you bracketed. If you take multiple bracketed shots of the same scene, I think that option 1 **[-, 0, +]** shows the separation a bit better because the overexposed shot from one sequence is right next to the underexposed shot from the next sequence.

C.Fn I-6 Safety Shift: Use this function for difficult exposure situations. If the camera is set for **Av** or **Tv** exposure mode and **[Enable (Tv/Av)]** is selected, the exposure is adjusted during shooting to produce proper exposure. For example, imagine you have selected **[Enable (Tv/Av)]** and you shoot in **Tv** mode with a 1/125 shutter speed. If the lens aperture can't open up to let in enough light, the camera changes the shutter speed in order to achieve a proper exposure.

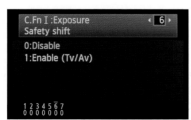

‹ Like a safety net for a trapeze artist, this function will override exposure settings if you try an take a picture with an exposure setting that camera can't use.

C.Fn I-7 Flash Synchronization Speed in Av Mode: This sets the flash sync in Aperture-Priority Av mode either to automatic adjustment or to a fixed setting. When this is set for **[Auto]** (the default), you can use flash for slow shutter speeds, which may cause blurred elements in your scene. The **[1/250-1/60 sec. auto]** option limits shutter speed to no slower than 1/60 second, so there is less blurring. To lessen blur even more, the **[1/250 sec. (fixed)]** option forces the 60D to always use 1/250 second when a flash is engaged, but exposure for the background elements is sacrificed.

> Remember that this custom function only affects exposure when in Av mode.

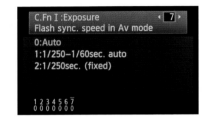

HINT: While it might seem that options 1 and 2 are the most useful, you can get some creative images by using a slow shutter speed with flash.

C.FN II: IMAGE

Image processing is the main focus of this Custom Function group. In particular, it offers control over Noise Reduction and image detail in high brightness situations.

> This custom function grouping affects how the 60D processes the image.

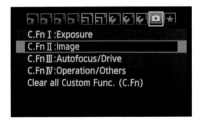

C.Fn II-1 Long Exposure Noise Reduction: This setting engages automatic Noise Reduction for long exposures. When Noise Reduction is used, the processing time of the image is a little more than twice that of the original exposure. For example, a 20-second exposure takes a total of about 40 seconds to complete.

- ○ 0: **[Off]**: Long Exposure Noise Reduction is turned off.
- ○ 1: **[Auto]**: Noise Reduction is applied to noise detected on exposures of one second or longer.
- ○ 2: **[On]**: Noise reduction is turned on for all exposures one second or longer, even if no noise is detected.

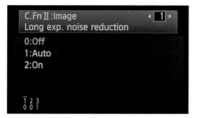

< The Auto option works well at reducing noise.

HINT: When using high ISO speed settings, you will usually get better results with option 1.

C.Fn II-2 High ISO Speed Noise Reduction: Although the DIGIC 4 image processor in the 60D always reduces noise when it processes an image, as you increase the apparent sensitivity of the 60D by using high ISO settings, you increase the noise in the image. This Custom Function cranks up the DIGIC 4 processor's Noise Reduction.

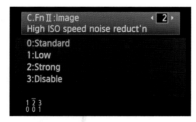

< Always evaluate image noise on a display other than the LCD on the back of the 60D. The LCD is simply too small to make any good evaluation of noise reduction.

If you shoot RAW or RAW+JPEG, the camera doesn't actually apply the Noise Reduction to the RAW image; it only embeds Noise Reduction data in the RAW file so Canon's Digital Photo Professional software can use that data to reduce noise. This means that when you shoot RAW, you won't see the effect of this setting on the LCD, in prints made directly from the camera, or when you connect the camera to a TV for Image Playback. Even if you shoot RAW+JPEG, you won't see the effect because the camera uses the RAW file, not the JPEG, to display and print.

NOTE: When set to **[Strong]**, the number of shots that can be captured in a row is decreased.

C.Fn II-3 Highlight Tone Priority: This is one of the 60D's more interesting custom functions. Enable this option to expand dynamic range near the bright area of the tone curve. This means if you are shooting scenes filled with white objects, like bridal gowns or snowy landscapes, this Custom Function will help maintain details in those bright areas. When enabled, the available ISO speed range is limited to 200 – 6400. Also, you may see more noise in the dark areas of the image when you use this Custom Function.

> The dynamic range of a digital camera is less than what our eyes can see. This custom function increases the dynamic range of the camera at the expense of some added noise.

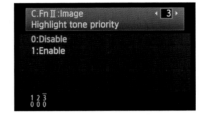

NOTE: When the 60D has Highlight tone priority enabled, D+ will be displayed in the viewfinder and on the LCD monitor.

C.FN III: AUTOFOCUS / DRIVE

This group contains a wide range of functions, from controlling how you adjust the focus systems to controlling the reflex mirror. With my photography, I probably change the mirror lockup Custom Function (in order to achieve sharp images at slow shutter speeds), more than any other Custom Function in this section.

> As the name implies, this group of Custom Functions is all about adjusting the focus operation of the 60D.

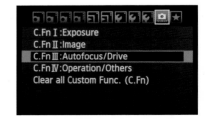

C.Fn III-1 Lens Drive when AF Impossible: If you are using autofocus and the lens keeps hunting for proper focus, this setting can stop the camera from trying to focus. If you use a long lens and autofocus produces an extremely out-of-focus setting, select **[Stop focus search]** to minimize the problem.

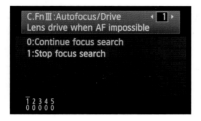

‹ You'll normally only need to change this if you are using very long (telephoto) lenses.

C.Fn III-2 AF Point Selection Method: When you start controlling which AF point the 60D is going to use to lock focus, there are two ways to get into the AF point setting mode. With the default setting, you first press ⊞ and then use ✳ to select the point. If you want to switch back to auto selection in this mode, you must push **SET** twice.

The second option in this Custom Function allows you to quickly set an AF point by using ✳ without first pressing ⊞. In this mode, ⊞ is used to switch to automatic AF point selection.

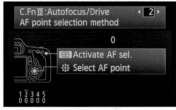

⌃ This is the default selection for C.Fn III-2, which requires selecting the ⊞ button in order to choose an AF point.

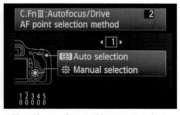

⌃ The other option enables you to select an AF point using just the Multi-Controller ✳.

When using either option, ✳ will enable you to pick any AF point except the center one. To select the center point, press **SET**.

> **NOTE:** When set to **[⊞ Auto selection / ✳ Manual selection]**, the C.Fn IV-2 setting, which controls the function of the **SET** button, is ignored.

C.Fn III-3 Superimposed Display: After focus has been locked, the viewfinder can illuminate the AF points that were used to set focus. If you find it distracting, you can disable this illumination. This does not affect illumination of AF points when you are in the process of setting focus.

> As you first start experimenting with focus on the 60D, use this function to see which AF point was used to set focus.

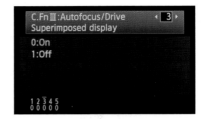

C.Fn III-4 AF-Assist Beam Firing: The AF-Assist beam is controlled through this Custom Function. The built-in flash and some Canon Speedlites offer a lamp that emits a series of rapid, low-powered flash bursts that are useful when operating autofocus in low-light situations. Some Canon Speedlites (i.e., the 580EX II) use an infrared (IR) AF-Assist beam instead.

- ○ 0: **[Enable]**: The AF-Assist beam is emitted whenever the camera deems it necessary.
- ○ 1: **[Disable]**: The camera will not emit the AF-Assist beam.
- ○ 2: **[Enable external flash only]**: In low light, an accessory Canon EX flash unit fires its AF-Assist beam. The built-in flash's AF-Assist feature is disabled.
- ○ 3: **[IR AF assist beam only]**: In low light, an accessory Canon EX flash unit that has an IR AF-Assist beam fires its beam. This is useful when even a low-power flash may distract your subject.

> How this Custom Function operates depends on if you are using an external Speedlite.

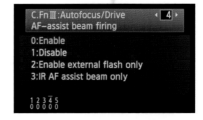

This Custom Function is ignored if your external flash's AF-Assist beam has been disabled through the flash's Custom Function settings.

C.Fn III-5 Mirror Lockup: When the 60D captures a still image in non-Live-View mode, the reflex mirror that sends the image to the viewfinder instead of the image sensor flips up when you press the shutter button. If you shoot with longer exposures, this small but violent mechanical action can cause a slight camera movement, thus introducing some blur to your image. Use this Custom Function to lock up the mirror. When the mirror is locked up, you will not be able to see an image in the viewfinder.

- 0: **[Disable]**: The mirror functions normally.
- 1: **[Enable]**: The mirror moves up and locks in position with the first full press of the shutter button. With the second full press of the shutter button, the camera takes the picture. After the exposure is made, the mirror returns to its original position.

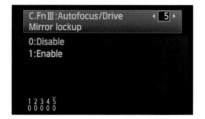

‹ This is a useful function to help keep your pictures sharp when using long exposures (and a tripod).

NOTE: If, after 30 seconds in the locked position, you have not taken a picture, the mirror flips back down.

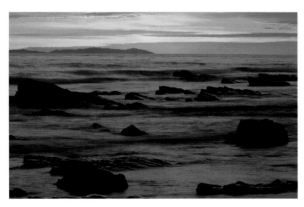

‹ Enabling the Mirror Lockup Custom Function can help reduce camera shake during long exposures, which are necessary to capture a shot like the one pictured here.

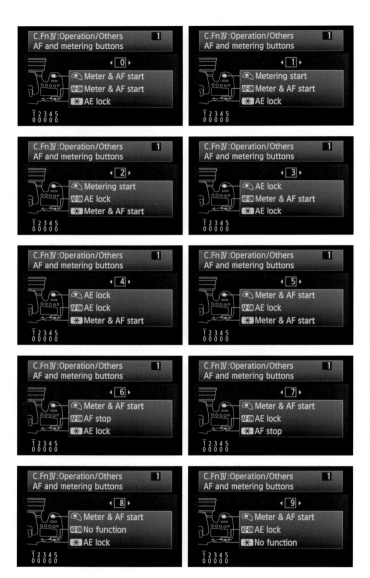

The 60D allows you to separate the action of starting focus lock and metering. This is accomplished by assigning focus and metering to separate buttons.

This group is partially about programming (or reprogramming) some of the buttons on the 60D. It also deals with optional focusing screens and provides functionality for forensic photography applications.

C.Fn IV-1 AF and Metering Buttons: Although this is a complicated setting (there are 10 different options!), it offers you precise control over when focusing and metering begin. To better understand it, follow the diagram on the LCD. Essentially, you are changing the function of three buttons: the shutter button, the **AF-ON** button, and the ✳ button.

Arguably more than any other Custom Function, how you set this really depends on how you want the 60D to work for your type of shooting. Sometimes you want to explicitly control when focus starts and exposure locks, and sometimes you don't. I think option 1 offers the most control because it separates metering, focus, and exposure lock onto three separate buttons. The shutter button just starts metering and **AF-ON** controls when autofocus happens. ✳ operates how you think it would, namely, to lock exposure.

NOTE: You can access this Custom Function via the Quick Control screen. Highlight the ▣ icon and press **SET**. Then use ⌂, ○, or ✳ to highlight the control you want to modify.

C.Fn IV-2 Assign SET Button: Somewhat surprisingly, the **SET** button really doesn't have a function on its own. Normally, you must first access a menu or press a button before you can, or need to, use **SET**. Rather than let it go to waste, you can use this Custom Function to make better use of the **SET** button.

○ 0: **[Default(no func)]**: The **SET** button is used to accept settings in menus, and to switch between the center AF point or automatic AF point selection; otherwise it has no direct function.

○ 1: **[Image quality]**: The **SET** button provides quick access to file-recording size and quality.

○ 2: **[Picture Style]**: The **SET** button accesses the Picture Style settings.

○ 3: **[White balance]**: The **SET** button brings up the White Balance options.

○ 4: **[Flash exp. comp.]**: The SET button accesses the Flash Exposure Compensation ⚡± setting. One key to good flash photography is controlling flash exposure. By dialing down the output of the flash, you reduce the "mugshot" look of many flash photographs. Unfortunately, ⚡± is buried in a submenu of a submenu. In fact, at a minimum, you need 5 button presses to access the setting—not counting first pressing MENU. This Custom Function allows Flash Exposure Compensation to be a single button press away.

○ 5: **[Viewfinder ⚙]**: Normally, the electronic level display only appears on the LCD monitor. When you select this option, whenever you press SET, the exposure scale in the viewfinder turns into a level display.

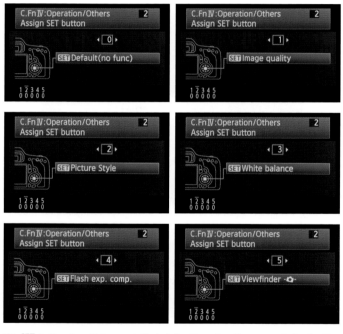

The SET button doesn't have a dedicated function when the camera is in shooting mode; therefore, you can assign a function to it.

NOTE: When the Custom Function for AF point selection (C.Fn III-2) is not set for its default setting, it will override any settings in this Custom Function. In this case, pressing SET changes the AF point to the center point.

C.Fn IV-3 Dial Direction During Tv/Av: When **[Reverse direction]** is selected in Manual mode (**M**), both the Main dial 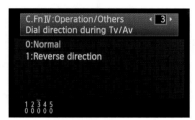 and the Quick Control dial ○ operate in reverse directions. In other words, normally, rotating clockwise shortens the shutter speed (1/60...1/250...1/1000) and rotating ○ clockwise closes down the aperture (f/4...f/8...f/22). When **[Reverse direction]** is selected, you'll need to rotate each control counter clockwise to achieve the same effect. When the exposure mode is set for **Av**, **Tv**, or **P**, this option has the same effect on . However, since ○ acts as an Exposure Compensation dial in these exposure modes and it is coordinated with the Exposure Compensation scale on the back of the camera, in the viewfinder, and on the LCD panel, its direction is not changed.

⟨ This setting, more than most, is about what feels natural to you. If you find yourself always rotating the dial the wrong way at first, try reversing the direction.

C.Fn IV-4 Focusing Screen: The 60D can accept accessory focusing screens. When you change the focusing screen you have to let the camera know what type of focusing screen has been installed, as the focusing screen does not do it for you. See page 55 for more information about focus screens.

- ○ 0: **[Ef-A]**: standard focusing screen
- ○ 1: **[Ef-D]**: focusing screen with grid
- ○ 2: **[Ef-S]**: Super Precision Matte screen

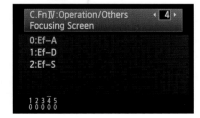

⟨ There isn't any way for the camera to sense if you have changed the focusing screen.

151

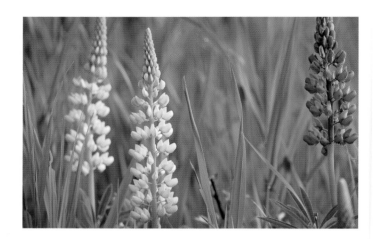

C.Fn IV-5 Add Image Verification Data: This function is used with the Original Data Security Kit OSK-E3, an optional Canon-designed software package. The software provides the necessary authentication of image data that forensic and other specialized applications use.

- O 0: **[Disable]**: The captured image is not embedded with any verification data.
- O 1: **[Enable]**: The image is embedded with verification data.

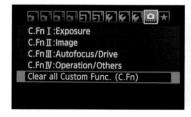

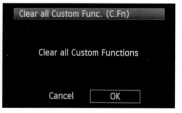

You can reset all of the Custom Functions to their default setting via this option.

This menu is color coded green. If you find yourself returning to certain menu items and custom functions on a regular basis, you can build your own customized menu, called My Menu. This is a powerful tool that you can use so camera adjustments are quick and easy. For example, I have built a menu that gives me quick access to [Mirror lockup] (C.Fn III-5), [Highlight tone priority] (C.Fn II-3), [Flash control], [ISO expansion] (C.Fn I-3), and [Long exp. noise reduct'n] (C.Fn II-1). Sometimes, I remove one or two items and add others. For instance, I might add [Protect], if I am using an Eye-Fi card and want to control when an image is transmitted; or I might load up the menu with video options if I am shooting video all day.

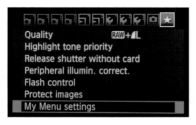

‹ My advice is don't try to fill the My Menu right away. Use the camera for awhile and see what controls you use most often.

NOTE: The My Menu items are not available in the Basic Zone shooting modes.

When you first use the 60D, the My Menu display only has one selection: [My Menu settings]. Use this selection to build a custom menu of any top-level selections in any of the menus, as well as any of the Custom Functions. My Menu can contain up to six selections.

To build a menu, first press MENU and move to the ★ tab. Highlight [My Menu settings], and then press SET. From the submenu that appears, scroll to highlight [Register to My Menu], and press SET again. A list of every top-level menu option and all the Custom Functions is displayed. Scroll to select a desired option and press SET again. Highlight [OK] and press SET to confirm the addition of the selected option. Once selected, the option will be grayed out so that you can't insert the same option twice. Repeat the process until you have selected the options you want, up to a maximum of six. Press the MENU button to exit the selection screen, then press MENU again to see the resulting My Menu you have created.

The [Sort] submenu under [My Menu settings] allows you to sort your menu items once you've added them. Select [Sort] and press SET. [Sort My Menu] is displayed, showing the current order of your menu items. Scroll to highlight an item you wish to move. Press SET and an up / down arrow appears to the right of the item. Use ⁜ to move the item up or down in the list. Press SET once the item is in the preferred position. You can then repeat these steps to change the position of other items, or press MENU to exit.

If you have filled ★ with six items, you must delete an item before you can insert a new one; there is no exchange function. Highlight [Delete item/items] in the [My Menu settings] submenu and press SET. Highlight an item you wish to delete. Press SET and a dialog asks you to confirm the deletion. Highlight [OK] and press SET. Repeat this process if you wish to delete other My Menu items, then press MENU to exit the [Delete My Menu] screen. Similarly, you can select [Delete all items] to start with an empty My Menu.

You can customize your 60D so that ★ is displayed every time you press MENU (no matter which menu you were last on). To do so, highlight [Display from My Menu] from the [My Menu settings] screen. Press SET, then highlight [Enable], and press SET.

NOTE: You can also use Canon's EOS Utility software that comes with the 60D to build your My Menu.

◢▬ *MOVIE 1 MENU*

This menu tab is the first of three Movie menus that are available when the Mode dial is set for Movie Shooting ▐▀. This menu contains a key option that wasn't even available when DSLRs first gained the ability to record video. Initially, exposure was set automatically with no option for manual control. Arguably, the most import menu item here is the first one.

MOVIE EXPOSURE

Video is not a single image and the lighting often changes when a subject (or the camera) moves, so the exposure must change with it.

○ **[Auto]**: The camera automatically controls all exposure adjustments (aperture, shutter speed, and ISO speed) in order to achieve proper exposure. You can still override the selected settings with Exposure Compensation.

○ **[Manual]**: This option allows for full manual control over exposure. Set shutter speed using ▧, aperture using ◯. Set ISO speed by pressing the ISO button and choosing a speed from the selections displayed on the LCD monitor.

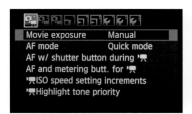
⌃ Besides setting AF mode, probably the most importing setting here is Movie exposure.

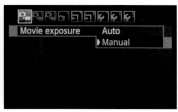
⌃ Manual exposure control requires that you change exposure when the lighting in your scene changes.

AF MODE

During movie recording, the AF sensor is blocked by the reflex mirror. This selection offers alternative AF modes.

○ AF▐Live▌ **[Live mode]:** Using the images coming from the image sensor, this selection measures contrasting edges in order to determine proper focus. This method of focusing is slower and not as accurate as AF▐Quick▌.

○ ⌣̈ **[Live mode]:** This focus mode detects faces in a scene where people are photographed and sets focus to ensure those people are in focus.

○ AF▣ **[Quick mode]**: This selection temporarily flips the reflex mirror down and uses the normal AF sensor for setting focus. While it sounds as if flipping the mirror down and then back up would be slow, it is actually the fastest method of achieving autofocus in Movie mode.

AUTOFOCUS WITH SHUTTER BUTTON DURING 🎥

While the 60D does not offer the continuous autofocus capability of a video camcorder, you can still refocus the camera while shooting video.

○ **[Disable]**: The camera is prevented from changing focus during recording.
○ **[Enable]**: You can change focus while recording by pressing the shutter release button halfway. Refocusing does not happen quickly, and that portion of the recorded video will likely need to be edited out. If the AF mode is set for AF▣, autofocus will operate as though the 60D is set for AF▣ mode.

AUTOFOCUS AND METERING BUTTON FOR 🎥

You can adjust how the shutter release button, the **AF-ON** button, and the ✳ autoexposure lock button work when shooting video. Since the shutter release button isn't used to start recording, and AF is a bit different when recording movies, this customization can be helpful. This is similar to the settings in C.Fn IV-1.

These settings are specifically for video shooting and override the settings in C.Fn IV-1 when you shoot movies. (Custom Functions are not accessible when the 60D is in 🎥 mode.) Because shooting video is pretty different from capturing a single frame, and because focus operates differently when you shoot video, you may find that you set this option quite differently than C.Fn IV-1.

🎥 **ISO Speed Setting Increments:** This is similar to C.Fn I-2—you can change the Movie mode ISO speed increment so that the steps are larger.

○ 0: **[1/3-stop]**
○ 1: **[1-stop]**

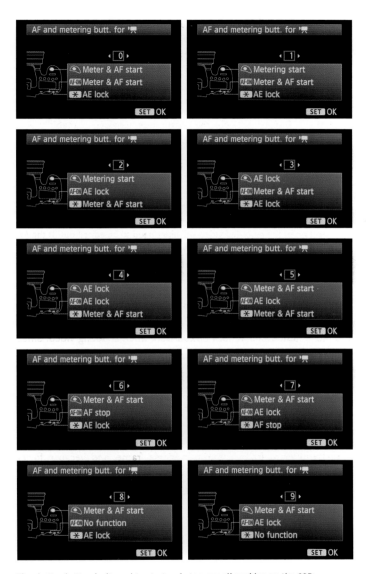

The shutter button isn't used to start and stop recording video on the 60D; therefore, you can assign it to other functions.

'🎥 Highlight Tone Priority: Just like Custom Function C.Fn II-3, enable this option to expand dynamic range near the bright area of the tone curve. So, if you are shooting scenes filled with white objects, like bridal gowns or snowy landscapes, this menu item will help maintain details in those bright areas. When enabled, the available ISO speed range is limited to 200 – 6400. Also, you may see more noise in the dark areas of the image when using this menu item.

- ○ 0: **[Disable]**
- ○ 1: **[Enable]**

NOTE: When the 60D has Highlight Tone Priority enabled, **D+** will be displayed in the viewfinder and on the LCD monitor.

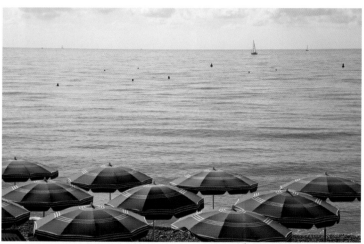

∧ Shooting on sunny days, especially around water, can be prime situations for overexposed highlights. Utilizing the Highlight Tone Priority setting can help minimize blown highlights.

This menu tab is only available when the Mode dial is set for Movie Shooting '▮. A critical option in this menu is Movie-Recording Size.

MOVIE-RECORDING SIZE

Whether the 60D video system is set for NTSC or PAL in ▮: (see page 131), there are three high-definition (HD) and two standard-definition settings for recording video.

Menu selections when the video system is set to NTSC:

○ **[1920x1080 30]**: Full HD. The "1920 x 1080" designation represents the number of pixels (horizontal x vertical), and "30" represents the frame rate of the video (30 frames per second, or fps). 30 fps is the normal frame rate for high-definition video (the actual frame rate being 29.97 fps).

○ **[1920x1080 24]**: This selection is available for both NTSC and PAL video systems. 24 fps is the typical frame rate used in shooting films that you see in a movie theater. Videographers often shoot at this frame rate to achieve a more cinematic look. Be aware, though, that since images are captured less frequently, fast motion can often have a stuttered look to it. (The actual frame rate for this selection is 23.976 fps.)

○ **[1280x720 60]**: This HD format offers a frame rate of 60 fps, which can capture scenes that contain a great deal of motion. It is also handy for movies you want to slow down as you edit them on a computer. In order to achieve the high frame rate, the resolution is reduced. (The actual frame rate is 59.94 fps.)

○ **[640x480 60]**: Also at 60 fps, this setting is approximately the size of standard-definition video (the television standard before the advent of HD recording and viewing). (The actual frame rate is 59.94 fps.)

○ **[Crop 640 60]**: This is a special type of recording that is available with the 60D. With all the other settings, the entire image output from the image sensor (5184 x 3456) is scaled down to the video format selected. With **[Crop 640 60]**, the center portion of the image sensor is used to create a 640 x 480 image. This results in an apparent 7x magnification of the image. (The actual frame rate here is 59.94 fps.)

Menu selections when the video system is set for PAL:

○ **[1920x1080 25]**: Full HD – 25 fps is the customary frame rate for countries outside of North America.

○ **[1920x1080 24]**: This selection is available for both NTSC and PAL video systems. 24 fps is the typical frame rate used in shooting films that you see in a movie theater. Videographers often shoot at this frame rate to achieve a more cinematic look. Be aware, though, that since images are captured less frequently, fast motion can often have a stuttered look to it. (The actual frame rate for this selection is 23.976 fps.)

○ **[1280x720 50]**: This HD format offers a frame rate of 50 fps for countries outside of North America. You can only access this frame rate when **[Video system]** is set for PAL in 🎥 (see page 131).

○ **[640x480 50]**: At 50 fps, this setting is for countries outside of North America and is available only when **[Video system]** is set for PAL in 🎥 (see page 131).

○ **[Crop 640 50]**: This setting is for use outside of North America where the frame rate is customarily 50 fps. You can only access this frame rate when **[Video system]** is set for PAL in 🎥 (see page 131).

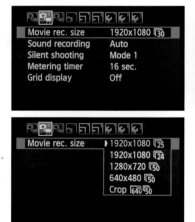

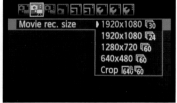

The options for frame rate depend on the video standard for which the camera is currently set.

NOTE: Only use 25/50 fps if you are creating video to be used outside of North America.

The 60D is capable of recording sound with the video. Audio comes from either the built-in microphone or an external microphone connected to the external microphone IN terminal on the left side of the camera. (Learn more about connecting a microphone on page 231.) This option brings up a submenu:

○ **[Sound rec.]:**

- **[Auto]**: The camera records sound using the mono built-in microphone or through an external microphone via the external microphone IN terminal. The level recorded is automatically adjusted by the camera.

- **[Manual]**: When this is selected, the **[Rec. level]** option becomes available. This allows you to adjust the audio level of the recording.

- **[Disable]**: No audio is recorded.

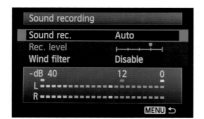

‹ It is important to check audio levels before each recording. Overdriving the audio levels can't be fixed later.

○ **[Rec. level]:** When available, use ○ to adjust the recording level. A meter is displayed on the LCD monitor showing the audio coming in to the 60D. This audio meter is called a peak hold meter in that it holds onto the loudest measurements for a few seconds so that you see when the levels are too loud. You should set the levels so that they average around the −10 or −12 mark. If levels reach the zero mark, your audio will be distorted.

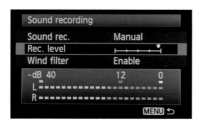

‹ You can only adjust audio levels when the Sound rec. option is set for manual.

○ **[Wind filter]:**

- ● **[Enable]:** Microphones are very susceptible to wind noise. Use this electronic filter to reduce the noise. However, it cannot remove all of the noise, and it will also remove some of the lower frequencies of sound that you meant to record.

- ● **[Disable]:** If you are not in an environment with wind (indoors), turn off the wind filter so you don't lose low frequency sounds.

SILENT SHOOTING

This is the same as the silent shooting option when the 60D is in Live View shooting mode. These options lessen noise when you take still photos while in Movie mode.

○ **[Mode 1]:** This resets the shutter right after the picture is taken.

○ **[Mode 2]:** The reset happens only after you take your finger off the shutter release, so there will be no reset sound as long as you keep the shutter depressed.

○ **[Disable]:** This option should be used when you shoot with tilt-shift lenses or close-up tubes. This is required to ensure that exposures are accurate. When you use the built-in flash or a Canon Speedlite, the 60D will not perform the silent shooting function. This option must be selected when using a third-party flash, or else the flash will not fire.

METERING TIMER

By default, the metering system stays engaged for 16 seconds when you tap the shutter release button. Use this option if you want the meter to shut off earlier or stay on longer. The range is from 4 seconds to 30 minutes. This is also how long exposure will remain locked when using exposure lock.

○ **[4 sec.]**

○ **[16 sec.]**

○ **[30 sec.]**

○ **[1 min.]**

○ **[10 min.]**

○ **[30 min.]**

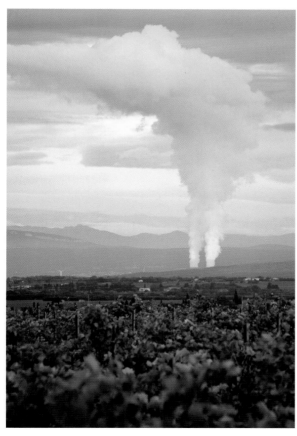

> The Rule of Thirds is a quick and easy way to elevate a so-so photo into an interesting composition. Practice this technique using the options listed below.

GRID DISPLAY

This option is useful for image composition.

- O **[Off]**: No grids are displayed.
- O **[Grid 1]**: A Rule of Thirds grid overlays the image on the LCD. For good composition, place your subjects at the intersections of these lines.
- O **[Grid 2]**: A denser grid displays. When you shoot scenes with a lot of geometrical shapes, like architecture, this is useful in making sure your camera is level and square to your subject.

EXPOSURE COMPENSATION

This is similar to Exposure Compensation when you take still photographs. It is a way to override the exposure that the 60D automatically sets. When the **[Exposure comp.]** option is selected, press **SET**. A scale from –5 to +5 is displayed on the LCD monitor (0 is the default). Press right or left on ⚬ to set the exposure brighter (+) or darker (–); you must press **SET** to apply the exposure adjustment. The compensation value will be displayed on the scale in the viewfinder and on the LCD monitor.

> When the 60D is in autoexposure for Movie mode, use this setting to correct for under- or overexposure.

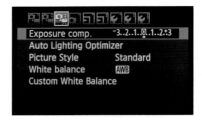

NOTE: Exposure Compensation is not reset when you power off the camera. Make sure you keep an eye on the scale to double-check that Exposure Compensation is not set for a previous shot.

HINT: You can also set Exposure Compensation without going into a menu by just turning ⚪.

AUTO LIGHTING OPTIMIZER

This recent introduction to EOS cameras is an exposure correction mode that makes use of the power and design of the 60D's DIGIC 4 image-processing chip. By evaluating the image, the camera can help brighten underexposed scenes while still maintaining image details. You can also access this setting in the Quick Control screen.

○ **[Disable]**: This option for brightness correction is disabled.

○ **[Low]**: A slight amount of correction is applied.

○ **[Standard]**: This is a good starting point if you want to experiment with the Auto Lighting Optimizer control.

○ **[Strong]**: The highest amount of correction is applied.

NOTE: If Highlight Tone Priority is enabled in ⏻, then this option will be disabled.

PICTURE STYLE

This is the same setting as for stills. The 60D allows you to customize the look of your videos via the [Picture Style] menu selections. There are six presets that you can use or modify, with [⊞ Standard] as the default. Additionally, there are three user-defined Picture Styles that allow you to create your own look. (Learn more about Picture Styles on pages 66-72.)

WHITE BALANCE

You can choose one of the nine white balance (WB) selections, including seven presets, ⏺ to set a precise color temperature, and ⏺ to set a custom WB. The default WB setting is ⏺ (Auto). Learn more about White Balance on pages 75-84.

CUSTOM WHITE BALANCE

If you use a custom White Balance ⏺ setting, you must tell the 60D which image to use as a basis for white balance (see page 79). Once you have captured an image, select this menu item, scroll to the image you want to use as a reference and press **SET**. The 60D can only set custom White Balance data via measuring a still image, so you won't be able to select a movie for reference.

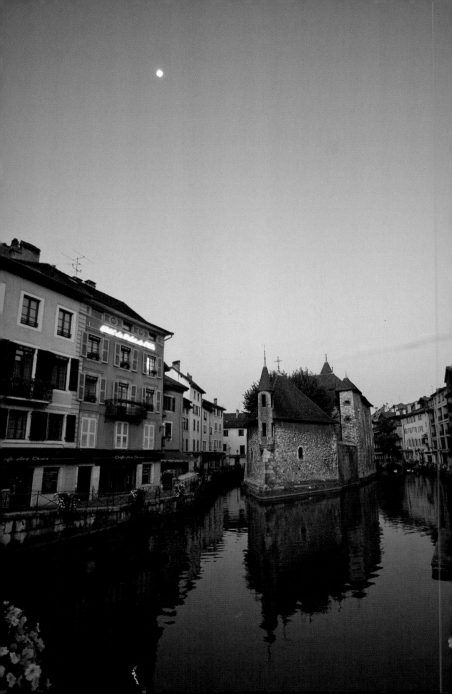

Shooting and Drive Modes

SHOOTING MODES

There are 13 shooting modes in the 60D, ranging from completely automatic to entirely manual. The shooting modes are divided into three areas: the Basic Zone, the Creative Zone, and a Movie mode that stands alone at the end of the Mode dial. The Basic Zone modes allow the camera to be matched quickly to various conditions and subjects. Fast and easy to manage, the Basic Zone modes let the camera predetermine a number of settings. The Creative Zone modes, as the name suggests, allow for complete creative control of the 60D. Lastly, the remaining mode is for Movie shooting. In this mode, the 60D can record both high-definition and standard-definition video.

All shooting modes are selected by using the Mode dial, located on top of the camera's left shoulder. Simply press and hold the lock on the top of the dial as you rotate it to the icon you wish to use. The Basic Zone includes full auto □, flash off ⊡ (essentially full auto, but with no flash), creative auto ⒸⒶ, portrait ⓐ, landscape ⌂, close-up ⚘, sports ⚔, and night portrait ⓐ. The five Creative Zone shooting modes are program autoexposure (AE) P, Aperture-Priority AE Av, Shutter-Priority AE Tv, Manual exposure M, and Bulb B. These are more advanced modes in that you, not the camera, must manage more of the camera settings to achieve the photographic results you're looking for. For most of these settings, the camera only pays attention to the exposure settings—specifically shutter speed, aperture, and sometimes ISO sensitivity. You have to do the rest.

BASIC ZONE SHOOTING MODES

☐ **Full Auto:** Turn your Mode dial to the green rectangle for completely automatic shooting. This mode essentially converts the 60D into a very sophisticated point and shoot. The camera chooses everything; you cannot adjust any controls except the file size/format (image quality) and the self-timers. This shooting mode is designed for photographers who aren't familiar with DSLRs. In ☐, the Picture Style is set to standard ⊞S, for crisp, vivid images; the white balance is set for AWB; ISO speed is auto, and focus is set for **AI FOCUS**. The built-in flash pops up automatically and fires if needed.

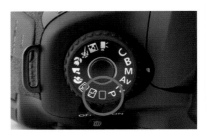

> The Full Auto mode is useful when just starting out with the 60D.

NOTE: Keep in mind that manual focus can be engaged on the lens if you wish to override the focus setting in any shooting mode, including ☐.

🚫 **Flash Off:** This shooting mode prevents the flash from firing. It operates the same as ☐ except that the flash will never fire. In fact, you can't even pop up the flash using the ⚡ button—pressing the button will simply display a message saying, "This function is not selectable in the current shooting mode." If the flash is popped up before you enter 🚫 mode, it won't fire. This is the mode to use when in museums and other sensitive locations that do not allow flash photography.

🅲🅰 **Creative Auto:** This mode is similar to ☐, but offers the opportunity to make more adjustments. Press the Quick Control button 🅀 to display the Quick Control screen, then scroll using ✦ to turn the flash on or off, set the drive mode, adjust background, and set the Shoot by Ambience setting.

The background setting is unique to 🅲🅰. Using the background control is another way of adjusting depth of field. Instead of having to worry about which aperture or shutter speed to use, press ⓠ and use ⁂ as a joystick to navigate to the desired background adjustment via a slider. You can choose whether you want the background in your image to be blurry or sharp. A blurry background can be useful when shooting portraits of people standing in front of a busy background. And if you set the background adjustment towards the sharp end, the 60D picks an appropriate aperture (f/stop) to increase depth of field so that a greater part of your photo is in focus.

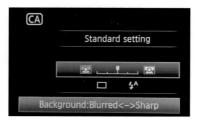

‹ In previous EOS cameras automatic modes offered little in the way of adjustments.

You can't change the Picture Style that is automatically selected for ⓒⒶ, but for the first time in an EOS camera you can modify the selected Picture Style by accessing the Shoot by Ambience selection in the Quick Control screen. The Picture Style set for ⓒⒶ is standard ᴾᵗˢ. Press ⓠ then use ⁂ to highlight the Shoot by Ambience parameter which is just above the Background parameter.

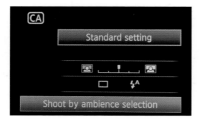

‹ The Shoot by Ambience feature is a relatively new feature in Canon cameras.

There are nine different settings to select from. This can be done with ⌇ but when you are first learning the camera you might want to first press **SET** to get a list of options, then use ⁂ or ○ to select an ambience. You can select from standard, vivid, soft, warm, intense, cool, brighter, darker, and monochrome. Once you have made a selection other than standard you can further modify the setting by adjusting the strength of the effect. For most ambience settings these adjustments are low, standard, and strong. With monochrome you can keep the image in pure black and white or apply a light tint of blue or sepia. You can see where to make this adjustment on the Quick Control screen as it is immediately under the ambience parameter.

> At first glance the CA mode looks like a typical automatic shooting mode, but it allows you some creative control of how your scene will look.

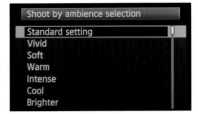

Shoot by ambience selection

Standard setting
Vivid
Soft
Warm
Intense
Cool
Brighter

The following drive modes are available in CA: Single shooting ☐, Low speed continuous shooting ☐, and Self-timer:10sec/Remote control ⏱. To set drive mode, highlight the parameter and press **SET**. Then use ✦ to select a drive mode.

The options for flash are Auto flash ⚡ᴬ, Flash on ⚡ and Flash off ⚡. Use ✦ or ○ to make this adjustment once you have selected the parameter and have pressed **SET**.

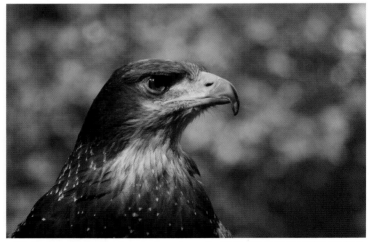

∧ **Whether you are shooting images of people or of animals, the Portrait setting can be a good place to start.**

Portrait: If you like to shoot portraits, this setting is for you. It makes adjustment choices that favor people photography. The drive mode is set to continuous ☳ so you can quickly shoot changing gestures and expressions, but you can also change it to ⟡ if you want to jump into the picture. AF mode is set to **ONE SHOT** so you can lock focus with a slight pressing of the shutter release. The meter favors wider f/stops (those with smaller f/numbers) because this limits depth of field, offering backgrounds that are softer, contrasting with the sharper focus of the subject. A wider f/stop also results in faster shutter speeds, producing sharper handheld images.

The Picture Style is set to Portrait ⊞⁼P for softer skin tones (see page 67 for more about the portrait Picture Style). Just as with ⒸⒶ you can adjust Shoot by Ambience to adjust the Picture Style. The flash will fire if needed.

While you can't adjust the white balance setting the way you would in Creative Zone shooting modes, the 60D (for the first time in an EOS camera) allows you to adjust the white balance using the Quick Control screen. Normally the camera is set for the default, which is the same as ⓐⓦⓑ. To adjust the white balance using the Shoot by Lighting or Scene Type setting, press ⓠ then use ❖ to highlight the Shoot by Lighting or Scene Type parameter and press **SET** to bring up a list of lighting conditions. The options are: Standard, Daylight, Shade, Cloudy, Tungsten light, Fluorescent light, and Sunset. (Tungsten means a normal light bulb found in a table lamp—tungsten is what the light bulb's filament is made of.) Use ❖ or ○ to make a selection and press **SET**. As you get more familiar with the 60D you can skip a step and just highlight the parameter on the Quick Control screen, and then use ⌂ to scroll through the options.

HINT: If you aren't sure which Shoot by Lighting or Scene Type to use (or even Shoot by Ambience), flip on Live View and look at the LCD as you make the adjustment.

Landscape: When shooting landscape photography, it is important to lock focus one shot at a time, so the 60D's landscape mode uses ONE SHOT AF and □ drive mode (though you can also select ⟨�⟩). The meter favors small f/stops (higher f/numbers like f/8 or f/11) for more depth of field, which is often important for scenic shots. The Picture Style is locked to Landscape ⌷⌷ for vivid greens and blues. You can modify the Picture Style by adjusting the Shoot by Ambience setting via the Quick Control screen. The flash will not pop up either automatically or manually. If it has already popped up from a previous setting it will still not fire. Just as with ◈ you can use Shoot by Lighting or Scene Type in the Quick Control screen to adjust white balance. However, since it is assumed that Landscape means outdoors, you don't have access to the Tungsten light and Fluorescent light settings.

Close-Up: This mode also uses ONE SHOT AF and □ drive mode (but ⟨◈⟩ is also selectable). It favors wider f/stops for faster shutter speeds, giving better sharpness with a handheld camera and far less depth of field in order to set off a sharp subject against a softer background. The Picture Style is set to Standard ⌷⌷, and can be adjusted via Shoot by Ambience. White balance can be set via Shoot by Lighting or Scene Type in the Quick Control screen and the flash fires if needed.

NOTE: Simply setting the 60D to ❀ does not make your lens more capable of close-up focusing. If you need to be able to get closer to fill the scene you may need to invest in a macro lens or extension tubes.

Sports: Designed for action and using fast shutter speeds to stop the motion of your subject, sports mode uses AI SERVO AF and High speed continuous drive mode ⌷H, both of which allow continuous shooting as action unfolds in front of you. You can switch the drive mode to ⟨◈⟩. In addition, the beep for AF confirmation is softer than other modes. The Picture Style is ⌷⌷, and can be modified by Shoot by Ambience. White balance is also adjustable with Shoot by Lighting or Scene Type. The flash does not fire.

Night Portrait: Despite its name, this setting is not limited to nighttime use. It is very useful, even for advanced photographers, to balance flash with low-light conditions. This mode uses flash to

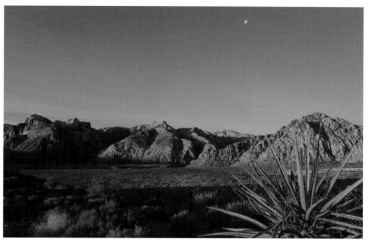

⌃ The landscape mode uses small f/stops to create the greatest depth of field, which is usually a must for landscape photography.

illuminate the subject (which may or may not be for a portrait) and selects exposure settings (shutter speed, ISO, and aperture) to balance the background and capture detail. The exposure settings allow what is called an ambient-light exposure (an exposure of the parts of the scene not illuminated by the flash). A good capture of detail in low-light conditions can require a very slow shutter speed and may result in a blurry background, so you may need a tripod if that is not the effect you are going for. The flash will always pop up and fire in this mode. The Picture Style is ⧉ and you can modify the setting with Shoot by Ambience. You can't adjust white balance via Shoot by Lighting or Scene Type—because it is assumed that the flash will be firing. Like most of the Basic Zone modes, night portrait mode defaults to ☐ drive mode, but can be switched to ⏱.

CREATIVE ZONE SHOOTING MODES

The appropriately named Creative Zone modes offer you more control over camera adjustments, thus encouraging a more creative approach to photography. In each mode other than manual exposure, the camera controls some aspect of the exposure equation, but settings such as white balance, file type (RAW or JPEG), metering method, focus method, Picture Style, ISO, and drive mode are set manually. Control is usually a good thing, but so many possible adjustments can be confusing at worst, and time consuming at best. However, once you become familiar with the 60D, you will probably want to use the Creative Zone shooting modes most of the time.

P Program AE: In P mode, the camera chooses the shutter speed and aperture combination. This gives the photographer less direct control over the image because no matter how appropriate, the settings are chosen by the camera—not by you. However, you can employ a technique known as program shift to alter the settings that are automatically selected, changing either the aperture or shutter speed, and the 60D will compensate the complementary value to maintain the same exposure value. To shift the program, simply press the shutter button halfway to turn on the camera's built-in light meter, then turn 🔘 until the desired shutter speed or aperture value is displayed on the LCD monitor or viewfinder.

NOTE: Program shift is not the same as exposure compensation, which actually changes the exposure value by under- or overexposing the scene in relationship to the camera's determination of the "correct" exposure. In contrast, program shift maintains the same exposure value by adjusting the shutter speed or aperture to match the corresponding value you have assigned.

NOTE: Program shift only works for one exposure at a time, making it useful for quick-and-easy shooting while providing some control over camera settings.

The flash will not pop up automatically in P mode when light levels are low. You must manually activate the flash by pressing the ⚡ button on the front of the camera above the lens release button. Also, when any flash is on (be it the built-in flash or an external flash unit), you cannot use the program shift technique.

P selects shutter speed and aperture values steplessly. This means that any shutter speed or aperture within the range of the camera and lens is selected, not just those that are the standard full steps. This has commonly been the case with most SLRs (both film and digital) for many years, and allows for extremely precise exposure accuracy thanks to the lens' electromagnetically controlled diaphragm and the camera's electronically timed shutter.

Tv Shutter-Priority AE: Tv stands for "time value." In this mode, you set the shutter speed using 🖐 and the camera sets the aperture. If you want a particular shutter speed for artistic reasons—perhaps a high speed to stop action, or a slow speed for a blur effect—this is the mode to use. Even if the light varies, the shutter speed does not. The camera keeps up with changing light by adjusting the aperture automatically.

If the aperture indicated in the viewfinder or the LCD monitor is constantly lit (not blinking), the 60D has picked a useable aperture. If the maximum aperture (lowest number) blinks, it means the photo will be underexposed. Select a slower shutter speed by turning 🖐 until the aperture indicator stops blinking. You can also remedy this by increasing the ISO setting. If the minimum aperture (highest number) blinks, this indicates overexposure. In this case, you should set a faster shutter speed until the blinking stops, or choose a lower ISO setting.

The 60D offers a choice of speeds, from 30 seconds up to 1/8000 second, in 1/3-stop increments. (You may also elect to use 1/2-stop increments via C.Fn I-1 **[Exposure level increments]**—see page 139.) For flash exposures, the camera syncs at 1/250 second or slower (which is important to know, since slower shutter speeds can be used to record the ambient or existing light in a dimly-lit scene).

Let's examine these shutter speeds by designating them as "fast," "moderate," or "slow." These divisions are somewhat subjective, so speeds at either end of a division can really be assigned to the groups on either side of it. I consider fast shutter speeds to be between 1/500 – 1/8000 second. It wasn't all that long ago that most film cameras could only reach 1/1000 second, so having this range of high speeds on a DSLR is quite remarkable. The obvious reason to choose a fast shutter speed is to stop action. The more the action increases in pace, or the closer it crosses directly in front of you, the higher the speed you will need to freeze it. As mentioned previously, the neat thing about digital cameras is that you can check your results immediately on the LCD monitor to see if the shutter speed has, in fact, stopped the action.

At these fast speeds, camera movement during exposure is rarely significant unless you try to handhold a super telephoto lens of 600mm (not recommended!). This means, with proper handholding technique, you can shoot using most normal focal lengths (from wide-angle to telephoto) up to about 300mm without blur resulting from camera movement. Besides stopping action, high shutter speeds also allow you to use your lens at its widest opening (such as f/2.8 or f/4) for selective focus effects (i.e., shallow depth of field). This is a useful technique. In bright sun, for example, you might have an exposure of 1/200 second at f/16 with an ISO setting of 200. You can get to f/2.8 by increasing your speed by five whole steps of exposure, to approximately 1/4000 second.

HINT: With exposure settings, there is a balance between shutter speed and aperture. In Tv, the camera takes care of aperture, according to how you set shutter speed. Try this yourself. Go outside and use 🗘 to set the shutter speed to 1/200. Now, look in the viewfinder, ignore the shutter speed, and just watch the aperture. Keep changing the shutter speed by rotating 🗘 until the aperture is at the widest setting that the lens will allow. Now look and see how short the shutter speed has become.

Moderate shutter speeds (1/60 – 1/250 second or so) work for most subjects and allow a reasonable range of f/stops to be used. They are the real workhorse shutter speeds, and they really do the job nicely... as long as there isn't any fast action. You have to be careful, though, when handholding cameras at the lower end of this range—especially with telephoto lenses—or you may notice blur in your pictures from camera movement during the exposure. Many photographers find that they cannot handhold a camera with moderate focal lengths (50 – 150mm) at shutter speeds less than 1/125 second without some degradation of the image due to camera movement. You can double-check your technique by taking a photograph of a scene while handholding the camera and then comparing it to the same scene shot using a tripod. Be sure to magnify the image to check for image blur caused by camera motion. (Even better, check it on the computer.)

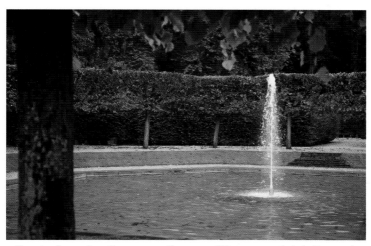

^ These two images have the same overall exposure. This one uses a fast shutter speed, which freezes the motion of the water. Because of the fast shutter speed, a large aperture (bigger opening) is needed. A large aperture means narrow depth of field. Notice the out-of-focus leaves in the foreground.

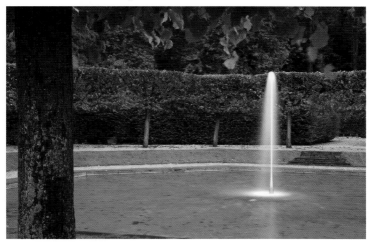

^ In this image, the shutter speed is slower and the aperture is smaller. With the slower shutter speed, the water becomes blurred. But, notice the increased depth of field: the foreground leaves are sharp.

Slow shutter speeds (1/60 second or slower) require something to stabilize the camera. Some photographers may discover they can handhold a camera and shoot relatively sharp images at the high end of this range, but most cannot get optimal sharpness from their lenses at these speeds without a tripod or another stabilizing mount. Slow shutter speeds are used mainly for low-light conditions, and to allow the use of smaller f/stops (higher f/numbers) for increasing depth of field.

A fun use of slow shutter speeds, such as in the 1/2 – 1/8 second range, is to photograph movement, such as a waterfall or runners, or to move the camera during exposure, panning it across a scene. The effects can be unpredictable, but again, image review using the LCD monitor helps. You can try different shutter speeds and see what your images look like. This is helpful when you try to choose the best shutter speed for the subject because each speed blurs action differently.

You can set really slow shutter speeds up to 30 seconds for special purposes, such as moonlit landscapes. Canon has engineered the sensor and its accompanying circuits to minimize noise (a common problem of long exposures with digital cameras) and the 60D offers remarkable results with these exposures. C.Fn II-1 **[Long exp. noise reduction]** can be used to reduce noise even more (see page 142).

In contrast to long exposures using film, long digital exposures are not susceptible to reciprocity—the condition in which, in film exposures beyond approximately one second (depending on the film), the sensitivity of the film declines, resulting in the need to increase exposure to compensate. A metered 30-second film exposure might actually require double or triple that time to achieve the desired effect. Digital cameras do not have this problem. A metered exposure of 30 seconds will perform at exactly the exposure and sensitivity settings you entered into the 60D, but there will still be increased noise.

Av Aperture-Priority: In **Av** (aperture value) mode, you set the aperture (the opening in the lens, measured in f/stops) and the camera selects the appropriate shutter speed for a proper exposure. This is probably the most popular automatic exposure setting among professional photographers. One of the most common reasons to use **Av** mode is to control depth of field (the distance in front of and behind a specific plane of focus that is acceptably sharp). While the f/stop, or aperture, affects the amount of light entering the camera, it also has a direct effect on depth of field. The three variables that affect depth of field are lens aperture, focal length, and focused distance.

A small lens opening (higher f/number), such as f/11 or f/16, increases the range of acceptable sharpness in the photograph. Hence, higher f/numbers are great for landscape photography. A wide lens opening, such as f/2.8 or f/4, decreases the depth of field. These lower f/numbers work well when you want to take a photo of a sharp subject that creates a contrast with a soft, out-of-focus background.

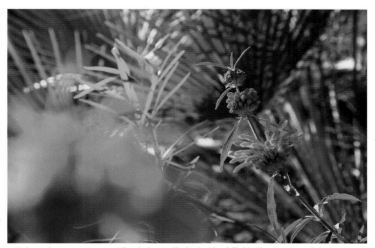

^ Using a large aperture setting helps to limit depth of field. The Aperture-Priority setting allows you to select the depth of field you desire while the camera selects the appropriate shutter speed to create a "good" exposure.

If the shutter speed blinks in the viewfinder (or on the LCD monitor), it means the shutter speed the camera wants to use is not available. In other words, good exposure is not possible at the selected aperture. Decide whether you need to change the aperture to let in less light (select a higher f/number) or more light (select a lower f/number). You can also choose to increase or decrease the ISO to change the sensitivity of the 60D's sensor to the light.

You can see the effect of the aperture setting on the depth of field by pushing the camera's depth-of-field preview button, located on the front of the camera on the opposite side from the lens release button. This stops the lens down to the taking aperture and reveals sharpness in the resulting darkened viewfinder. Using depth-of-field preview takes some practice due to the darkened viewfinder, but changes in focus can be seen if you look hard enough. Remember you are only evaluating depth of field; don't worry about how dark things look. You can also check focus in the LCD monitor after the shot (magnifying as needed).

HINT: If the viewfinder is too dark, consider using Live View mode and then checking depth of field. With Live View the 60D will keep the image bright when the depth-of-field preview button is pressed.

It may sound counterintuitive, but a sports or wildlife photographer might choose Av mode in order to stop action, rather than to capture depth of field. To accomplish this, he or she selects their widest lens opening—perhaps f/2.8—to let in the maximum amount of light. The camera automatically selects the fastest shutter speed possible for the conditions. Compare this with Tv mode, in which you can set a fast shutter speed, but the camera still may not be able to expose correctly if the light drops and the selected shutter speed requires an aperture larger than the particular lens can provide. (The aperture value blinks in the viewfinder if this is the case.) As a result, photographers typically select Tv only when they have to use a specific shutter speed. Otherwise they use Av both for depth of field and to gain the fastest possible shutter speed for the circumstances.

HINT: Another option is to use Tv and Auto ISO. For example, if you are shooting a sporting event and you discover that you need a shutter speed of 1/500, you could set that while in Tv and then, if the aperture is at the end of its range (largest opening that the lens allows), the Auto ISO function will kick up the camera's sensitivity, allowing you to use your selected shutter speed and still maintain a good exposure.

M Manual Exposure: With no autoexposure involved, this option is important for photographers who are used to working in full manual and for anyone who faces certain tricky situations. (However, since this camera is designed to give exceptional fully-automatic exposures, I recommend that everyone try the fully-automatic settings at times to see what they can do.) In M, you set both the shutter speed (using 🔲) and aperture (using ⚪).

You can use the camera's exposure metering system to guide you through the manual exposure settings. The current exposure is visible on the scale at the bottom of the viewfinder information display. "Correct" exposure is at the mid-point, and you can see how much the exposure settings vary from that point by observing the scale. The scale shows up to two stops over or under the midpoint, allowing you to quickly compensate for bright or dark subjects (especially when using partial metering). If the pointer on the scale blinks, the exposure is off the scale. (Of course, you can also use a handheld meter.)

The following examples of complex metering conditions might require you to use **M** mode:

O Panoramic shooting, since you need a consistent exposure, white balance, and focus across the multiple shots taken

O Lighting conditions that change rapidly around a subject, such as in a theatre performance

O Close-up photography where the subject is in one light but slight movement of the camera dramatically changes the light behind it

O Any shooting situation where you need a consistent exposure throughout varied lighting conditions

B Bulb Exposure: This mode allows you to control long exposures because the shutter stays open as long as you keep the shutter button depressed. Let go, and the shutter closes. A dedicated remote switch, such as the Canon RS-60E3, is helpful for these long exposures. It allows you to keep the shutter open without touching the camera (which can cause movement). It attaches to the camera's remote terminal (on the left side). You can use the RC-1, RC-5, or RC-6 wireless remote switches for bulb exposures, as well.

Since the shutter speed is directly controlled by how long the shutter is depressed, both 🖾 and ○ set the aperture. When you use **B**, the camera shows the elapsed time (in seconds) for your exposure as long as you keep the shutter release or remote switch depressed, which is a helpful feature. Currently with digital camera technology, exposures beyond a few minutes start to produce excessive noise. Still, the 60D allows longer exposures than most cameras of this type. It is a good idea to use C.Fn II-1, **[Long exp. noise reduction]**, to apply added in-camera noise reduction (see page 142). Remember that long exposure noise reduction doubles the apparent exposure time, so make sure you have enough battery power.

C **Camera User Settings:** This isn't a setting like the others in the Creative Zone—designed by Canon. This is your setting; you design how the 60D will operate. Imagine you want to shoot your daughter's soccer match. You will no doubt set your camera differently than if you are going to record an autumn morning landscape. The exposure mode (or even aperture and shutter speed), plus the ISO setting, white balance, saturation and/or sharpness levels, etc. will be different for each type of photo.

Once set to record the soccer match, the camera can memorize and save those settings so it is ready to shoot soccer action every time there is a match—you don't have to remember the settings and reprogram them each time you get to the field.

You accomplish this by using the Camera User Settings. **C** stores more than just shooting modes; it remembers many menu settings and even custom functions. Once you get used to your 60D, you'll find that **C** is a powerful tool for quickly setting up your camera for different shooting situations. The possibilities are endless.

To set up **C**, first pick a shooting mode (not **C**) on the Mode dial, then make adjustments to other settings, configure your custom functions and then go into ♥ to register the Camera User Setting (page 135). When you want to use the registered settings, just set the Mode dial to **C** and you're ready to go. Note that even when you select the Camera User Setting, you are still able to temporarily override any of the camera's settings.

> As you get used to shooting with the 60D don't forget about using Camera User Settings to create a quick camera setup.

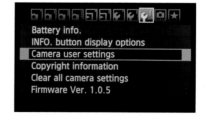

HINT: Don't try to set up the camera user settings right away. Instead, after you've used your camera for awhile, start paying attention to the modes and settings you keep using. Then create the camera user settings based on those settings.

DRIVE MODES AND THE SELF-TIMER

The term "drive mode" is a throwback to film days when a photographer had to advance the film after every shot. Professional photographers would add a "motor drive" to their camera so that they could take photos in rapid succession without having to manually cock the shutter and advance the film. Even though the film is gone, shutter mechanics are still needed in any DSLR. The 60D offers several different drive modes.

To select a drive mode, press DRIVE and use , , or to select from Single shooting □, High speed continuous H, Low speed continuous, Self-timer:10sec/Remote control, and Self-timer:2sec/Remote control 2.

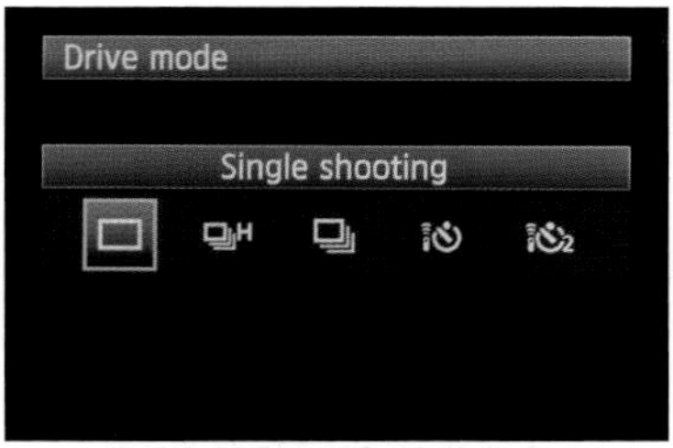

‹ Pick your drive mode wisely. If you use the continuous shooting modes all the time, you will end up with a lot of images to go through when you download them to your computer.

NOTE: You can also set the drive mode using the Quick Control screen (see page 58).

□ SINGLE SHOOTING

This is the standard shooting mode. One image is captured each time you press the shutter release. You'll probably use this mode most of the time. While memory cards are increasing in capacity, you still have to manage all those image files, so you might want to stay in this mode, rather than using continuous as your default and taking a burst of shots each time you press the shutter button.

H HIGH-SPEED CONTINUOUS

When the shutter button is held down, the camera captures at a rate of 5.3 images per second for approximately 58 consecutive JPEG images at the highest JPEG resolution and best quality. When the in-camera buffer (or the memory card) fills up, the camera stops capturing images. The

60D resumes taking pictures when the buffer has space again. When you shoot RAW images, a maximum of about 16 consecutive images can be captured before the buffer fills up. With RAW+JPEG shooting it drops to about 7 images.

🖳 LOW-SPEED CONTINUOUS

High-speed continuous shooting can fill up a memory card very quickly, and with the image size the 60D records, that can mean a lot of storage on your computer too. Low-speed continuous shooting gives you the ability to capture multiple images, but at a slower rate. When the shutter button is held down, the camera captures at a rate of three images per second.

NOTE: The speed for continuous drive modes is dependent on memory card speed, battery charge, and shutter speed.

🖳 SELF-TIMER:10SEC./REMOTE CONTROL

There are actually two parts to this setting: (1) self-timer and (2) remote control. When you want to be in the picture, the 10-second self-timer is the function to use. Press the shutter button halfway and make sure you have achieved focus. Then, press the shutter release button the rest of the way down. A self-timer lamp (located on the front of the camera next to the handgrip) flashes once per second to count down the seconds. By default, a beep is enabled and sounds during the countdown. Two seconds before the picture is taken, the lamp is solidly on and the camera beeps more frequently to let you know the shutter is about to be released. To cancel the countdown, press DRIVE.

🖳 SELF-TIMER:2SEC.

The 2-second self-timer operates similarly to the 10-second timer in that it takes the picture after a set time. When you shoot with a tripod and have longer shutter speeds, 1/60 and slower, use this quick timer, along with C.Fn III-5, [Mirror lockup], to reduce camera motion blur.

NOTE: Remember that the only way to cancel the self-timer once it has started counting down is to press DRIVE.

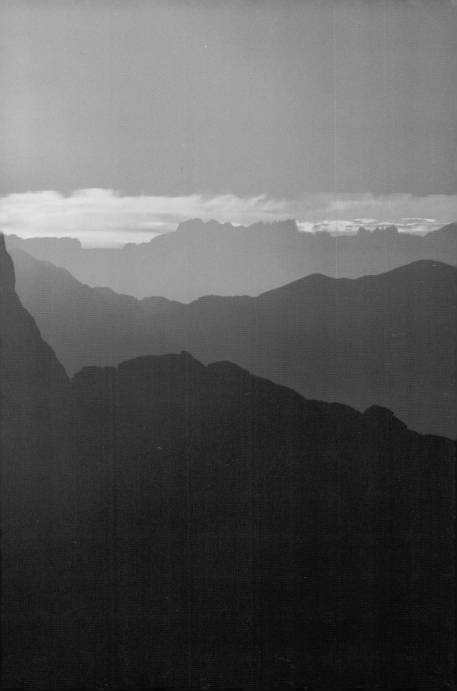

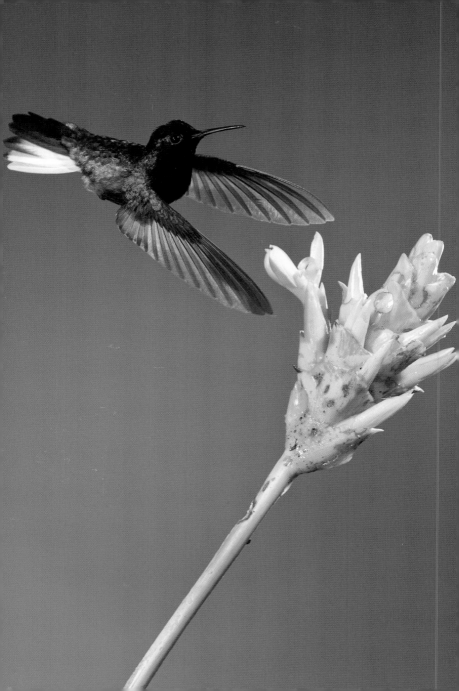

Focus and Exposure

You have in your hands a marvel of digital photography. The innovation, thought, and technology that have gone into the 60D become evident as soon as you begin to operate the camera's various systems and utilize its many functions. From finding focus on moving subjects, to capturing great exposures in low light, the 60D offers a number of options that enhance your ability to take excellent photographs.

AUTOFOCUS

The 60D uses an AI (artificial intelligence) AF (autofocus) system based on a special CMOS sensor dedicated to autofocus. The nine AF points give the camera nine distinct spots where it can measure focus. Eight points are positioned in a diamond pattern around a central ninth point. This diagonal arrangement makes for improved focus tracking of moving subjects. The center AF point is a very precise, cross-type point that works best at f/2.8.

The AF points work with an EV (exposure value) range of EV −0.5 to +18 (at ISO 100), and are superimposed in the viewfinder. They can be used automatically (the camera selects them as needed), or you can choose one manually.

This camera smartly handles various functions of autofocus through the use of a high-performance microcomputer, along with improvements in the AF system design. Its ability to autofocus while tracking a moving subject is quite good.

When light levels are low, the camera activates AF-assist with the built-in flash and produces a series of quick flashes to help autofocus. (External dedicated flashes can also do this. See C.Fn III-4 on page 146.) The range with the built-in flash is up to approximately 13.1 feet (4 m) in the center of the frame, and 11.5 feet (3.5 m) at the other AF points. The 580EX II Speedlite includes a more powerful AF-assist beam, effective up to 32.8 feet (10 m).

AF MODES

The camera has three AF modes: **ONE SHOT**, **AI SERVO**, and **AI FOCUS**. Each is used for a specific purpose, as described below. With the exception of the Basic Zone shooting modes where the AF mode is set automatically, you can choose among all three settings. They are accessed by pressing **AF**, which displays the AF mode menu on the LCD monitor. Use ☁, ○, or ☀ to select the mode you want. Once selected, press **SET** or tap the shutter button to accept the selection. The selected AF mode is indicated on the camera settings display on the LCD monitor.

> Which focus mode to use really depends on the subject matter of your shot.

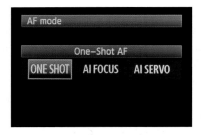

NOTE: You can also set the AF mode using the Quick Control screen (page 58).

ONE SHOT: This is ideal for capturing stationary subjects. The camera finds and locks focus on the important part of a subject when you aim and press the shutter button halfway. In this mode, once the camera achieves focus, it locks on that point. After focus is set, the camera beeps, and the viewfinder briefly shows the AF point or points that were used for the task. The focus confirmation light ● glows steadily in the viewfinder when you have locked focus. It blinks when the camera can't achieve focus. Since this camera focuses very quickly, a blinking light is a reminder that you need to change something (you may need to focus manually).

If the camera doesn't focus on the right spot, simply release the shutter button, change the framing slightly, and press the shutter button halfway to lock focus. Once you have found and locked focus, you can move the camera to set the proper composition. The 60D is designed to take clear pictures so that if it can't achieve focus lock it won't let you take a picture.

> **NOTE:** If you want to separate the focus from the shutter button you can reprogram the 60D so that focus starts only when you press **AF-ON**. This is done with C.Fn IV-1 (page 149). Also note that if you take the focus start function away from the shutter button, the 60D will allow you to take a picture without first achieving focus lock.

AI SERVO: If you do a lot of action photography you might find that ONE SHOT is not an AF mode to use. When subjects are in motion, AI SERVO becomes active when you press the shutter button halfway, but it does not lock focus. It continually looks for the best focus as you move the camera or as the subject travels through the frame. Focus and exposure are set only at the moment the shutter opens. This can be a problem when it is used for motionless subjects because the focus continually changes as the camera perceives changes within the frame, which is especially troublesome if you are handholding the camera. However, if you use AI SERVO on a moving subject, it is a good idea to start the camera focusing (depress the shutter button halfway) before you actually need to take the shot, so the system can find the subject.

If the camera is set for automatic AF point selection then AI SERVO will first use the center AF point for focus. Once the subject moves away from the center, the focus system will track the subject as long as it can be covered by one of the eight other focus points.

> **NOTE:** Since the camera is continually adjusting focus, it will not beep to indicate focus lock nor will the focus confirmation indicator ● light up.

> AI Servo can help
you track fast-
moving objects to
keep them in focus.

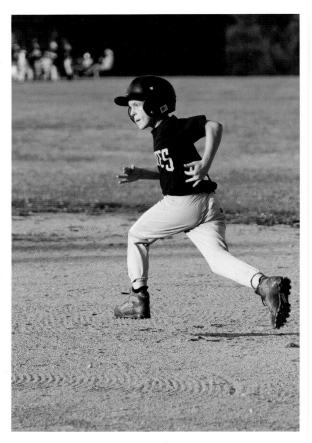

AI FOCUS: This mode allows the camera to choose between **ONE SHOT** and **AI SERVO**. It can be used as the standard setting for the camera because it switches automatically from **ONE SHOT** to **AI SERVO** if your subject should start to move. Note, however, that if the subject is still (like a landscape), this mode might detect other movement (such as a tree blowing in the wind), so it may not lock on the non-moving subject. When focus has been achieved in **AI FOCUS** mode the camera will give an indication based on the focus mode it has used. If lock was achieved via **ONE SHOT** mode the camera will beep and the focus confirmation indicator ● will light. If lock is set using **AI SERVO** mode there will be a quieter beep and the focus confirmation indicator ● will not light.

> **NOTE:** Focus during Live View shooting and movie shooting is handled differently. See page 215.

SELECTING AN AF POINT

You can let the 60D select the AF point automatically, or you can manually select a desired point. Manual AF point selection is useful when you have a specific composition in mind and the camera won't focus consistently on the desired area. To manually select an AF point, simply push the ⊞ button (on the back of the camera in the upper right corner; it is also ⚲ during Playback), and use ⌒, ○, or ✳ to make the selection. Points light up in the viewfinder and on the LCD monitor as they are selected.

If all points are lit, the camera automatically makes the AF point selection. You can press **SET** to jump directly to the center AF point. Once there you can use **SET** to toggle between the center AF point and automatic selection. You can also turn on automatic selection by pressing ✳ twice in the same direction. For example if you press ✳ left once it will select the left AF point, if you press left again it will select automatic selection—all the points are selected.

Turning ⌒ and ○ rotates through all of the points and is not as direct as selecting points with ✳. However, some photographers find ⌒ is easier to use while looking through the viewfinder. You can return to shooting mode at any time during AF point selection by either pressing the shutter halfway or pressing ⊞. You do not need to press **SET** to have the camera accept your selection.

AUTOFOCUS LIMITATIONS

With its impressive AF sensitivity, the 60D is able to autofocus in conditions that are quite challenging for other cameras. Still, as the maximum aperture of lenses decreases, or tele-extenders are used, the camera's AF capabilities change. AF works best with lenses that have wide maximum apertures (f/2.8 or wider). This is normal, and not a problem with the camera.

It is possible for autofocus to fail in certain situations, requiring you to focus manually. This is most common when the scene is low contrast or has a continuous tone (such as sky), in conditions of extreme low light, with subjects that are strongly backlit, and with compositions that contain repetitive patterns. A quick way to deal with these situations is to focus on something else at the same distance, lock focus on it (keep the shutter button pressed halfway), then move the framing back to the original composition. This only works while the camera is in **ONE SHOT** Mode.

EXPOSURE

When recording your digital images, it is always preferable to have the best possible exposure. A properly exposed digital file is one in which the right amount of light has reached the camera's sensor and produces an image that corresponds to the scene, or to the photographer's interpretation of the scene. This applies to color reproduction, as well as tonal values and subject contrast.

ISO

ISO (sensitivity) is one control worth knowing so well that its use becomes intuitive. The first step in getting the best exposure is to provide the camera's meter with information on how it should respond to light. The meter can then determine how much exposure is required to properly record the image. Digital cameras adjust the sensitivity of the sensor's circuits to settings that can be compared to film ISO speeds. (This is an "apparent" change in sensitivity; in reality the electronic sensor data is amplified.)

The 60D offers ISO speed settings of 100 – 6400. This range can be expanded from 100 up to 12800 by using C.Fn I-3 (see page 140). When the ISO range is expanded, the 12800 ISO speed is represented by the letter "H." The H setting is not a free ride, however, as additional noise is present in the image. (To counteract this, extra noise reduction can be applied by using C.Fn II-2, see page 143.)

The full ISO range (expanded or not) is only available in Program **P**, Shutter-Priority **Tv**, Aperture-Priority **Av**, Manual **M**, and Bulb **B** shooting modes. In most Basic Zone modes, ISO is set automatically from 100 – 3200, and you cannot override it. In ⚘, ISO is fixed at 100. There is also an auto ISO setting that lets the 60D select which ISO setting to use (see below).

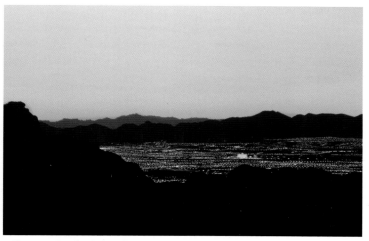

^ If you are shooting in any of the Basic Zone modes, the camera will automatically choose the ISO setting.

Setting the ISO: To set the ISO speed, use the ISO button located on the top right shoulder of the camera behind 🔄. The ISO speed menu displays on the LCD monitor and in the viewfinder. Use 🔄, ○, or ☼ to choose the sensitivity that you want, and confirm by pressing **SET**, ISO, or the shutter button. The selected ISO setting appears on the camera settings display on the LCD monitor. You can also look in the viewfinder while changing ISO as the speed will be displayed in the information bar at the bottom of the viewfinder.

ISO speed					
		Auto			
AUTO	100	125	160	200	250
320	400	500	640	800	1000
1250	1600	2000	2500	3200	4000
5000	6400	H(12800)			

‹ There are a range of ISO options to choose from in order to achieve a good exposure. Lower ISOs will result in less digital noise in your images.

NOTE: By default, the ISO settings occur in 1/3-stop increments (100, 125, 160, 200 etc.). You can change the steps to 1-stop increments by using C.Fn I-2.

Most of the time you will want to choose among several key ISO settings: 100 to capture detail in images of nature, landscape, and architecture; 400 when more speed is needed, such as handholding for portraits when shooting with a long lens; 800 and 1600 when you really need the extra speed under low-light conditions.

Auto ISO: You can also let the 60D select the ISO. One of the options in the ISO menu is [AUTO]. When selected, the camera chooses an ISO from 100 to 6400. When you use bulb B, the ISO is set to 400. When you use flash, auto ISO uses 400 unless the 60D determines there will be overexposure, and then a lower ISO is selected. With a Speedlite set for bounce, the ISO is set in the range of 400 – 1600.

Auto ISO can be used in combination with Aperture-Priority Av and Shutter-Priority Tv shooting modes to give you enhanced control of exposure settings. For example, if you want to shoot with a high shutter speed, set the mode to Av, open the aperture to its widest setting, and turn on auto ISO. The 60D will set both shutter speed and ISO speed, with emphasis on high shutter speed.

ISO speed can be set quickly from shot to shot in the P, Tv, Av, M, and B shooting modes. Since sensitivity to light is easily adjusted using a DSLR, and since the 60D offers clean images with minimal noise at any standard setting, ISO is a control you can use freely to rapidly adapt to changing light conditions.

Low ISO settings give the least amount of noise and the best color, while high ISO settings can lead to noise in your pictures. Traditionally, film would increase in grain and decrease in sharpness with increased ISO. This is not entirely true with the 60D because its image is extremely clean. Noise is virtually nonexistent at ISO settings of less than 800. Some increase in noise may be noticed as settings of 800 or 1600 are used, but there will be little change in sharpness. (Check the image on a computer to see if the noise is acceptable.) If you use speeds beyond 1600, the noise level in the image will increase, but it may be the only way to get the shot.

You can also set the ISO speed using the Quick Control screen. Press ⊡ and use ✣ to highlight the current ISO setting. Then use ⌂ to scroll through the ISO options. If you want a list of possible ISO settings to choose from, use the same first two steps: press ⊡ and use ✣ to highlight the current ISO setting, then press SET to bring up a list of ISO options and then use ⌂, ○, or ❖ to make your selection. Next, tap the shutter release or press **SET** to exit.

> **NOTE:** If you use Highlight Tone Priority (C.Fn II-3, see page 144) to expand the dynamic range of the 60D, the ISO range is 200 – 6400 and **D+** shows up next to the ISO number in the settings display.

Maximum Auto ISO: In ◻︎ᶠ, the **[ISO Auto]** option allows you to limit the maximum ISO speed. This is useful if you still want to use auto ISO but object to the amount of noise present at the highest ISO speeds. The maximum ISO speed allowed ranges from 400 to 6400. The ISO Auto setting only affects Creative Zone shooting modes. Basic Zone shooting modes will still use an ISO range of 100-3200. (❀ uses ISO 100).

METERING

The 60D uses Canon's iFCL (intelligent Focus Color Luminance) system. This new technology works in conjunction with the nine-point AF system to produce well-exposed images even in difficult lighting situations. The 63-zone iFCL sensor is made up of two layers, one that is sensitive to blue and green light, the other that is sensitive to red and green light. The two layers are compared to minimize errors due to color. Together, they evaluate the color and luminosity (brightness) of light surrounding the active AF point. In addition, the AF points transmit distance information to the metering system to help achieve accurate exposures.

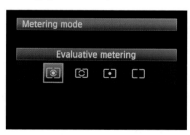

‹ While the 60D offers a sophisticated metering system, you can still use metering modes that photographers have been using for years.

To select a metering mode, press 🔲 and use ⌂, ○, or ❖ to select the mode you want. Once selected, press either **SET** or the shutter button. The symbol or icon for the type of metering in use appears on the camera settings display on the LCD monitor. The camera offers four user-selectable methods for measuring light (metering modes):

○ ⊛ evaluative (linked to any desired AF point)

○ ⊡ partial

○ ⊡ spot

○ ⊡ center-weighted average

NOTE: Use the Quick Control screen for a faster method of setting the metering mode. With the shooting settings displayed on the LCD monitor, press ⊙ and use ✵ to highlight the current metering method. Then use ⌂ or ○ to scroll through the metering options, or you can press **SET** to bring up the metering mode screen and then use ⌂, ○, or ✵ to make your selection. Tap the shutter release or press **SET** to exit.

⊛ **Evaluative Metering:** The 60D's evaluative metering system divides the image area into 63 zones, "intelligently" compares them in conjunction with the AF system, and then uses advanced algorithms to determine exposure. The zones come from a grid of carefully designed metering areas that cover the frame and complement the nine AF points. Basically, the system evaluates and compares all of the metering zones across the image, noting things like the subject's position in the viewfinder (based on focus points and contrast), brightness of the subject compared to the rest of the image, backlighting, and much more.

As mentioned above, the 60D's evaluative metering system is linked to autofocus. The camera actually notes which autofocus point is active and emphasizes the corresponding metering zones in its evaluation of the overall exposure. If the system detects a significant difference between the main point of focus and the different areas that surround this point, the camera automatically applies Exposure Compensation. (It assumes the scene includes a backlit or spot-lit subject.) However, if the area around the focus point is very bright or dark, the metering can be thrown off and the camera may underexpose or overexpose the image. When your lens is set to manual focus, evaluative metering uses the center autofocus point.

NOTE: With ⊛, after autofocus has been achieved, exposure values are locked as long as the shutter button is partially depressed. However, meter readings cannot be locked in this manner if the lens is set for manual focus. In this case, use the AE lock button ✳ to lock exposure (see page 45). It is located on the back of the camera toward the upper right corner.

It is difficult to capture perfect exposures when you shoot subjects that are extremely dark or light, that are backlit, or that have unusual reflectance. Because the meter theoretically bases its analysis of light on an average gray scene, it tends to overexpose or underexpose when subjects or the scene differ greatly from that average. Luckily, you can check exposure information in the viewfinder, or check the image itself—and its histogram—on the LCD monitor, and make adjustments as needed.

The main advantage of evaluative metering over the other methods is that the exposure is biased toward the active AF point, rather than the center of the picture. Plus, ⊚ is the only metering mode that automatically applies Exposure Compensation based on comparative analysis of the scene.

⊡ **Partial Metering:** The ⊡ metering selection covers about 6.5% of the frame, utilizing the exposure zones at the center of the viewfinder. It allows the photographer to selectively meter portions of a scene so that the 60D can evaluate the readings in an effort to select the right overall exposure. To compare exposures, fill the viewfinder with the area you want to meter and press ✳ to lock exposure, then reframe and press ✳ again and compare exposure settings. This can be an extremely accurate way of metering, but it requires some experience to do well. When you shoot with a telephoto lens, partial metering acts like spot metering.

⊡ **Spot Metering:** Use this mode to further reduce the area covered for metering. The metering is weighted to the center area (about 2.8%) of the viewfinder. This can give you an extremely accurate meter reading of a single object in your scene. This "spot" is indicated by the circle in the viewfinder.

> **NOTE:** Just because ⊡ only measures the center of the frame, it doesn't mean your subject has to stay in the center. Use ✳ to lock exposure and then reframe.

⊡ **Center-Weighted Average Metering:** This method averages the readings taken across the entire scene. In computing the average exposure, however, the camera puts extra emphasis on the reading taken from the center of the horizontal frame. It can be very useful with quickly changing scenes that have an important central subject, such as an outdoor portrait.

Since most early traditional SLR cameras used this method exclusively, some photographers have used center-weighted average metering for such a long time that it is second nature and they prefer sticking with it. It can be very useful with scenes that change quickly around the subject.

HINT: Be aware of the effect the viewfinder eyepiece can have on exposure! The 60D's metering system is sensitive to light coming through an open eyepiece. If you shoot a long exposure on a tripod and do not have your eye to the eyepiece, there is a good possibility that your photo will be underexposed. To prevent this, Canon has included an eyepiece cover on the camera strap. It can be slipped over the viewfinder to block the opening in these conditions. It is necessary to remove the rubber eyecup on the viewfinder to attach the cover. You can quickly check the effect by watching the camera settings on the LCD monitor as you cover and uncover the eyepiece—you'll see how much the exposure can change.

✳ AE LOCK

AE lock is a useful tool for the P, Tv, and Av shooting modes. Under normal operation, the camera continually updates exposure as you move it across the scene or as the subject moves. This can be a problem if there is strong light in the scene that may cause the camera meter to underexpose the shot. For example, if you want to take a photo of a person standing next to a bright window, the meter will overcompensate for the window light, causing the person to be underexposed. In this case, point the camera at the subject, so the window is not in the frame, press ✳, then reframe the shot so both the person and window are in it. (If you have a zoom lens mounted, you could zoom in to a particular area of the scene, as well.)

AE lock on the 60D is similar to that used for most EOS cameras. The ✳ button is located on the back of the camera to the upper right, easily accessed with your thumb. Aim the camera where needed for the proper exposure, then push ✳. The exposure is locked or secured, and it won't change, even if you move the camera. ✳ appears in the viewfinder on the left of the information display until the lock is released.

The exposure stays locked until you take a picture or the camera's metering system shuts down (which takes about four seconds). You can tell that the metering system has shut down when the information display turns off in the viewfinder. If you want to keep the exposure locked longer—even through multiple shots—press and hold ✶. The meter stays on and the exposure stays locked until about four seconds after you let go.

EXPOSURE COMPENSATION

The existence of Exposure Compensation, along with the ability to review images in the LCD monitor, means you can quickly override exposures without using the M shooting mode. Exposure Compensation cannot be used in M or B mode; however, it makes P, Tv, and Av shooting modes much more versatile. Compensation is added (for brighter exposure) or subtracted (for darker exposure) in f/stop increments of 1/3 for up to +/− five stops (1/2-stop increments with C.Fn I-1; see page 139).

To use the Exposure Compensation feature, tap the shutter to turn on the light meter. Rotate ◯ to change the compensation amount. The exact Exposure Compensation appears on the scale at the bottom of the viewfinder information display, as well as on the LCD monitor. You can also adjust Exposure Compensation by activating ⊚ to navigate the Quick Control screen. There is also the **[Expo.comp./AEB]** option in ◻. Adjusting Exposure Compensation via this method allows access to exposure bracketing, too (see page 102).

NOTE: The Exposure Compensation scale in the viewfinder and the LCD panel on top of the camera can't display the full range of +/- 5 stops, so the Exposure Compensation pointer will change to an arrow if the setting has exceeded the capability of the display. Refer to the LCD monitor to see the actual Exposure Compensation setting.

It is important to remember that once you set your Exposure Compensation control, it stays set even if you shut off the camera. Check your exposure setting (by looking at the bottom scale in the viewfinder information display or checking the LCD monitor's camera settings screen) as a regular habit when you turn on your camera to be sure the compensation is not inadvertently set for a scene that doesn't need it. Turn Exposure Compensation off by rotating ◯ to set the scale in the LCD monitor or viewfinder back to zero.

With experience, you may find that you use Exposure Compensation routinely with certain subjects. Since the meter wants to increase exposure on dark subjects and decrease exposure on light subjects to make them both closer to middle gray, Exposure Compensation may be necessary.

For example, say you are photographing a baseball game with the sun behind the players. The camera wants to underexpose in reaction to the bright backlight, but the shaded sides of the players' bodies may be too dark. So you add exposure with the Exposure Compensation feature. Or maybe the game is in front of densely shaded bleachers. In this case, the players would be overexposed because the camera wants to react to the darkness. Here, you subtract exposure. In both cases, the camera consistently maintains the exposure you have selected until you readjust the exposure settings.

The LCD monitor can come in handy when you experiment with Exposure Compensation. Take a test shot, and then check the photo and its histogram (see page 205). If it looks good, go with it. If the scene is too bright, subtract exposure; if it's too dark, add it. Again, remember that if you want to return to making exposures without using compensation, you must move the setting back to zero!

NOTE: Because ◎ controls Exposure Compensation without the need to press another button, you might find yourself accidentally turning on Exposure Compensation when you don't need it. The 60D allows you to lock ◎ so that you will need to press the UNLOCK button before you can adjust Exposure Compensation. This can be done with the **[Lock ◎]** option in ❡².

AUTOEXPOSURE BRACKETING (AEB)

This control offers another way to apply Exposure Compensation: AEB tells the camera to make three consecutive exposures that are different: (1) A standard exposure or "base-line" shot (even a shot that already has Exposure Compensation applied); (2) An image with less exposure; and (3) One with more exposure. The last two shots are said to bracket the base-line exposure.

The difference between exposures can be set up to +/- two stops in 1/3-stop increments. (C.Fn I-1 allows you to change this to 1/2-stop increments—see page 139.) When you use AEB, the 60D brackets using the shutter speed in **Av** mode and aperture in **Tv** mode.

NOTE: If the 60D is in auto ISO mode and AEB needs to use an exposure setting beyond the range of the camera, the ISO speed is adjusted. So you could pick a shutter speed where the aperture doesn't change through the bracketed shots, but the ISO speed does.

AEB is set using ◖▪. Scroll to **[Expo.comp./AEB]** and press **SET**. The submenu gives you to the ability to adjust both Exposure Compensation and bracketing. Use ○ or ✷ to adjust Exposure Compensation on the center shot (between the under- and overexposed images), then use ◠ to set the bracketing amount. The short outer lines show the exposure setting for "under" and "over" shots, and the long line is the "center" exposure. Make sure you press **SET** to accept the changes or they will be ignored. If C.Fn I-1 is set for 1/2-stop increments, the bracket amount will also use 1/2-stop increments.

HINT: Put the Quick Control screen to work for you. It is the quickest way to access AEB. Press ▣ and use ✷ to highlight the Exposure Compensation scale. Use ○ to set Exposure Compensation for the center shot and rotate ◠ to set the bracket amount. If you forget which control affects which parameter, press **SET** to bring up a more intuitive display. Another advantage to using this method is that it is not necessary to press **SET** to accept the setting, you can just make the adjustment and start shooting.

When in ☐ drive mode, you must press the shutter button for each of the three shots. The three indicators on the exposure scale will blink as long as there are shots left to be taken for the bracketing sequence. When you turn on the meter by pressing the shutter release button, a single point appears that indicates which shot in the bracket sequence will be captured next. In � or 535H drive mode, when you press and hold the shutter release button, the camera takes the three shots and stops. When you use ▷◷ or ▷◷2 drive modes, all three shots are taken after the time counts down.

NOTE: When set to AEB, the camera continues to bracket exposures until you reset the control to zero or turn the camera off. Also, AEB is turned off for flash, but when you stop using flash, the AEB setting is restored.

AEB can help ensure that you get the best possible image files for later adjustment using image-processing software. A dark original file always has the potential for increased noise as it is adjusted, and a light image may lose important detail in the highlights. AEB can help you determine the best exposure for the situation. You won't use it all the time, but it can be very useful when the light in the scene varies in contrast or is complex in its dark and light values, or if you don't feel confident with your exposure setting.

> **NOTE:** The default order for exposure is normal exposure, underexposed, overexposed. With C.Fn I-5 you can change the order to underexposed, normal, overexposed. See page 141.

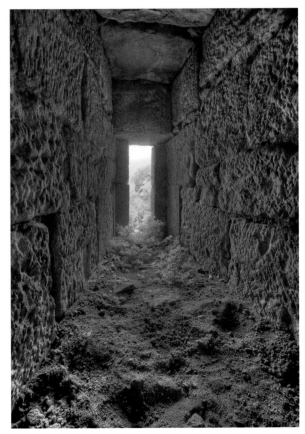

> Autoexposure bracketing can be used to create HDR images. HDR is used to capture scenes that have a dynamic range greater than the camera can record.

AEB is also important for a special digital editing technique called high dynamic range (HDR) photography. This allows you to put multiple exposures together in the computer to gain more tonal range from a scene. You can take the well-exposed highlights of one exposure and combine them with the better-detailed shadows of another. (This works best with 1/2-stop bracketing.) If you carefully shoot the exposures with your camera on a tripod, you can put the images on top of one another as layers using image-processing software so that they line up exactly, making the different exposures easy to combine. (You may even want to set the camera to ⏣ or ⏣H —in this mode it takes the three photos for the AEB sequence and then stops.)

NOTE: There are software applications that can merge these files and help you choose which parts of which image to use. In order for HDR to be successful, a tripod is a necessity. You'll also need to record using **Av** (so depth of field doesn't change) or **M** shooting modes. Also, use a Preset White Balance and not **AWB** (so color doesn't change), and use manual focus or a locked focus (so that focus doesn't change). HDR works best with images that have little or no movement.

You can combine Exposure Compensation with AEB to handle a variety of difficult situations. But remember, although AEB resets when you turn off the camera, Exposure Compensation does not.

JUDGING EXPOSURE

Examine your recorded images on the LCD monitor during Playback. Though it is possible to be fooled, with a little practice you will soon be able to use this small image to evaluate your exposure. Recognize that because of the LCD monitor's calibration, size, and resolution, it only gives an indication of what you will actually see when the images are downloaded into your computer.

The 60D includes two features—highlight alert and the histogram—that give you a very good indication of whether or not each exposure is correct. These features can be seen on the LCD monitor once an image is displayed there. Push INFO. repeatedly (located on back of the camera to the right of the LCD monitor) to cycle through a series of four displays: (1) The image plain; (2) the image with exposure information (shutter speed and aperture), Exposure Compensation value (if any), protection icon (if the image is protected), the image rating (number of stars, if any), the file and folder number, the Playback number, and total number of images on the card; (3) a small image with a histogram (brightness or RGB depending on the histogram setting in ⊡), as well as extended image information (including ISO speed, file size, Picture Style, and color space); and (4) a small image with the Brightness Histogram, the RGB Histogram, and reduced image information.

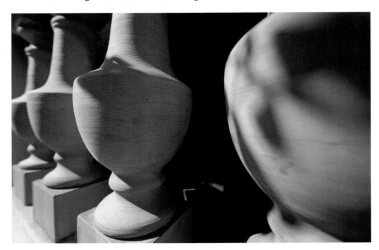

Highlight Alert: The camera's highlight alert is straightforward: Overexposed highlight areas blink when an image is displayed on the LCD monitor. These areas have so much exposure that only white is recorded, no detail. To turn on this useful exposure tool, go to ⊡ and use ○ or ⁙ to select [Highlight alert], then press SET. Use ○ or ⁙ to select [Enable] and press SET.

> Start with the highlight alert enabled. This will help you watch for overexposure.

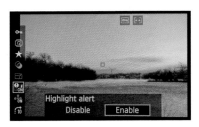

Although it is helpful to immediately see what highlights are getting blown out, some photographers are distracted by the blinking. But blinking highlights are simply information, and not necessarily bad. Sometimes the less important areas of the frame become washed out when the most important parts of the scene are exposed correctly. However, if you discover that significant areas of your subject are blinking, the image is likely overexposed and you need to reduce exposure in some way.

The Histogram: The 60D's histogram, though small, is an extremely important tool. It is the graph that appears on the LCD monitor next to the image when selected with INFO. during Image Review or Playback. The 60D can display two different kinds of histograms: Brightness and RGB. The Brightness Histogram allows you to judge the overall exposure of the image, while the RGB Histogram focuses on the individual color channels.

The horizontal axis of the Brightness Histogram represents the level of brightness—dark areas are at the left, bright areas are at the right. The vertical axis indicates the pixel quantity of the different levels of brightness. If the graph rises as a slope from the bottom left corner of the histogram and then descends towards the bottom right corner, all the tones of the scene are captured.

Consider the graph from left to right (dark to bright). If the graph starts too high on either end (i.e., so the slope looks like it is abruptly cut off at either side), then the exposure data is also cut off at the ends (also known as being clipped) because the sensor is incapable of handling the areas darker or brighter than those points. An example would be a dark, shadowed subject on a bright, sunny day.

Or, the histogram may be weighted towards either the dark or bright side of the graph (wider, higher "hills" appear on just one side or the other). This is okay if the scene is naturally dark or bright, as long as detail is not lost. However, be careful of dark scenes that have all the data in the left half of the histogram. Such underexposure tends to overemphasize any sensor noise that may be present. You are better off increasing the exposure, even if that makes the LCD image look too bright. You can always darken the image in the computer, which will not affect grain; however, lightening a very dark image usually has an adverse effect and results in added noise.

If highlights are important, be sure that the slope on the right reaches the bottom of the graph before it hits the right edge. If darker areas are important, be sure the slope on the left reaches the bottom before it hits the left axis.

If the scene is low in contrast, the histogram appears as a rather narrow hill in the middle of the graph, leaving gaps with no data toward both left and right axes. To help this situation, check the 60D's Picture Styles. Boosting contrast expands the histogram—and you can create a customized Picture Style with contrast change and tonal curve adjustment that addresses such a situation. This means better information is captured—it is spread out more evenly across the tones—before bringing the image into your computer to use image-processing software. You could also experiment with the **[Auto Lighting Optimizer]** option in ◘ (see page 103). Or, you could record using RAW, since results are best in RAW (versus JPEG) when the data has to be "stretched" to make better use of the tonal range from black to white.

NOTE: When shooting RAW, the effects of the Auto Lighting Optimizer will only be apparent if the RAW file is processed through Canon's Digital Photo Professional software.

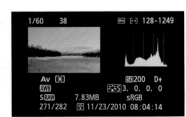

∧ The brightness histogram can quickly show you overall under- or overexposure.

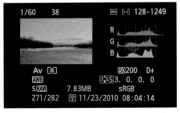

∧ The RGB histogram can show which color channel (red, green or blue), is under- or overexposed.

RGB Histogram: You can check to see if any of the individual color channels is oversaturated when you use the RGB histogram. Similar to the Brightness Histogram, the horizontal scale represents each color channel's brightness level. If more pixels are to the left, the color is less prominent and darker; to the right, the color is brighter and denser. If the histogram shows an abrupt cut-off on either end of the histogram, your color information is either missing or oversaturated. In short, by checking the RGB Histogram, you evaluate the color saturation and white balance bias.

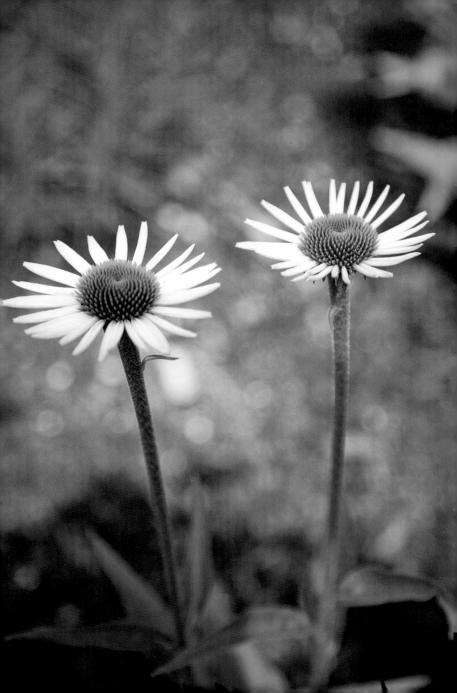

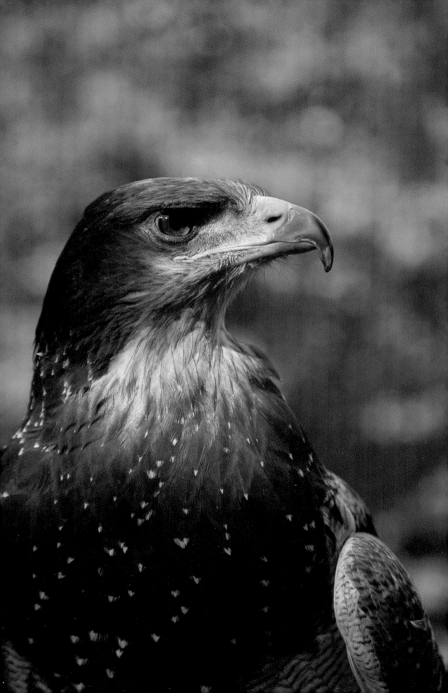

Live View and Movie Shooting

LIVE VIEW

Canon was one of the first manufacturers to offer Live View shooting in a DSLR. It wasn't long ago that people who were stepping up to a DSLR from a point-and-shoot camera were asking, "Why can't I see the image on the LCD before I take the shot? My little camera that is one-fourth of the price can do it!" Live View in DSLRs has changed all that.

This technology, which displays an image on the LCD monitor before you shoot, allows you to frame shots when it is difficult to look through the viewfinder. It also permits you to check exposure, composition, color, and focus on a computer display: When you connect the 60D to a computer and run Canon EOS Utility software, you view images live on the computer.

> **NOTE:** Since Live View and movie shooting share the same technology and some of the same camera settings, this chapter deals with both in tandem. But keep in mind that when I refer to Live View shooting, I am talking about capturing stills; movie shooting refers to the 60D's operations when the Mode Dial is set for 🎥.

To enable Live View shooting, go to ◻️⠿, scroll to highlight **[Live View shoot.]**, and press SET. Then use ○ or ⠿ to highlight **[Enable]** and press SET to confirm the setting. Once Live View shooting is enabled, press the ◻️ button—to the right of the viewfinder—at any time to turn it on.

› All the settings for Live View are found in the fourth Shooting menu tab.

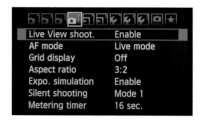

To shoot movies, set the Mode dial to '🎥. Once the switch is set, the image displays immediately on the LCD monitor. ◻️ is used to start and stop recordings. Movie mode does not require **[Live View shoot.]** to be enabled.

All the menu items for Live View mode are found in the ◻️⠿ menu. When the 60D is set for '🎥, three new menu items (◻️🎥, ◻️🎥⠄, ◻️🎥⠄) are added to the front of the menu tabs. In addition, Shooting 2 ◻️⠄, Shooting 3 ◻️⠄, and Shooting 4 ◻️⠄ menus are removed and various options in ◻️⠄ are eliminated.

NOTE: Although the Live View and movie-shooting menus appear in two different places, they share some of the same settings. For example, if you set the metering timer for one minute in the Live View options in ◻️⠿, it will also be set to one minute in ◻️🎥⠄ menu.

LCD MONITOR

The LCD monitor is the key to Live View and movie shooting. It doubles as a viewfinder for composing your scene, yet it still acts as a status display to show you many of the 60D's settings. New with the 60D is the articulating feature of the LCD monitor. This allows you to shoot in awkward positions—low or high angles, for instance—while still being able to see the display. The image will flip if the LCD is positioned to the front of the camera, which is useful for self-recordings like video blogs.

Depending on your camera's settings, you can cycle through up to five display modes (four when in movie mode) by pressing INFO.. The default (or first) display is simply the image with the AF point. The AF point's appearance changes depending on the AF mode for which the camera is set. The AF point might not be displayed at all if the AF mode is set for AF ⛄.

Press INFO. to add a status display at the bottom of the LCD, including some exposure setting information, an exposure level indicator (with exposure compensation and bracketing indicators if engaged), flash status, shots remaining, ISO speed, Highlight Tone Priority indicator, and battery level.

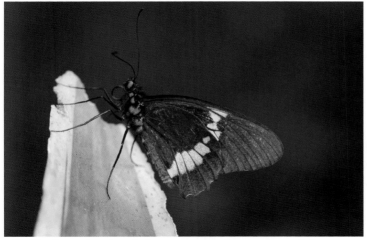

⌃ Live View is a good way to evaluate exposure even before you take the shot.

The exposure setting display depends on which shooting mode the camera is in and whether the exposure meter is on. For example, if the camera is set for aperture priority **Av**, then the aperture setting will be displayed. Later, when the meter is engaged (by tapping the shutter button), the current shutter speed (set by the camera's metering system) will be added to the display. When you use autoexposure lock by pressing ✳, the status display will indicate that exposure is locked by displaying ✳.

If the camera is in a Basic Zone shooting mode, the information is reduced. In movie shooting, this status display is similar except there is no flash status.

NOTE: If there is no SD card in the camera or the card is full, the movie-recording size will appear along with the remaining recording time of 00:00 displayed in red. At the top of the screen will be the warning "No card in camera".

Press INFO. again in Live View shooting to add information about drive mode, AF mode, white balance, Picture Style, Auto Lighting Optimizer, image-recording quality, flash exposure compensation, autoexposure bracketing (AEB), external flash exposure bracketing (FEB), Eye-Fi status, and exposure simulation (covered later in this chapter).

In movie shooting, this display is slightly different. Beneath the image-recording quality are the movie-recording size and the remaining recording time. The available recording time switches to elapsed time when you start recording; and instead of exposure simulation status Exp.SIM there is an exposure mode indicator (manual vs. auto). Missing from this display in movie shooting is flash-ready and AEB, since flash cannot be used while shooting movies and bracketing is also disabled.

> You can overlay a lot of camera setting information simply by pressing the INFO. button.

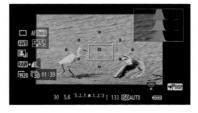

Press INFO. again to display a histogram. It displays brightness or RGB, depending on the **[Histogram]** setting in ▤². The histogram display mode will only be available when the 60D is set for Exp.SIM (exposure simulation) when in Live View mode or in movie mode when manual exposure mode is set. If those modes aren't set, then this display mode is skipped. One last press of INFO. displays the electronic level.

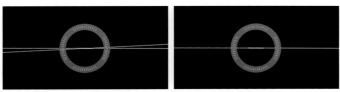

The level display helps with keeping your 60D level. The horizontal line turns green when the camera is level.

QUICK CONTROL SCREEN

When shooting in Live View, you can adjust exposure, AF mode, drive mode, and ISO speed with their dedicated buttons. But just as with non-Live View, you can quickly access many shooting settings via the Quick Control screen. Press ⊙ to bring up the Quick Control screen on the left side of the LCD monitor.

With Live View shooting, the Quick Control screen allows you to adjust autofocus mode, drive mode, white balance, Picture Styles, Auto Lighting Optimizer, image-recording quality, and flash exposure compensation. Use ☼ to highlight the parameter you want to change. Then use ☼, ○, or ⌒ to change the value. If you want to bring up a list of possible settings for the parameter you are adjusting, press **SET**. Note that Auto Lighting Optimizer is disabled when C.Fn II-3 **[Highlight tone priority]** is enabled.

For movie shooting, the Quick Control screen operates similarly except that drive mode setting and image-recording quality only relate to any stills that you capture while shooting movies. There is also a separate setting to adjust movie resolution and frame rate. Additionally, flash exposure compensation is not available since this feature is disabled when you are in movie mode.

> **NOTE:** If the 60D is in one of the Basic Zone shooting modes, the Live View Quick Control screen will only let you adjust the same parameters as the non-Live View Quick Control screen.

Since ⊞/🔍 is used to magnify the image on the LCD monitor when you are in Live View, you cannot use it to pick AF points. Instead, you use the Quick Control screen to pick AF points when the 60D is set for AF Quick. While in the Quick Control screen, first use ☼ to highlight AF mode. Then press up on ☼ to enter the AF point selection mode. The currently selected AF points will be highlighted in blue on the LCD monitor. Use ○ or ☜ to move through the AF points. Use ◙ or tap the shutter to exit. The AF-point selection options are the same as non-Live View shooting. When all the AF points are highlighted, the 60D will select the AF point automatically based on the subject.

NOTE: With other AF modes, the Quick Control screen is not necessary.

CAMERA SETTINGS

When you are shooting in Live View, you still have access to many of the same settings that are used for non-Live View shooting, with a few exceptions. The biggest change is that metering is always evaluative ▣. Otherwise, you still have access to white balance, autofocus, drive mode, ISO, flash exposure compensation, Picture Styles, and exposure compensation. Since the Quick Control screen has fewer options in Live View, a number of settings (i.e., autoexposure bracketing) are accomplished via menus.

When you shoot movies, you have access to white balance, autofocus, and exposure compensation. Drive mode relates only to taking still images. Metering is center-weighted average ▢, and ISO can only be set when the movie exposure mode is set to manual (see page 223).

NOTE: Live View and movie shooting use a lot of power, so make sure you have fully charged batteries on hand. The 60D is good for about 350 shots using Live View (320 when flash is used about half the time). When you record movies, the battery lasts about two hours. (Battery runtime figures assume a temperature of 73°F or 23°C.)

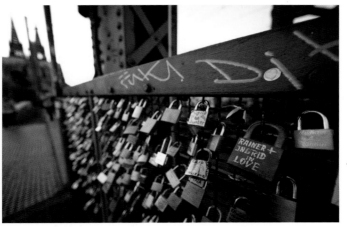

∧ The immediate feedback with Live View can help with troublesome exposure situations.

FOCUS DURING LIVE VIEW SHOOTING

As mentioned previously, when Live View shooting is turned on, the reflex mirror pops up, rendering the viewfinder unusable. Since the autofocus sensors are part of the viewfinder, which is blocked by the mirror, the 60D's traditional autofocus method is not immediately functional. Autofocus is accomplished by either flipping the mirror back down or evaluating the image coming from the sensor. You choose the AF mode via the Live View Quick Control screen ⃞. There are three autofocus options:

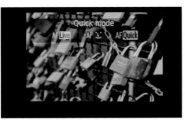

‹ You can use the Live View Quick Control screen to set AF mode.

AF⃞Quick⃞ QUICK MODE AF

You might wonder why this is called Quick mode since it takes a bit of time to achieve focus. In reality, this is often the fastest and most accurate way to achieve focus. The method uses the same autofocus sensors that are used during non-Live View still photography. Remember that during Live View, the reflex mirror (reflex is the "R" in DSLR) is in the up position; light lands on the image sensor and creates an image. But because the AF sensors are located in the viewfinder, the reflex mirror must be in the down position so that the light hits them. In other words, if you use AF⚙Quick, the Live View image is temporarily interrupted while the camera sets focus.

When you use AF⚙Quick, you must select AF point(s), just as you would if you were not using Live View; however, you must use the Live View Quick Control screen. Press ◉ to activate the Quick Control screen. Use ✴ to highlight AF mode then press up once to put the 60D into Live View AF point selection mode. The AF⚙Quick AF points will be highlighted in blue on the LCD monitor. Use ⌂ or ○ to move through the AF points. Once you have highlighted the AF point(s) you want to use, press ◉ or tap the shutter to exit AF point selection. The AF point(s) selected are overlaid on the LCD monitor as gray points. The selected AF point also carries over from non-Live View shooting. For example, if you have selected the center AF point during normal shooting, the selected AF point is still the center point when you switch to Live View with AF⚙Quick, until you change it.

Once the AF point is selected, press the shutter release button halfway and hold it to start the autofocus process. The mirror flips down, interrupting the Live View image on the LCD monitor. The camera then sets focus and confirms the focus with a beep (unless the beep was disabled in ◻'). Once focus is set, the mirror flips back up and you can see the Live View image again. The AF point(s) used to set focus is highlighted in green. If the camera isn't able to achieve focus, the mirror will stay down and the AF point(s) will flash red.

> **NOTE:** It is critical that you make sure the 60D has set focus before you take the picture. Unlike non-Live View shooting, the focus process takes time. You can't just press the shutter button all the way down to take a picture without setting focus first by pressing the shutter button halfway.

To check the focus once it has been set, a white rectangular magnifying frame can be moved anywhere in the scene with ✴. Once in place, press 🔍 to magnify the image in that frame. Press once to magnify 5x, press again to magnify 10x, and press a third time to return to normal view. Use ✴ to scroll around the magnified image or press 🗑 to reset the magnifying frame to the center of the screen.

Once focus has been set, press the shutter to take the picture. If you let go of the shutter button before you take the picture, the 60D attempts autofocus again when you press the shutter release button. So, when shooting with Live View, get into the habit of keeping your finger down on the shutter release button (halfway) after focus is achieved.

The 60D has a separate autofocus button **AF-ON** that is useful to separate engaging autofocus from exposure and from taking the picture. It is especially useful when shooting with Live View. It is comfortably placed near where your right thumb lands when you hold the camera. Use this button to start the Live View autofocus process; simply press and hold the button to set focus, and keep pressing it while you take the picture. You can also continue to hold it if you want to keep the same focus setting for multiple shots.

HINT: Consider using **AF-ON** in order to lock focus on objects that aren't near the AF point(s) you have selected. Instead of changing the AF point selection, simply temporarily frame the subject so that it is covered by the selected AF point and set focus by pressing and holding **AF-ON**. Then reframe and take the picture.

AF🄻🄸🅅🄴 *LIVE MODE AF*

In this mode, the 60D sets focus by evaluating the image coming from the sensor. The camera uses contrast detection to examine edges in the scene, continually measuring the image while focus is adjusted. This feedback loop takes a bit longer to set focus compared to AF🄀🅄🄸🄲🄺, but it does not interrupt the Live View image.

With AF🄻🄸🅅🄴, you first need to set the 60D's AF🄻🄸🅅🄴 focus point. In AF🄻🄸🅅🄴 the white frame overlay becomes the AF point. Use ✲ to move the AF point to the area of the image on which you want to focus. For quicker and more accurate results, pick an area with high contrast. You can move the AF point around more than 60% of the image with ✲ but you won't be able to get to the far edges. If you press 🗑 you can reset the AF point to the center of the screen.

When the AF point is correctly located, press the shutter release button halfway to start autofocus. The camera indicates that focus is achieved by beeping and turning the AF point green. If the camera fails to find focus, the AF point turns red and there is no beep. You can magnify the image using ⊕ to check the focus. Press ⊕ once to magnify 5x, twice for 10x, and a third time to return to normal view. Unfortunately, magnifying the image might change the focus setting.

Once AF is set, the picture can be taken. It is critical that you make sure the 60D has set focus before you take the picture. If you let go of the button you used to achieve focus before you take the picture, the 60D attempts focus again when you press the shutter release button.

HINT: AF-ON can be used for setting focus just as with AF Quick.

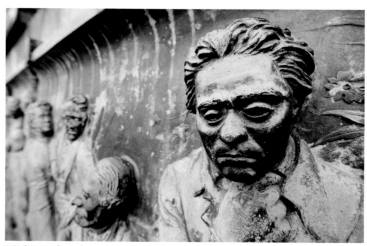

^ Make sure focus is locked on the right subject before taking the picture.

NOTE: There is a difference between the AF Live AF point and the magnification point displayed when the 60D is in AF Quick AF mode. The magnification point has a horizontal orientation (it is wider than it is tall) and the AF Live AF point is vertical.

AF ☺ FACE DETECTION AF

The last Live View AF mode uses face detection technology built into the DIGIC 4 chip. The 60D can detect up to 35 different faces in the scene. Once detected, the camera chooses either the largest or the closest face in the scene and sets the AF point at that location.

When AF ☺ is selected, simply frame the scene and the camera detects the faces in it. A special face detection AF point ⸢ ⸣ appears over the largest or the closest face on the LCD monitor. If there are multiple faces in the scene, the face detection AF point changes to ❮ ❯. Use ✤ (press left or right) if you want to move the AF point to a different face. Once a face has been selected, press the shutter release button halfway (or press **AF-ON**) to engage autofocus. When focus is achieved, the face detection AF point turns green and the camera beeps. If focus cannot be achieved, the AF point turns red. Once focus has been set, you can take the picture.

NOTE: You cannot magnify the live image to evaluate the focus in Face Detection AF mode.

If a face cannot be detected in the scene, an AF point will not be displayed. Pressing the shutter or **AF-ON** will switch the camera to AF⟦Live⟧ mode; the AF⟦Live⟧ AF point will appear in the center of the screen, and the 60D will use it to lock focus. You will not be able to move this point. To temporarily leave AF ☺ so that you can have more control over the AF point, press ⟦🗑⟧. This toggles the AF mode to AF⟦Live⟧. Then you can use ✤ to move the AF point and set focus by pressing the shutter button halfway or pressing **AF-ON**. Then take the picture. Press ⟦🗑⟧ again to return to AF ☺. This is a useful technique to remember if you want to quickly switch between AF⟦Live⟧ and AF ☺.

Face detection is an impressive technology, but it is not perfect. Faces will be difficult to detect if they are at an angle to the camera, are tilted, are too dark or too bright, are close to the edge of the frame, and are too small. Don't expect the face detection AF point to completely overlay the face all the time. Also, if the lens is way out of focus to begin with, the camera will have difficulty detecting faces. If the lens supports manual focusing (via turning the focus ring), manually set the focus while the lens is in AF mode. Once the Live View image is in better focus, the 60D may detect faces.

AF in Live View only occurs near the center area of an image. If the camera detects a face near the edge of the frame, the face detection AF point turns gray. If you attempt autofocus at that time, the center Live View AF point is used instead.

NOTE: AF in Live View mode is limited to about 60% of the image displayed on the screen, so this is another good reason to use **AF-ON**. If a subject is near the edge of the frame, reframe so that the subject is covered by the AF point, press and hold **AF-ON** to set focus, and then recompose the shot and press the shutter button to capture the scene.

MF *MANUAL FOCUS*

Manual focus is still a good option for Live View shooting. When you switch the manual focus switch on the lens, the camera displays a magnification frame. One of the best ways to ensure accurate focus is to use ○ to position the magnification frame over the area of your scene that you want in focus. Then press ⊕ to magnify the image either 5x or 10x. You can center the magnification frame by pressing 🗑. Use the lens' focus ring to set focus; then press ⊕ once or twice to restore the normal image size.

HINT: Even if you don't normally shoot stills using Live View, this manual focus procedure is a useful way to check your focus when you shoot in situations that make focus hard to judge—like at dusk.

FOCUS DURING MOVIE RECORDING

Since movie shooting uses the same technology as Live View, the AF modes are the same. You can use AF〔Quick〕 before you start shooting movies, but once recording starts, AF〔Quick〕 is no longer accessible. Pressing the shutter release button halfway attempts focus using AF〔Live〕. AF〔Live〕 can be used during movie shooting just like with Live View shooting: Use ⊹ to move the AF point, then press and hold the shutter release button halfway to set focus. AF ☺ also works for recording movies the same way it does for still shooting.

Don't expect AF〔Live〕 or AF ☺ to be as smooth as if you had a Hollywood-style focus puller—the person whose sole job on a movie set is to adjust lens focus when the camera moves. Since there is a feedback loop, the focus setting hunts a little when it gets close to the right setting. Also, the brightness level of the scene will usually temporarily change while focus is set.

If you are used to the autofocus of camcorders, it will take some time to adjust to the autofocus of the 60D. In short, I don't recommend that you try to autofocus while the 60D is recording, unless you don't mind if the video image is disturbed (focus and exposure) while the camera sets focus. For best results, consider using manual focus when recording movies. It may be the fastest method to achieve focus. And, with a gentle touch, it can be done while recording.

> **NOTE:** The built-in microphone (or a close external microphone) will pick up the sound of the focus motors in the lens when the camera adjusts focus.

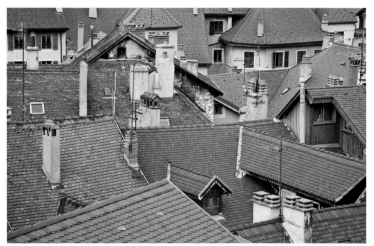

^ Using autofocus in Movie Recording mode is a less than gratifying experience, especially when there are many focus points for the camera to choose from.

While it is tempting to just watch the LCD and set exposure by eye, you should use the same techniques for setting proper exposure that you use while not in Live View: look at the review image and its histogram, and pay attention to the exposure scale when you are in **M** shooting mode.

ISO IN LIVE VIEW

During Live View shooting, the ISO speed setting operates the same way as during normal still shooting: Press ISO and use ☼, ○, or 🖰 to select the ISO speed from the overlay on the LCD monitor.

NOTE: When Highlight tone priority has been activated (C.Fn II-3), it is indicated by **D+** next to the ISO speed display at the bottom of the LCD monitor during Live View still shooting.

ISO IN MOVIE SHOOTING

There is no direct control over the ISO setting when shooting movies, except when **[Movie exposure]** is set for **[Manual]** in ☐'🎥'. In manual exposure mode, press ISO and use ☼, ○, or 🖰 to select the ISO speed from the overlay on the LCD monitor. If you set ISO to Auto, the 60D automatically adjusts the ISO for the best exposure while shooting.

EXPOSURE MODES IN LIVE VIEW

When you capture stills during Live View shooting, the **P**, **Tv**, **Av**, **M**, and **B** modes operate the same way as during non-Live View shooting. Exposure compensation is accessed using ○ as with normal shooting. Apply AEB through ☐'.

NOTE: Exposure compensation as currently set for non-Live View shooting carries over into Live View shooting.

In ﹐🎥, the 60D automatically sets ISO speed, aperture, and shutter speed when **[Movie exposure]** is set for **[Auto]** in ▭🎥. The shutter speed is set in a range from 1/30 – 1/125 second. The exposure settings change as needed—even during recording—to maintain a good movie image. Exposure compensation is available using ○, and exposure can be locked with ✳. But be careful! If you lock exposure, it stays locked even if the scene gets darker or lighter. In that case you'll need to press ✳ to lock a new exposure. If the change is drastic you may need to press ✳ twice.

NOTE: If you adjust the zoom while recording, the image may flicker as the 60D adjusts the exposure.

The 60D offers manual exposure control when **[Movie exposure]** is set for **[Manual]** in ▭🎥. Just as in still shooting, use 🖾 to set shutter speed and ○ to set aperture. ISO is set using ISO. The shutter speed must be equal to or faster than the frame rate that you are using to record. For example, if the 60D is set for 1920 x 1080 at 30 frames per second, the shutter speed can only be set for 1/30 of a second or faster. If you use 1280 x 720 at 60 frames per second, the shutter speed will be 1/60 or faster.

HINT: Consider using Auto ISO for video shooting in manual exposure mode. If your lighting changes, the exposure will be adjusted by the 60D. However, the adjustment will be less noticeable because it will be an ISO speed change, not an aperture change (which would affect depth of field) or shutter speed change (which would affect motion). Instead, the image will have slightly less or more noise depending on the direction in which the ISO speed changes.

Metering during Live View shooting is preset to ▣ because it is linked to the Live View AF point. It cannot be changed. You can still use all of the exposure and drive modes that would normally be available, depending on whether you are in the Creative or Basic Zone shooting modes. Adjust ISO, aperture, shutter speed, and exposure compensation just as you would when shooting normally.

When you use a Speedlite external flash unit, E-TTL II metering uses the normal meter in the viewfinder, so the mirror must drop down briefly.

When you take a picture with flash, the 60D sounds like it is taking two pictures. Flash units other than Canon's do not fire. Also, flash exposure lock (FEL) is not available.

> **NOTE:** If you use one of the continuous drive modes, the exposure for all of the images shot is locked to the first image captured.

METERING IN MOVIE SHOOTING

Movie shooting exposure metering is automatically set for center-weighted average metering ⎣⎦. The one exception is if you use AF ⚄. When a face is detected, the metering is ⊛, and it is linked to the face detection AF point. If you shoot a still in movie shooting mode it will use the same center-weighted average metering ⎣⎦ for exposure.

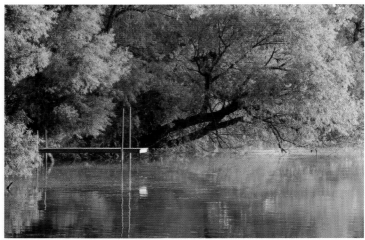

^ A scene with an overall, even light source will meter well, but pay attention to exposure metering when you shoot in movie mode, since the 60D is automatically set for center-weighted metering. This is especially true if you are shooting a high-contrast scene.

EXPOSURE SIMULATION INDICATOR

Normally the 60D tries to display a good image on the LCD monitor, no matter how the exposure is set. In Live View, Exp.SIM displays to indicate that the image presented on the LCD monitor (in terms of exposure) is close to the actual exposure that will be captured when the shutter release button is pressed. If this icon blinks, it means the image on the screen does not represent the exposure that will be used for the actual image. If you are using flash or **B**, Exp.SIM will be grayed out since the LCD can't represent flash illumination or an unknown shutter speed length. When the 60D is shooting movies, the camera always displays a representation of the video exposure.

> **NOTE:** Heat can be a problem when you use Live View and movie shooting. Thermal build-up on and near the image sensor causes the function to shut down. This is particularly true when you shoot under hot studio lights or outdoors in direct sun. If heat becomes a problem, the temperature icon is displayed. While you can keep shooting, image quality may suffer, so it is best to turn off Live View shooting for a while.

One 60D feature that is improved with Live View shooting is Depth-of-Field preview. Depth-of-Field preview normally produces an image that is dim in the viewfinder, making it difficult to see the image. With Live View shooting, the Depth-of-Field preview has a brighter display that allows you to better check depth of field, as long as a reasonably correct exposure is set.

MOVIE SHOOTING

There are ten things you should do to record movies successfully with your 60D. These steps are important because the process of recording movies can be very different than that of shooting stills. However, these are just starting points. As you get used to the camera, you'll develop your own steps.

1. Make Sure You Have Plenty of Power: If you use batteries, make sure they are charged and make sure you have spares. Running Live View and recording movies can use up battery power quickly. Better yet, use the optional AC adapter (ACK-E8).

2. Use a Large SDHC or SDXC Class 6 or Higher (High-Speed) SD Memory Card: For optimum performance when recording high-definition movies, make sure that you format the card in the 60D. If you shoot stills and record movies, consider using different cards for

each scenario. This also helps organize files when you download to the computer.

3. Pick the Movie Resolution: Press ⌨, highlight the movie-shooting size parameter on the Quick Control screen, and use 🎛 to make your choice. The options are **[1920 x 1080 30/25 fps]**, **[1920 x 1080 24 fps]**, **[1280 x 720 60/50 fps]**, **[640 x 480 60/50 fps]**, or **[Crop 640 60/50 fps]**.

NOTE: 30/25 and 60/50 indicate different frame rates depending on whether the camera is set for NTSC or PAL video system in 🔧.

---

4. Enable Audio Recording and Set Level: To reduce camera handling noise picked up by the microphone, make sure that you make all camera adjustments before you start recording, or use an external microphone. Decide if you want to use automatic or manual level control. If you choose the latter, adjust the level before recording. Adjust audio in 🎙.

5. Select a Picture Style: Press ⌨ and use ✴ to highlight the Picture Style parameter. Use 🎛 to choose from ⬚⬚S, ⬚⬚P, ⬚⬚L, ⬚⬚N, ⬚⬚F, ⬚⬚M, or one of the three User-defined Picture Styles ⬚⬚1. To make adjustments, press **SET** to bring up the Picture Style list, then press down on ✴ to adjust any of the following: Sharpness, Contrast, Saturation, and Color tone. Once the specific parameter is highlighted, use 🎛 or ✴ to adjust. Press **INFO.** to reset the parameter to its default setting. If ⬚⬚M is selected, the adjustable parameters are Sharpness, Contrast, Filter effect, and Toning effect. (For more on Picture Styles, see pages 66-72.)

6. Make a White Balance (WB) Selection: If in doubt, use **AWB**, but the image displayed on the LCD monitor can help you choose the best white balance setting. To set, press ⌨ and highlight the current white balance setting on the LCD monitor. Use 🎛 to scroll through the white balance options: Auto **AWB**, Daylight ☀, Shade 🏠, Cloudy ☁, Tungsten light 💡, White fluorescent light 💡, Flash ⚡, Custom 📷, and color temperature **K** (see pages 75-84).

7. Choose a Focus Mode: Decide if you want to set focus manually or via one of the three special movie AF modes. If you opt for an AF mode, first make sure your lens is not in manual focus mode. Next, press ⌨ and use ✴ to highlight the current AF mode. Use 🎛 to select one of the AF options: AF Quick, AF Live, or AF ☺ (see pages 188-191).

8. Set Focus: The 60D does not automatically set focus before movie recording. Press and hold the shutter release button halfway until you receive a confirmation that focus has been achieved. Depending on the AF mode you have set, this might involve momentary loss of the Live View image display on the LCD monitor.

9. Adjust Exposure: Use manual or automatic exposure mode via ▣🎥. For manual exposure, set the shutter speed with ⬙. Adjust the aperture with ○. Set ISO with ISO. To adjust exposure in the automatic mode, use exposure compensation via ○ to add or subtract up to 5 stops of exposure compensation.

10. Make a Test Recording: Press ▣ to start recording. Since you can't monitor audio from the 60D's audio/video out terminal while you record movies, make sure that you do a test recording. Listen to the recorded audio to make sure it sounds good, then look at the movie to check exposure. Exposure compensation can be adjusted by rotating ○ before and during recording.

MOVIE-RECORDING QUALITY

There are four parameters that are important in any digital movie specification: resolution, frame rate, scanning type, and compression. The first two you can control; the last two cannot be changed.

Resolution: Much like still photography, digital video is captured in pixel form. Unlike stills, however, movies cannot "print" at various sizes and resolutions. Instead, movies are locked into displays that have fixed pixel counts. Rather than talking about how many megapixels a camera has, you specify exactly how many pixels there are in the horizontal and vertical direction.

The 60D has four digital movie resolution options: **[1920 x 1080]**, **[1280 x 720]**, **[640 x 480]**, and **[Crop 640]**. **[1920 x 1080]** and **[1280 x 720]** are the two resolutions that comprise High-Definition video. It is typical to refer to the resolution by its vertical dimension, so the 60D can shoot 1080 or 720 HD video.

[640 x 480] and **[Crop 640]** are close to the standard-definition digital video specification (which is typically 720 x 486). While **[Crop 640]** is the same resolution as **[640 x 480]** it takes a center cut of the image sensor rather than scaling down the image from the entire sensor. This means that the image will appear to be magnified almost 7 times.

The 60D is a true 1080 camera. Some camcorders (including high-level professional cameras costing thousands more) use pixels that are rectangular. The actual count of their pixels is 1440 x 1080, which is later stretched out to create a 1920-wide image. The 60D uses square pixels.

> The 60D supports recording of two of the most popular high-definition frame sizes.

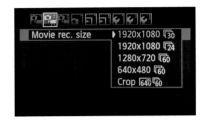

HINT: While it is easy to print a vertical (portrait format) still image and hang it on the wall vertically, you don't see many televisions mounted on a wall vertically. So avoid shooting movies when the camera is in a vertical position.

Frame Rate: The second parameter is frame rate—the number of frames that the camera can capture per second. This should not be confused with shutter speed or maximum burst rate. In the case of the 60D, the camera records 30 or 24 frames per second (fps) in 1080, and 60 fps in 720 and standard definition. 24 fps is the standard frame rate for movies and it is used in video cameras to approximate a "film look." In reality, more than just frame rate is involved in creating a film look (i.e., lighting, depth of field, and camera movement) but the 60D can produce some great film-like moving images.

NOTE: The frame rates given are rounded up. The true frame rates for HD video are 29.97, 23.976 and 59.94.

HINT: If you live outside of North America, the frame rates may be changed. In ⚙, set [Video system] to PAL. This changes your recording options to [1920 x 1080 25fps], [1920 x 1080 24fps], [1280 x 720 50fps], [640 x 480 50fps], and [Crop 640 50fps]. 50 and 25 are not rounded up.

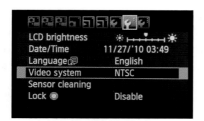

‹ The video system setting is also responsible for setting the frame rate of the recording.

Scanning Type: Another parameter important in movies is the scanning type. There is nothing similar to it in still cameras. In the early days of television, bandwidth was a big problem. Transmitting lines of video (think of a line of video as a row of pixels) every 1/30 second required a great deal of bandwidth. Using lots of bandwidth meant fewer television channels, so a system was devised to transmit every other line of video at 1/60 second. This "interlace" scanning scheme has been used for decades and it fit in very nicely with televisions based on CRTs (cathode ray tubes).

With the advent of computers and computer displays like LCDs, the concept of interlace scanning became problematic. LCDs are more efficient if they get each line sequentially, rather than every other line. LCDs use a type of scanning that is called progressive. The 60D is a progressive scanning capture device and so the high-definition output is sometimes referred to as 1080p or 720p—"p" for "progressive." There exist other movie recorders that are 1080i ("i" for "interlace").

Compression: Lastly, because movies—particularly high-definition movies—take up a lot of space on memory cards and hard drives, they are usually compressed. Just as the JPEG compression that is used for still images is of a high quality, so is the 60D's video compression—don't think web movie compression. In video parlance, the compression is referred to as a codec, which stands for compressor/decompressor. The 60D uses an MPEG4 compression scheme that is most commonly referred to as h.264. There are a variety of quality levels of h.264, from very low file size and low image quality, to large file size and high image quality. This camera uses a very high quality version of h.264 for all resolutions.

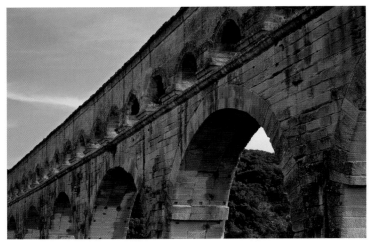

^ When the 60D is shooting video the minimum shutter speed is determined by the frame rate of the recording.

SHUTTER

When you shoot movies, the 60D does not use the mechanical shutter that is used for taking still photos. Instead, it uses an electronic shutter on the image sensor. This type of shutter is sometimes referred to as a "rolling shutter." A rolling shutter does not capture the entire image at one time. This can lead to motion artifacts where fast-moving objects become skewed. If you move the camera quickly—for example, a rapid pan—the image can appear to wobble.

To minimize these effects, be careful with panning speed and use a faster shutter speed if it is available. It should be noted that cinematographers face similar challenges with panning speeds when shooting motion picture film at 24 fps.

AUDIO

Audio is recorded simultaneously with the movie. The 60D records two digital audio channels (stereo) at a sampling rate of 48 kHz, which is the normal rate used for video. (CDs use 44.1 kHz.) It uses a linear PCM audio format, which is uncompressed. The audio can be recorded via the built-in microphone (located on the front of the camera above the

60D logo) or from an external audio source plugged into the external microphone jack. You can also turn off audio recording if it is not needed.

The built-in microphone is mono and picks up a lot of the camera noise, such as focus motors, stabilization, lens zooming, and any adjustments you make to a camera control. So, the built-in microphone isn't the answer for good audio recording. It is more for background recording, where audio isn't that important. The external microphone connection (located on the left side of the camera) is a stereo mini jack (3.5mm). It is important that a stereo plug is used; otherwise you may end up with a noisy recording or no audio at all. The microphone input supports condenser or dynamic microphones, but it does not supply power for microphones that require phantom power (+48v).

Much like setting the 60D for automatic exposure, the default setting for audio level control is automatic. In the **[Sound recording]** option in ⌂'🎥 you can choose from **[Auto]**, **[Manual]**, and **[Disable]**. When **[Manual]** is selected there is an additional menu option call **[Rec. level]**. Highlight this option and press **SET**. Then use ⁕ or ○ to adjust the audio recording level. It is important that you set this level while there is sound being produced at a volume that is similar to the volume when you record. There is an audio level meter on this screen. For best results set the level so that most of the main sounds reach about -12 or -10 on the scale. Make sure that any loud sounds do not reach the zero level.

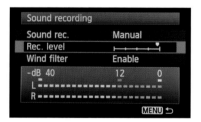

‹ When you are recording sound with the 60D, make sure to test your sound levels so that you can adjust the recording level appropriately.

NOTE: If you don't set the audio level properly, the sound will either be too low to hear or too loud, which results in permanent audio distortion in your recording.

RECORDING LENGTH

As mentioned before, a large SDHC or SDXC memory card with a speed class of 6 or higher should be used for recording movies.

MOVIE REC. SIZE	FILE SIZE	4GB CARD	8GB CARD	16GB CARD
1920 x 1080	330MB/min.	12 minutes	22 minutes	44 minutes
1280 x 720	330MB/min.	12 minutes	22 minutes	44 minutes
640 x 480	165MB/min.	24 minutes	46 minutes	92 minutes
Crop 640 x 480	165MB/min.	24 minutes	46 minutes	92 minutes

The maximum size for a single file is 4GB. The maximum recording time of one movie is 29 minutes, 59 seconds. If you have installed, say, a 16GB card, the camera will stop recording when the file size of the current recording reaches 4GB or 29 minutes, 59 seconds. Even though the 16GB card has a 49-minute HD capacity (see the chart above), those 49 minutes must be in several discrete files. The LCD monitor displays movie-recording size information and the amount of time left on the memory card. During recording, it indicates the elapsed shooting time.

If the card you are using is slow, a buffer capacity indicator appears on the LCD monitor. As the buffer fills up, waiting to write to the card, the icon indicates when the buffer is close to reaching capacity. When the memory card is full (or not present) the file recording size on the LCD appears in red.

MOVIE PLAYBACK

To access recorded movies, press ▶. Movies are indicated in the upper-right corner of the LCD by ≞ SET; the movie's duration in minutes and seconds is displayed as well, depending on the status display set via the INFO. button. Once a movie is selected via ❖, press SET to enter movie playback mode. A set of VCR-style playback controls appears at the bottom of the screen:

> Canon designed
the movie playback
interface in easily
understandable icons
for quick movie
viewing.

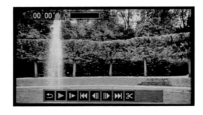

- Exit: Returns LCD to single-image display.
- Play: This button is highlighted by default. Press **SET** to begin playback; press it again to pause playback.
- Slow Motion: Once engaged, use ◀▶ to change the playback speed.
- First Frame: Returns to the first frame of the recorded movie.
- Previous Frame: Highlight this button and press **SET** to move back one frame. If you keep holding down **SET**, the rate increases until you reach rewind speed.
- Next Frame: Operates exactly like "Previous frame" above, except it advances through frames rather than going backward.
- Last Frame: Skips to the last frame of the movie.
- Edit: Allows you to trim the beginning or end of the movie (see below).

While movies are playing back, rotate to adjust the volume of the audio coming out of the camera's speaker. The control will not affect the volume when the 60D is connected to a TV. In that case, use the TV's volume control.

✂ MOVIE TRIMMING

While you would normally transfer your movie to a computer for editing, there is a tool built into the 60D that allows you to remove (trim) some footage at the beginning or end of the movie. To trim your movie:

- Select the movie you want to edit.
- Press **SET** to bring up the Playback controller.
- Highlight ✂ and press **SET**. A timeline appears at the top of the display and the trimming controls appear.
- Use ✳ to select whether you want to **[Cut beginning]** or **[Cut end]**, and press **SET**.
- Use ✳ to move the trimming pointer a frame at a time, or hold ✳ down to shuttle through the movie.
- Press **SET** to stop moving the pointer. If you want to trim the other end of your movie, the previous two steps.
- Highlight ▶ and press **SET** to preview your edit.
- Highlight ⮫ and press **SET** to save your edit. You can overwrite the original movie or save it as a new file. If there is not enough room on the memory card, the only option is to overwrite the original file.

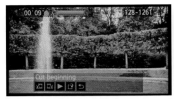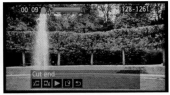

You can trim (shorten) the beginning and end of your movie clip, right in the camera.

NOTE: If you are interested in learning more about HD Video, check out *Digital Photographer's Complete Guide to HD Video* (978-1-60059-699-5).

STILL CAPTURE WHILE RECORDING MOVIES

While you can extract a still image from a movie using the Canon software that came with the 60D, the still will only be the resolution of the movie (i.e., a maximum of 1920x1080 pixels or about 2MP).

However, you can capture a higher resolution still while shooting: Just press the shutter release button while recording a movie. The image quality/size, white balance, and Picture Style will be determined by the current settings on the Quick Control screen. The drive mode will be whatever you set before shooting. A self-timer can be set but won't be used while recording; instead, single shooting will be used.

While the still image is being captured, the movie records a still frame without audio and then will resume video recording once the high-resolution still image has been written to the memory card. When you play back the movie you'll see the 1-second freeze frame and a jump in the recording.

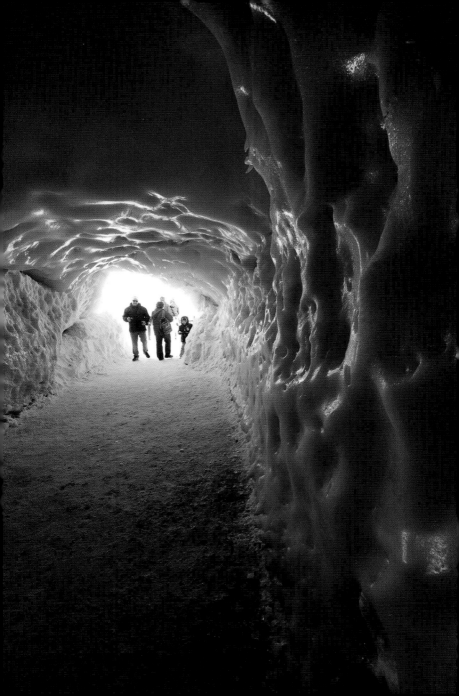

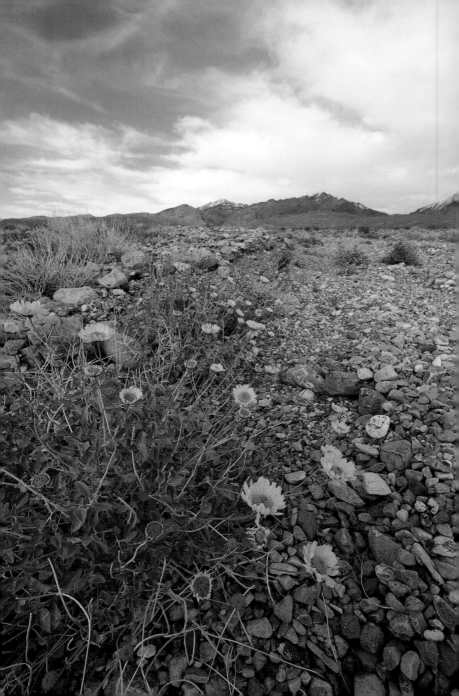

Flash

There will be times when there just isn't enough light to capture an image. But electronic flash is not just a supplement for low light—it can also be a wonderful tool for creative photography. Flash is highly controllable, its color is precise, and the results are repeatable. However, the challenge is getting the right look. Many photographers shy away from using flash because they aren't happy with the results. This is because on-camera flash can be harsh and unflattering, and taking the flash off the camera used to be a complicated procedure with less-than-sure results.

The Canon EOS 60D's sophisticated flash system eliminates many of these concerns and, of course, the LCD monitor gives instantaneous feedback, eliminating much of the guesswork. With digital, you take a picture and you know immediately whether or not the lighting is right. You can then adjust the light level higher or lower, change the angle, soften the light, color it, and more. Just think of the possibilities:

Fill Flash: Fill in harsh shadows in all sorts of conditions and use the LCD monitor to see exactly how well the fill flash works. Often, you'll want to decrease the maximum output of an accessory flash to make sure the fill looks natural.

Off-Camera Flash: Putting a flash on a dedicated flash cord allows you to move the unit away from the camera, yet still have it work automatically. Using the LCD monitor, you can see exactly what the effects are so you can move the unit around for the best light and shadows on your subject.

Close-Up Flash: This used to be a real problem because the light from the flash could overwhelm a close subject. Now you can see exactly what the flash does to the subject. This works amazingly well with off-camera flash, as you can "feather" the light (aim it so it doesn't hit the subject directly) to gain control over its strength and how it lights the area around the subject.

Multiple Flash Setups: Modern flash systems make exposure with multiple flash units easier and more accurate. However, since the flash units are not providing continuous light, they can be hard to place so that they light the subject properly. Luckily, with the 60D it is easy to set up the various flash units and then take a test shot. Does it look good, or not? Make changes as required. In addition, certain Canon EX-series flash units (and independent brands with the same capabilities) offer wireless exposure control with the 60D. This is a good way to learn how to master multiple-flash setups.

Colored Light: Because the light from a flash is cooler than daylight, many flash photos look better, and more natural, with a slight warming filter. With multiple light sources, you can attach colored filters (also called gels) to the various flashes so that different colors light different parts of the photo. (This can be a very trendy look.)

Balancing Mixed Lighting: Architectural and corporate photographers have long used flash to even the lighting when different sources are present. With digital, you can double-check the light balance on your subject using the LCD monitor. You can even be sure the added light is the right color by attaching the proper gels to match lights (such as a green filter to match fluorescents).

THE BASICS OF FLASH

Flash is a highly versatile photography tool, but before we talk specifically about using flash with your 60D, it is helpful to look at a few basic concepts.

THE INVERSE SQUARE LAW

This defines how the light from a flash unit is affected as it travels over distance. The Inverse Square Law states that the power of light is inversely proportional to the square of the distance that light travels. This is a very technical way of saying: as light travels twice the distance from its source, its intensity is quartered. This is due to the fact that the light spreads out as it travels.

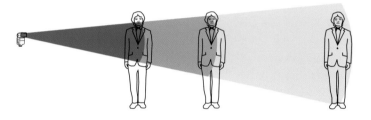

⌃ As light travels twice the distance from its source, its power is quartered.

GUIDE NUMBERS (GN)

A GN is a simple way to state the power of the flash unit. In the early days of flash photography, guide numbers were part of the formula that photographers used to determine the proper flash exposure setting for a given subject distance. While automation has eliminated that necessity, guide numbers are still used to quantify power output, and it is helpful to compare them when you shop for a flash unit. Guide number is computed as the product of aperture value and subject distance, and is usually included in the manufacturer's specifications for the unit. High numbers indicate more power; however, this is not a linear relationship. Guide numbers act a little like f/stops (because they are directly related to f/stops). For example, a GN of 56 is half the power of a GN of 80, and 110 is twice the power of 80 (see the relationship with f/5.6, f/8, and f/11?).

Since distance is part of the formula, guide numbers are expressed in feet and/or meters. Also, guide numbers are usually based on ISO 100. This can vary, however, so check the ISO reference (and the measurement system in use) when you compare different flash units. If you compare units that have zoom heads (special diffusers built into the flash units to match flash angle of view with the focal length in use), make sure you compare the guide numbers for similar zoom-head settings.

FLASH SYNCHRONIZATION

The 60D is equipped with an electromagnetically timed, vertically traveling, focal-plane shutter that exposes the sensor to light. The shutter works via two "curtains." The first curtain opens at the start of the exposure. The second curtain closes at the end of the exposure. With shorter shutter speeds (those shorter than the camera's "flash sync" rating) the second curtain starts to close before the first curtain has finished opening. This means that the entire surface of the image sensor is never completely exposed by the flash.

When you use a flash to illuminate the scene, the extremely short duration of the flash only reaches the sensor when it is entirely exposed. The fastest shutter speed where the entire image sensor is exposed at once—when the first curtain is completely open and the second curtain hasn't started to close—is called the maximum flash-sync speed.

The 60D's maximum flash sync speed is 1/250 second. If you use a flash and set a shutter speed faster than that in Shutter-Priority **Tv** or Manual **M** autoexposure modes, the camera automatically resets the speed to 1/250. In Aperture-Priority autoexposure mode **Av**, the 60D won't go above 1/250. Instead, if the aperture setting will cause overexposure, the shutter speed flashes, showing 1/250 in the LCD and viewfinder displays.

The 60D uses a flash autoexposure system that measures light coming through the lens (TTL). Canon's first evaluative flash metering system was called E-TTL; the latest version, which is used on the 60D, is called E-TTL II. E-TTL II has improved algorithms and, compared to E-TTL, can better use distance information obtained from the lens to improve control over flash exposure.

> **NOTE:** The terminology can be confusing at times. E-TTL II refers to the evaluative flash metering system available on the 60D. E-TTL refers to the earlier version of Canon's flash metering system, but it also refers to Canon's wireless flash system, something altogether different (see page 257). Unless noted otherwise, for the remainder of this chapter E-TTL will be used to refer to the wireless flash system.

It is important to understand that E-TTL II is a system—it won't work unless you are using both a flash unit that supports E-TTL II (any Canon Speedlite with EX in the name and some non-OEM units) and a Canon EOS camera that also supports E-TTL II. If you are not sure, speak with your authorized Canon dealer.

To understand the 60D's flash metering, it is helpful to know how regular E-TTL (non-E-TTL II) flash metering works with a Canon digital camera. When you first start pressing down on the shutter release button, the camera starts metering the ambient light. Once you fully press the shutter button, the camera stores the last ambient metering data, and it tells the flash to emit a pre-flash. During the pre-flash, the camera's metering system measures the pre-flash exposure. The camera also makes note of which AF point is being used to focus the lens. The camera takes these two sets of metering data and calculates the proper exposure placing emphasis on the AF point. All of this happens in a split second, of course.

With E-TTL II, the 60D ignores the AF point and instead uses all the metering zones in the camera to evaluate the ambient light and pre-flash. Any areas in the metering zones with dramatically different readings are given less weight in the overall exposure calculation, since they are likely to come from highly reflective surfaces that may skew the reading and cause underexposure. In addition, E-TTL II considers lens distance information in the exposure calculation in order to determine the location of the subject in the scene. Once the exposure has been calculated, the shutter is triggered, and the Speedlite is fired. The amount of flash that hits the subject is controlled by the duration of the flash emission; close subjects receive shorter flash bursts than more distant subjects. E-TTL II can produce some remarkably accurate flash exposures.

SETTING FLASH EXPOSURE

Though flash can sometimes be confusing when you are trying to set exposure, a few key concepts will help you understand how to adjust exposure when using it. First, shutter speed has no effect on flash exposure other than determining flash sync. The flash burst only occurs for a fraction of a second. Keeping the shutter open longer won't let in any more light from the Speedlite because it has already finished lighting up the scene. Thus, shutter speed only affects exposure for ambient light in the scene.

Second, aside from controlling the Speedlite power output on the unit itself, the only way to control the amount of flash illumination is to change the aperture. If you open up the aperture, you allow more of the light from the flash to reach the sensor. You will also allow more ambient light in, but since the ambient light is generally at a much lower level, the exposure change may not be as noticeable.

So remember: Adjust the shutter speed to control the amount of ambient light, especially in areas not lit by flash, and adjust the aperture to control the amount of flash illumination. Try it out yourself. Photograph a scene with some ambient light. Use M exposure mode and adjust only the shutter speed (in both directions). What changes do you see in your image? Now repeat the exercise but only adjust the aperture.

FLASH WITH SHOOTING MODES

With the exception of Creative Auto mode ⒸⒶ, you have no control over flash when the camera is set to any of the Basic Zone selections. This means you have no say in whether the flash is used for an exposure or how the exposure is controlled. The camera determines it all, depending on how it senses the scene's light values. Depending on the mode selected, when the light is dim or there is a strong backlight, the built-in flash automatically pops up and fires. In ⒸⒶ, you can use the Quick

Control screen to force the flash mode to always be off ⊕ (a useful setting when in a museum), to always be on ⚡, or to let the camera decide ⚡ᴬ.

NOTE: Never assume the flash will always fire if it is popped up (or an external flash is mounted and turned on) when in any of the Basic Zone modes. The flash will only fire if the mode requires it, and some modes will never require it.

In the Creative Zone shooting modes, you either pop up the built-in flash by pushing the flash ⚡ button (located on the front of the camera, on the upper left of the lens mount housing), or you attach an EX Speedlite accessory flash unit and simply switch it to the ON position. The flash operates in the various Creative Zone shooting modes as detailed below:

P Program AE: Flash photography can be used for any photo where supplementary light is needed. All you have to do is turn on the flash unit—the camera does the rest automatically. Canon Speedlite EX flash units should be switched to E-TTL II and the ready light should be on, indicating that the flash is ready to fire. When you are ready to take your picture, you must pay attention to make sure ⚡ is visible in the viewfinder, indicating that the flash is charged. The 60D picks a shutter speed in the range of 1/60 – 1/250 second automatically in P mode, and also selects the correct aperture.

Tv Shutter-Priority AE: This mode is a good choice in situations when you are using flash and want to control the shutter speed, which affects how ambient light is recorded. In Tv mode, you set the shutter speed before or after a dedicated accessory flash is turned on. All shutter speeds between 30 – 1/250 second synchronize with the flash. With E-TTL II flash in Tv mode, synchronization with longer shutter speeds is a creative choice that allows you to control the ambient-light background exposure. If you use a fast shutter speed to take a flash portrait of a person in front of a building with its lights on, you would expose the person correctly, but the background would be very dark. However, the ability to set slower shutter speeds using this mode allows you to control background exposure. If you set a shutter speed slower than 1/30 second, the camera automatically uses a "Slow sync" mode. You can turn this feature off using C.Fn I-7, however. (A tripod is recommended to keep the camera stable during long exposures.)

If the aperture value flashes on the LCD or in the viewfinder, the current shutter speed is forcing an aperture value beyond what the lens can produce, indicating that the flash exposure will not be adequate for the focused distance. Adjust the shutter speed until the aperture value stops blinking.

Av Aperture-Priority AE: Using this mode allows you to balance the flash with existing light and control the distance that the flash can reach. The camera calculates the lighting conditions and automatically sets the correct shutter speed for the ambient light. If the shutter speed value flashes on the LCD or in the viewfinder, the camera wants to choose a shutter speed beyond the sync speed of the flash. Either use an external Speedlite that can be set for high-speed sync (see page 250), or close down the aperture. When using an external Speedlite, you can adjust aperture (using 🖎) until you see the desired distance range in the external flash's LCD panel (if available).

M Manual Exposure: Using **M** mode gives you the greatest number of choices in modifying exposure. The photographer who prefers to adjust everything manually can determine the relationship of ambient light and electronic flash by setting both the aperture, which affects the flash exposure range, and the shutter speed, which affects the ambient light exposure. Any aperture on the lens and all shutter speeds between 30 – 1/250 second can be used. If a shutter speed above the normal flash sync speed is set, the 60D switches automatically to 1/250 second to prevent partial exposure of the sensor, unless you are using an external Speedlite capable of high-speed sync.

M mode also offers a number of creative possibilities for using flash in connection with long shutter speeds. You can use zooming effects that produce a smeared background and a sharply rendered main subject, or take photographs of objects in motion with a sharp "flash core" and indistinct outlines.

B Bulb: In **B** mode, you are effectively controlling the shutter speed by how long you keep the shutter release button depressed. The aperture setting controls the flash exposure, just as with **M** mode.

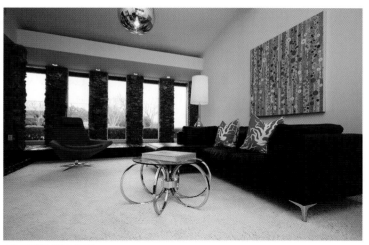

^ © Jessica Anne Baum

USING THE BUILT-IN FLASH

The 60D's built-in flash pops open to a higher position than the flash on many other cameras. This reduces the chance of red-eye in your photos and minimizes problems with large lenses blocking the flash. The flash supports E-TTL II, covers a field of view up to a 17mm focal length, and has a guide number of 43 feet (13 meters) at ISO 100. Like most built-in flashes, it is not particularly high-powered, but its advantage is that it is always available and is useful as fill flash to modify ambient light. This flash, as well as many Canon Speedlites, has the ability to send color temperature data to the camera's processor each time it fires. Just like flash output changes due to exposure needs, the color temperature of the flash can change. By communicating color temperature information to the camera, the 60D can better maintain consistent color.

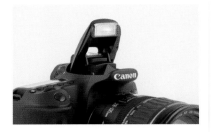

The flash pops up automatically in low-light or backlight situations in the fully automatic exposure modes, □ and CA; and in 🐦, ♨, and 🎨. In CA, you can force the flash mode to always be off ⊕ or always be on ⚡ using the Quick Control screen. In P, Tv, Av, M, and B you can choose to use the flash (or not) at any time. Just press the ⚡ button (located on the front of the camera, on the upper left of the lens mount housing) and the flash pops up. To turn it off, simply push the flash down.

NOTE: You cannot use the built-in flash while an external flash is mounted in the hot shoe of the 60D.

The P, Tv, Av, M, and B exposure modes do not all use the same approach with the built-in flash. In P mode, the flash is fully automatic, setting both an appropriate shutter speed and the aperture. In Tv, it can be used when you need a specific shutter speed up to the maximum sync speed (1/250 second). In Av, if you set an aperture that the flash uses for its exposure, the shutter speed controls how much of the ambient (or natural) light appears in the image.

In M, you set the aperture to control flash exposure, then choose a shutter speed that is appropriate for the ambient light in the scene (see flash metering below). Remember, you can use any shutter speed of 1/250 second and slower. With B you are setting a shutter speed based on how long you hold the shutter button down, so flash exposure is controlled by aperture.

↯* FE (FLASH EXPOSURE) LOCK

Just as Autoexposure lock (AE lock ✳, see page 198) on the 60D is a useful tool for controlling exposure in difficult natural light situations, Flash Exposure lock **FEL** offers the same control in difficult flash situations. When either the built-in flash or an attached flash is turned on, you can lock the flash exposure by pressing the ✳ button (on the back of the camera toward the upper right corner).

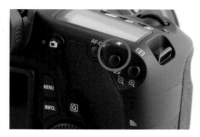

< This button is conveniently placed so that you can quickly press it with your thumb to lock exposure while still looking through the viewfinder.

With a charged external or built-in flash active, pressing ✳ causes the camera to emit a pre-flash, and the 60D calculates the exposure without taking the shot. **FEL** appears briefly in the viewfinder (replacing the shutter speed) during the pre-flash. ↯ changes to ↯*, indicating the flash exposure has been locked. You can press ✳ repeatedly as you change framing. If the subject is beyond the illumination of the flash, ↯ blinks.

> **NOTE: FEL** can also be used to reduce people's reactions to the pre-flash. They may keep their eyes open during the actual exposure for a change!

To use FE lock, pop up the flash with the ↯ button (or turn on an external flash unit), and then lock focus on your subject by pressing the shutter button halfway. Next, aim the center of the viewfinder at the important part of the subject and press ✳ (↯* appears in the viewfinder). Now, reframe your composition and take the picture. FE lock produces quite accurate flash exposures.

Using the same principle, you can make the flash weaker or stronger. Instead of pointing the viewfinder at the subject to set flash exposure, point it at something light in tone or a subject closer to the camera. This causes the flash to provide less exposure. For more light, aim the camera at something black or far away. With a little experimenting, and by reviewing the LCD monitor, you can very quickly establish appropriate flash control for particular situations.

FLASH EXPOSURE COMPENSATION

When you first start using the flash on the 60D, this control should be learned quickly. This function can go a long way to preventing overexposure by flash. Use the EOS 60D's flash exposure compensation feature to adjust flash exposure by up to +/− three stops in 1/3-stop increments (or 1/2-stop increments if selected in C.Fn-1). Flash exposure is accessed via the Shooting 1 menu ⬛: First, highlight [Flash control] and confirm with SET. Next, highlight [Built-in flash func. setting] for the built-in flash, or [External flash func. setting] for an external flash, and press SET again. Confirm that [Flash mode] is set to [E-TTL II], then select [⬜exp. comp] and press SET yet again. A flash exposure compensation scale—which operates similarly to the exposure compensation scale—is displayed. Press ✸ to the left or right, or turn ◯ to adjust the compensation +/− three stops. The viewfinder displays 🔆 to let you know flash exposure compensation is enabled.

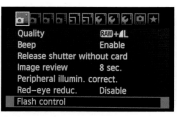
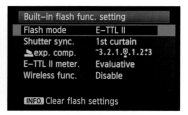

Flash exposure compensation is located in the Flash control sub menu. You might want to consider adding the function to your My Menu.

For the most control over flash, use the camera's **M** exposure setting. Set an exposure that is correct overall for the scene, and then turn on the flash. (The flash exposure is still E-TTL II automatic.) The shutter speed (as long as it is 1/250 second or slower) controls the overall light from the scene (and the total exposure). The f/stop controls the flash portion of the exposure. So, to a degree, you can make the overall ambient exposure of the scene lighter or darker by changing shutter speed (up to 1/250 second), with no direct effect on the flash exposure. (Note, however, that this does not work with high-speed sync.)

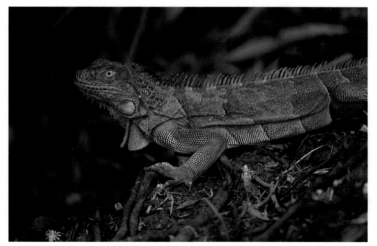

^ Use flash exposure compensation to dial down the flash output so that the flash is used just to fill in shadows rather than provide all the illumination for the scene.

RED-EYE REDUCTION

In low-light conditions, when the flash is close to the axis of the lens—which is typical for built-in flashes—the light from the unit can reflect back from the retina of people's eyes because their pupils are wide open.

This reflection appears as red-eye in the photo. You can reduce the chances of red-eye by using an off-camera flash or by having the person look at a bright light before you shoot (to cause their pupils to constrict). In addition, many cameras offer a red-eye reduction feature that causes the flash to fire a burst of light before the actual exposure, resulting in contraction of the subject's pupils. Unfortunately, this may also result in less than flattering expressions from your subject.

Although the 60D's flash pops up higher than most, red-eye may still be a problem. The 60D offers a red-eye reduction feature for flash exposures, but the feature works differently than red-eye reduction on many other cameras. The 60D uses a continuous light from a lamp on the front of the camera next to the handgrip—be careful not to block it with your fingers. This continuous, lower-power light (versus a brief bright flash) closes the subject's iris somewhat and helps your subject pose with better expressions. Red-eye reduction is enabled in the ☐ menu under **[Red-eye reduc.]**. Since the lamp is lower power, it takes a little longer to do the job. The 60D provides a visual countdown in the viewfinder, where the exposure compensation scale would normally display. Once the indicator decrements to nothing and the exposure compensation scale reappears, you can take the picture. In reality, you can take the picture at any time, but for best results you should wait for the countdown.

NOTE: Don't confuse red-eye reduction with the AF-assist beam (see page 188). The AF-assist beam uses a series of brief flashes to help the 60D achieve focus. This function is turned on/off via the Custom Function menu, not the red-eye reduction setting. However, the 60D is smart enough that if the AF-assist beam is fired, it knows that the red-eye reduction lamp doesn't have to be used.

HIGH-SPEED SYNC

If you want to use flash beyond the maximum sync speed of 1/250 second, you'll need to use Canon EX-series flash units that allow flash at all shutter speeds up to 1/8000. This mode is called high-speed sync. Instead of one burst of flash illumination, the Speedlite emits light in several short bursts as the shutter slit moves across the sensor. High-speed synchronization must be activated on the flash unit itself or by using [Flash control] in ◻︎ˈ (see page 101). It is indicated by the ⁴ₕ symbol on the flash unit's LCD panel and in the 60D's viewfinder. The 60D's built-in flash does not offer high-speed sync.

FIRST AND SECOND CURTAIN SYNC

When you use flash with longer shutter speeds and mixed with ambient light, the timing of the firing of the flash can lead to unnatural effects with moving subjects. Imagine a baseball pitcher throwing a ball during a night game. The sequence for a flash picture is: first curtain opens, flash fires, shutter remains open for rest of exposure, second curtain closes. While the shutter remains open, the image sensor still records ambient light in the scene.

When you look at the picture, it will look as though the ball player is pulling the ball back towards himself. This is because the flash fires at the beginning of the exposure, "freezing" the action of his arm. Then the pitcher's arm travels forward, lit by ambient light. So the final image has a blurry trail preceding the moving arm. This is the opposite of what we are used to seeing—motion expressed as trails following a moving object. To correct this anomaly, the 60D can be set to fire the flash just before the second curtain closes. This is called second curtain sync. It can be used with the built-in flash and external Speedlites. Use ◻︎ˈ, and select [Flash control] and press SET. Select either [Built-in flash func. setting] or [External flash func. setting] and press SET. Select [Shutter sync.] and press SET. Select [2nd curtain] and press SET.

NOTE: Second curtain sync is only necessary at slow shutter speeds (1/30 and below) and only when there is lighting in the scene in addition to the flash. If the 60D uses a shutter speed faster than 1/30, first curtain sync is used.

CANON SPEEDLITE EX FLASH UNITS

Canon offers a range of accessory flash units in the EOS system, called Speedlites. While Canon Speedlites don't have the power of studio strobes, they are remarkably versatile. These highly portable flash units can be mounted in the camera's hot shoe, used off-camera with a dedicated cord, or used wirelessly via Canon's wireless Speedlite system.

The 60D is compatible with the EX-series of Speedlites. Units in the EX-series offer a wide range of features to expand your creativity. They are designed to work with the camera's microprocessor to take advantage of E-TTL II exposure control, extending the abilities of the 60D considerably. Speedlite EX-series flash units vary in power from the Speedlite 580EX II, which has a maximum ISO 100 GN of 190 feet (58 m), to the small and compact Speedlite 270EX, which has an ISO 100 GN of 72 feet (22 m).

I strongly recommend Canon's off-camera OC-E3 shoe-mounted extension cord for your Speedlite. When you use the off-camera cord, the Speedlite can be moved away from the camera for more interesting light and shadows. You can aim light toward the side or top of a close-up subject for variations in contrast and color. If you find that your subject is overexposed, rather than dialing down the light output (which can be done on certain flash units), just aim the Speedlite a little farther away from the subject so it doesn't get hit so directly by the light.

CANON SPEEDLITE 580EX II

Introduced with the Canon EOS 1D Mark III professional camera, the 580EX II replaces the popular 580EX. This top-of-the-line flash unit offers outstanding range and features adapted to digital cameras. Improvements over the 580EX include a stronger quick-locking hot shoe connection, stronger battery door, better dust and water resistance, a shorter and quieter recycling time, and an external metering sensor. The tilt/swivel zoom head on the 580EX II covers focal lengths from 14mm to 105mm, and it swivels a full 180° in either direction.

The zoom positions (which correspond to the focal lengths 24, 28, 35, 50, 70, 80, and 105mm) can be set manually or automatically (the flash reflector zooms with the lens). In addition, this flash knows what size sensor

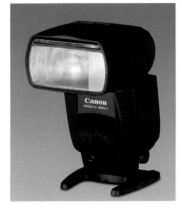

> The 580EX II comes with a stand so that you can set the flash apart from the camera and remotely trigger it.

is used with a DSLR and it varies its zoom accordingly. With the built-in retractable diffuser in place, the flash coverage is wide enough for a 14mm lens. It provides a high flash output with an ISO 100 GN of 190 feet (58 m) when the zoom head is positioned at 105mm. The guide number decreases as the angular coverage increases for shorter focal lengths, but is still quite high with an ISO 100 GN of 145 feet (44 m) at 50mm, or an ISO 100 GN of 103 feet (32 m) at 28mm. When used with other flashes, the 580EX II can function as either a master flash or a slave unit (see page 263).

The 580EX II offers flash exposure bracketing that you can access via the 60D flash control menu. Flash exposure bracketing (FEB) is similar to exposure bracketing (page 200). The camera takes three exposures, all at different flash output settings. The adjustment scale looks just like the one for exposure bracketing.

The 580EX II also has a PC terminal for use with PC cords. PC cords were the way external flashes were connected to cameras before the hot shoe was developed. The 60D does not have a PC connector, but PC terminals are still used for flash accessories like wireless remotes. For external power, the 580EX II uses the LP-E4 power pack that is dust- and water-resistant.

The large, illuminated LCD panel on the 580EX II provides clear information on all settings: flash function, reflector position, working aperture, and flash range in feet or meters. The flash also includes a dial for easier selection of these settings. When you press the 60D's depth-of-field preview button (on the front of the camera, to the lower right of the lens mount housing), a one-second burst of light is emitted. This modeling flash allows you to judge the effect of the flash. The 580EX II also has 14 user-defined custom settings that are totally independent of the camera's custom functions. Don't hesitate to study the flash manual for more information.

Although the LCD panel on the 580EX II provides a lot of information, it can be a little complicated if you try to adjust the various settings and custom functions when you don't use the flash every day. Canon came up with a great solution: You can use the 60D's menu system to access the 580EX II's controls. The custom functions appear as numeric codes on the Speedlite's LCD, but within the 60D's external flash control system, those custom functions have names and descriptions, just like the 60D's own custom functions. The same is true when you adjust other flash functions such as flash exposure mode, flash exposure compensation, shutter sync, flash exposure bracketing, and many more. You can also adjust the flash zoom head setting and wireless E-TTL II setting from the camera. With this new intelligence, it has never been easier to learn how to use Canon Speedlites to capture great images.

CANON SPEEDLITE 430EX II

Much as the 580EX II improved on the 580EX, the 430EX II, introduced in June 2008, improved on the 430EX. While the ISO 100 GN stayed the same—141 feet (43 m)—the recycle time decreased by 20%. It is also quieter than the 430EX and can be controlled from the 60D, just like the 580EX II. It offers E-TTL II flash control, wireless E-TTL operation, flash exposure compensation, and high-speed synchronization. It does not offer flash exposure bracketing.

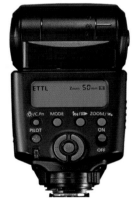

The tilt/swivel zoom reflector covers focal lengths from 24mm to 105mm and swivels 180° to the left and 90° to the right. The zoom head operates automatically for focal lengths of 24, 28, 35, 50, 70, 80, and 105mm. A built-in, wide-angle pull-down reflector extends flash coverage making it wide enough for a 14mm lens.

An LCD panel on the rear of the unit makes adjusting settings easy, and there are six custom functions. Just like the 580EX II, you can control most of the settings and custom functions from the 60D's menus. Since the 430EX II supports wireless E-TTL, it can be used as a remote (slave) unit. A new quick-release mounting system makes it easy to securely attach the 430EX II to the 60D.

CANON SPEEDLITE 270EX

If you are looking for a simple, small flash that fits into just about every camera bag or even your pocket, the 270EX is it. It is a compact basic flash unit that offers a lot of features despite its size. Rather than have a zoom reflector, it has a 2-step selection of 28mm and 50mm. At the 28mm setting it has an ISO 100 GN of 72 feet (22 m). At the 50mm position the ISO 100 GN is 89 feet (27 m). Unlike its predecessor (220EX), the 270EX has a bounce feature, so the flash head can rotate to point straight up. It can also be controlled from the 60D's menu system.

OTHER SPEEDLITES

The Speedlite 220EX is an economy EX-series flash. It offers E-TTL flash and high-speed sync, but does not offer wireless E-TTL flash, or bounce, and it can't be controlled by the camera's menu. Like the 270EX, it has an ISO 100 GN of 72 feet.

CLOSE-UP FLASH

There are also two specialized flash units for close-up photography that work well with the 60D. Both provide direct light on the subject.

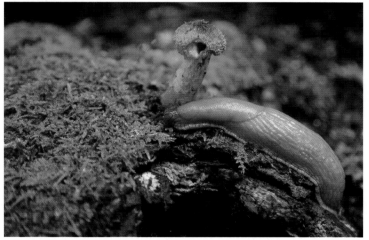

⌃ Close-up flashes can help bring out detail in macro photography.

Macro Twin Lite MT-24EX: The MT-24EX uses two small flashes affixed to a ring that attaches to Canon macro lenses. These can be adjusted to different positions to alter the light and can be used at different strengths so one can be used as a main light and the other as a fill light. If both flash tubes are switched on, they produce an ISO 100 GN of 72 feet (22 m), and when used individually, the ISO 100 GN is 36 feet (11 m). The MT-24EX does an exceptional job with directional lighting in macro shooting.

Macro Ring Lite MR-14EX: Like the MT-24EX, the MR-14EX uses two small flashes affixed to a ring. It has an ISO 100 GN of 46 feet (14 m), and both flash tubes can be independently adjusted in 13 steps from 1:8 to 8:1. It is a flash that encircles the lens and provides illumination on axis with it. This results in nearly shadowless photos because the shadow falls behind the subject compared to the lens position, though there will be shadow effects along curved edges. The MR-14EX is often used to show fine detail and color in a subject, but it cannot be used for varied light and shadow effects. This flash is commonly used in medical and dental photography so that important details are not obscured by shadows.

The power pack for both of these specialized flash units fits into the hot shoe of the camera. In addition, both macro flash units offer some of the same technical features as the 580EX II, including E-TTL II operation, wireless E-TTL flash, and high-speed synchronization.

NOTE: When the 60D is used with older system flash units (such as the EZ series), the flash unit must be set to manual, and TTL does not function. For this reason, Canon EX Speedlite system flash units are recommended for use with the camera.

BOUNCE FLASH

Direct flash can often be harsh and unflattering, causing heavy shadows behind the subject or underneath features such as eyebrows and bangs. Bouncing the flash softens the light and creates a more natural-looking light effect. The Canon Speedlite 580EX II, 580EX, 430EX II, 430EX, and 270EX accessory flash units feature heads that are designed to tilt so that a shoe-mounted flash can be aimed at the ceiling to produce soft, even lighting. The 580EX II also swivels 180° in both directions, so the light can be bounced off something to the side of the camera, like a wall or reflector. However, the ceiling or wall must be white or neutral gray, or it may cause an undesirable colorcast in the finished photo.

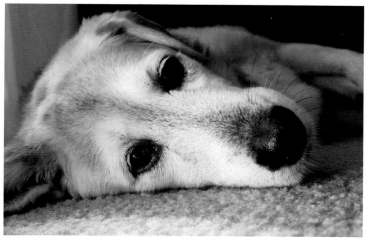

^ Keep an eye open for white surfaces—like walls and ceilings—that allow you to bounce light onto your subject. © Jessica Anne Baum

WIRELESS E-TTL FLASH

Canon's Speedlite system allows the Speedlites to communicate with each other via light. A single main controller called the master sends out pulses of light to transmit information on light output (including the ratio between multiple Speedlites) and also triggers the remote Speedlites to fire when the shutter is tripped. You can use up to two groups of Speedlite 580EX IIs, 430EX IIs, 430EXs, or the now discontinued 580EXs, 550EXs and 420EXs, for more natural lighting or emphasis. (The number of flash groups is limited to two, but the number of actual flash units is unlimited.) When set for E-TTL, the master unit and the camera control the exposure.

NOTE: All references to E-TTL in this wireless section refer to Canon's wireless technology, not the earlier version of E-TTL II.

Canon makes four devices that the 60D can use as master controllers: the Speedlite 580EX II, the Macro Twin Lite MT-24EX, the Macro Ring Lite MR-14EX, and the ST-E2 master controller. The ST-E2 doesn't illuminate a scene but simply controls the remote Speedlites. When one of the

Speedlites is used as a master controller and is mounted on the 60D, you can use the 60D's menu system to control the wireless setup of the master. (The 430EX II and 430EX can only be used as remote, or slave, units, and the 60D's built-in flash can also act as a master controller.)

CHANNELS

In the event that you are shooting with other Canon photographers and with multiple Speedlites, the wireless Speedlite system runs on transmission channels. There are four channels (1 – 4) to choose from, which is helpful when others around you are also shooting with flash. All of your Speedlites must be on the same channel in order to operate. Channels can be set via the control buttons on the back of each Speedlite. If you forget how to set the channels, an easy method to set up a newer Speedlite is to mount it on the 60D. Then use the 60D's menu system to set the channel.

To set the channel on a Speedlite mounted on the hot shoe, select **[Flash control]** from the ◻ menu, and press SET. Select **[External flash func. setting]** and press SET. Select **[Wireless func.]** and press SET. Select **[Enable]** and press SET. Then select **[Channel]** and press SET. Choose a channel using ✦ and press SET.

GROUPS

The wireless system divides the Speedlites into groups. Groups can be used to set up ratios between Speedlites. This enables you to have brighter light on one side of your subject and weaker fill light on the other. With E-TTL II, you don't have to worry about setting specific power output. The 60D's metering system handles all the calculations; you just set up how much brighter one flash group should be, compared to the other. This is known as setting the lighting ratios.

Groups can also be used when you want to control the power output of the Speedlites manually. By assigning each Speedlite to a different group, you can dial in each one's output from the camera, rather than

FLASH

from each unit. This makes it easy to take a quick shot, evaluate the exposure, make adjustments from the back of the camera, and quickly make another shot.

When using the built-in flash there are two groups labeled A and B. When you first start to use wireless Speedlites (particularly when using ratios), it is helpful to consider group A as your main light and group B as the fill. With external Speedlites there is access to a third group, C, which can be thought of as a background light.

WIRELESS E-TTL FLASH VIA INTERNAL FLASH

Since the built-in flash on the 60D can act as a master controller, it has some special groupings. To change the function, use ◻⁺, [Flash control], and press SET. Make sure [Flash firing] is set to [Enable]. Choose [Built-in flash func. setting] and press SET. Set [Flash mode] to [E-TTL II]. Using [Wireless func.] you can then choose between [Disable] and three wireless functions.

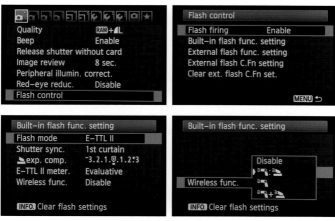

The flash control sub-menu gives you access to the wireless features of Canon's Speedlite system.

> NOTE: You must manually pop up the built-in flash. Also, if you want the 60D to control the remote flashes via E-TTL II, make sure that each remote flash is set to E-TTL and not to Manual or Multi.

[³⬛:⬛]: This wireless flash function's icon denotes the setting's purpose: to set up a ratio between any external Speedlite ³⬛ and the built-in flash ⬛ where they both contribute to exposing the scene. In this case there are no groups, so any slave Speedlite will be controlled no matter what "group" the slave is set for. (For example, if you are using two 580EX II Speedlites and one is set for slave group A and the other is set for group B, the two flashes will be controlled as one group.)

In this mode you can control the ratio of light via the **[⬛: ⬛]** selection. The ratio can be from 8:1 to 1:1, with the external group always being the left number (indicated by the setting's icon). This represents a three-stop difference. Because the GN of the built-in flash is weaker than the external Speedlites, this mode is most useful when the camera is close to the subject. In addition, the **[Flash exp. comp]** adjustment in this menu can control the flash exposure compensation for the overall flash illumination. It is important that you press **SET** to accept both ratio and exposure compensation settings.

[³⬛]: This wireless flash mode allows the built-in flash to control multiple external Speedlites, and is similar to mounting an ST-E2 to your 60D. The built-in flash simply becomes a wireless controller for the slave flashes, rather than contributing to lighting the scene. Although light comes from the built-in flash, it is at a level that is too low to illuminate the scene. The built-in flash is used strictly for communicating to the slave flashes. One benefit of the built-in flash vs. the ST-E2 is that the built-in flash can control three groups (A, B, and C) but the ST-E2 can only control two (A, B).

There are two firing group options when the 60D is set to [³⬛]. **[⬛All]** treats all the external Speedlites as one group. It doesn't matter which group the individual Speedlites are set for; as long as they are set for slave mode, they will be controlled as if they were all in one group. You can also control the flash exposure compensation (+/- 3 stops) for the entire group with the **[⬛exp. comp]** selection.

With the **[⬛ (A:B)]** selection, the built-in flash controls two groups of slave flashes: A and B. This allows you to set up light ratios from 8:1 to 1:8 using the **[A:B fire ratio]**. When set to 8:1, the A group produces three stops more light than the B group. Just like **[⬛All]**, there is control of the entire flash exposure compensation with the **[A,B exp. comp]** selection.

[³◥+³◢]: This is probably the most flexible wireless E-TTL mode. It operates similarly to ³◥ but it also adds the built-in flash as a light source for illuminating the scene. Keep in mind when setting ratios and flash exposure compensation that the light output of the built-in flash is significantly lower than an external flash.

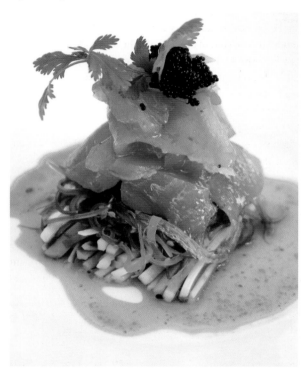

< Multiple Speedlites along with wireless control give you flexibility in controlling the lighting ratios in your scene. © Jessica Anne Baum

Just like [³◥], the [³◥+³◢] setting has two firing group options. The [◥All and ◢] selection treats all the external Speedlites as one group—hence the ◥All icon. It doesn't matter which group the remote slaves are set for. The built-in flash is a second group. You can control the flash exposure compensation of the remote group with the [◥exp. comp] selection. The built-in flash is controlled by [◢exp. comp].

With the [◥ (A:B) ◢] firing group option, the built-in flash controls two groups of slave flashes—A and B—and the built-in flash has its own separate output control—in essence, its own group. This allows you to set up light ratios from 8:1 to 1:8 using the [A:B fire ratio]. When set to 8:1, the

A group produces three stops more light than the B group. Just like $^{\exists}$▙, there is control of the entire remote flash exposure compensation with the [A,B exp. comp] selection. Since the built-in flash is not part of a group, you can control its exposure compensation via [▙exp. comp].

NOTE: Do not use this mode if you only have one remote Speedlite. The meter expects to see a group B flash illumination and won't expose properly.

WIRELESS MANUAL FLASH VIA BUILT-IN FLASH

There are times when E-TTL doesn't offer consistent performance. Sometimes you'll end up with underexposures and overexposures. Manually controlling the Speedlite power output can offer great results, particularly in environments where levels don't need to change once they have been set.

Instead of running around to each Speedlite and setting its output, you control all of the units wirelessly from the 60D. To run in manual mode, use ▢▪ [Flash control] and press SET. Make sure [Flash firing] is set to [Enable]. Choose [Built-in flash func. setting] and press SET. Change [Flash mode] to [Manual flash]. The [Wireless func.] now offers [Disable] and two options.

[$^{\exists}$▙]: When the manual mode is set for $^{\exists}$▙, the built-in flash is only used to control the slave Speedlites. While you will see the built-in flash illuminate, it is at a low level—just for controlling the slave flashes and not really contributing any light to the scene. Also remember that this is manual mode: you must set all output levels on the external flash units. The 60D does not control the output of the flash via any type of metering.

There are two firing group options. With the [▙All] selection, all of the remote slaves are adjusted to the same manual output setting, from 1/128 to 1/1 (full power) via the [▙flash output] setting. The slaves are controlled no matter what group they are set for—A or B. If you use firing group option [▙ (A:B)], then you can control the output of group A Speedlites separately from the group B Speedlites using [Group A output] and [Group B output].

NOTE: Since the 60D is not evaluating exposure of the Speedlites, you are setting flash output of each group separately, rather than setting a ratio between the groups.

[³⁣ᴹ+⌐ᴹ]: With this setting, the built-in flash participates in lighting the scene. Two groups are created, the remote slaves and the built-in flash. There are two firing group options. The **[ᴹAll and ⌐ᴹ]** option treats all the external Speedlites as one group. It doesn't matter which group the remote slaves are set for. The built-in flash is a separate group. The remote slaves are set via **[ᴹ flash output]**, with a range of output from full power (1/1) to 1/128 power. The built-in flash is adjusted by the **[⌐ᴹflash output]** selection. Since part of the built-in flash output is being used to communicate with the remote units, the power level range is from 1/4 to 1/128.

With the **[ᴹ (A:B) ⌐ᴹ]** firing group option, the built-in flash controls two groups of slave flashes—A and B—and the built in flash has its own separate output control. This allows you to manually set the flash output of each group using **[Group A output]** and **[Group B output]**. The built-in flash is controlled by **[⌐ᴹflash output]**. The output levels for the groups can be set from full power (1/1) all the way down to 1/128 power. Just as with the **[ᴹAll and ⌐ᴹ]** setting, the built-in flash can't be set for full power because part of its output is being used to communicate with the other Speedlites. Its range is from 1/4 to 1/128.

NOTE: While the remote slaves are considered a group, **[Group A output]** sets the output value for each individual Speedlite in the group. You do not set the output value for all the Speedlites combined. In other words, if you have two Speedlites in group A, setting **[Group A output]** to 1/4 means that each Speedlite will be set to 1/4 power. If you have four Speedlites in group A, each Speedlite will be set to 1/4. There is no compensation for a particular group having more Speedlites.

WIRELESS E-TTL FLASH VIA EXTERNAL SPEEDLITE

When you mount an external Canon Speedlite on the 60D to act as a master controller, you need to set up the groups. To set up the groups, use ◻ᶦ, **[Flash control]**, and press **SET**. Make sure **[Flash firing]** is set to **[Enable]**. Choose **[External flash func. setting]** and press **SET**. Set **[Flash mode]** to **[E-TTL II]**. Make sure the **[Wireless func.]** option is set to **[Enable]**.

The master flash (an external Speedlite mounted on the 60D) can be used to illuminate the scene and control the slave Speedlites or it can be set as a controller and not contribute to lighting the scene. If you don't want the mounted Speedlite to contribute to illuminating the scene, set [Master flash] to [Disable]. In this mode you will see the flash go off when you take a picture, but the light level will be low, just enough to communicate with the slave units. Just as with the built-in flash, there are several firing groups:

Firing Group [All]: This wireless firing mode treats all of the Speedlite groups as one flash. It doesn't matter which group the individual Speedlites are set for; as long as they are set for slave mode, they will be controlled. For example, if you are using two 580EX II Speedlites, and one is set for slave group A and the other is set for group B, the two flashes will be controlled as one group. You can control the flash exposure compensation for the entire group with the [Flash exp. comp.] selection. If [Master flash] is set to [Enable] then the master flash will be controlled as part of the group.

> **NOTE:** Controlling a flash means not only triggering it to fire, but also controlling the light output and flash duration.

Firing Group [A:B]: The camera-mounted Speedlite (or ST-E2 controller) allows you to set up light ratios from 8:1 to 1:8 using the [A:B fire ratio] setting. This represents a three-stop difference. When set to 8:1, the A group produces three stops more light than the B group. Just like [ALL], there is control of the entire flash exposure compensation with the [Flash exp. comp] selection. The master Speedlite is part of the A group.

Firing Group [A:B C]: This third firing mode builds on [A:B] by adding a third group: C. Notice the icon doesn't say that the C group has the same ratio setting as A and B. The C group should be used for backgrounds or accent lights. If the C group is used to light the main subject, the E-TTL system may cause overexposure. The ratio between A and B is set using the same function mentioned previously: [A:B fire ratio].

The C group is adjusted using a special control called [Grp C. exp. comp] which allows a +/- three-stop adjustment. The A and B groups, together, have their own exposure compensation setting.

> **NOTE:** Do not use this mode if you only have one remote Speedlite. The meter expects group B to provide illumination and won't expose properly.

There are times when E-TTL doesn't offer consistent performance. Sometimes you'll end up with underexposures and overexposures. Manual control of Speedlite power output can offer incredible control, particularly in situations where levels don't need to change once they have been set. Instead of running around to each Speedlite, you control all of the units wirelessly from the 60D. To operate in manual, use ❏´, [Flash control] and press SET. Make sure [Flash firing] is set to [Enable]. Choose [External flash func. setting] and press SET. Change [Flash mode] to [Manual flash]. The [Firing group] now offers three options.

Firing Group [All]: When the firing group is set for [All], all of the remote slaves (and the master) are adjusted to the same manual output setting, from 1/128 to 1/1 (full power). The slaves are controlled no matter what group they are set for—A, B, or C. Remember that this is manual mode: you have to set the output level according to how much flash illumination you think the scene needs. The 60D does not control the output of the flash via any type of metering.

Firing Group [A:B]: While this option looks similar to a ratio setup, in reality it allows you to set the manual output setting of the A and B groups separately, from 1/128 to 1/1 (full power). The 60D does not control the output of the flash via any type of metering.

Firing Group [A,B,C]: This gives you three groups, each individually controlled from 1/128 to 1/1 output. The 60D does not control the output of the flash via any type of metering.

> **NOTE:** While the remote slaves are considered a group, you set the output value for each individual Speedlite in the group. You do not set the output value for all the Speedlites in the group combined.

Remember to consult the manual that comes with each Speedlite unit to fully understand the features and operations of Canon's accessory flashes.

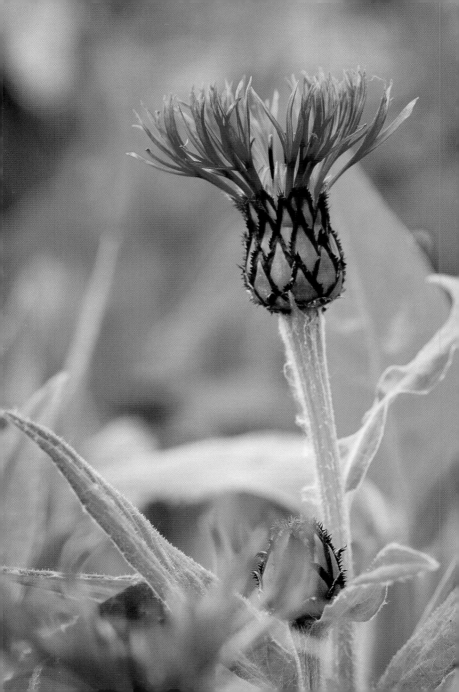

Lenses and Accessories

You might have bought your EOS 60D as a kit with an extra lens or two so that it is capable of capturing great images right out of the box. However, it also belongs to an extensive family of Canon EOS-compatible equipment, including additional lenses, flashes, and other accessories. With this wide range of available options, you can expand the capabilities of your camera quite easily. Canon has long had an excellent reputation for its optics, and offers over 60 different lenses from which to choose. Several independent manufacturers offer quality Canon-compatible lenses as well.

LENSES FOR CANON DSLRS

The EOS 60D can use both Canon EF and EF-S lenses, ranging from wide-angle to telephoto. The lens lineup includes zoom lenses that can change focal length, and prime lenses that offer a single focal length and high performance. Keep in mind, however, that standard 35mm focal lengths act differently on many DSLRs than they did with film. This is because many digital sensors are smaller than a frame of 35mm film, so they crop the area seen by the lens, essentially creating a different format. Effectively, this makes the subject appear comparatively larger within the frame. As a result, the lens acts as if it has been multiplied by a factor of 1.6 compared to how it would look on a 35mm film camera or a full-frame digital camera.

So, both the widest angle and the longest zoom focal lengths are multiplied by the 60D's 1.6x focal length conversion factor. The EF 14mm f/2.8 L lens, for example, is a super-wide lens when used with a 35mm film camera or a full-frame sensor like that found in the EOS 5D Mark II; but it offers the 35mm-equivalent of a 22mm wide-angle lens (14 multiplied by 1.6) when attached to the 60D—wide, but not super-wide. On the other hand, put a long 400mm lens on the 60D and you get the equivalent of a 640mm telephoto—a big boost with no change in aperture. (Be sure to use a tripod for these focal lengths and heavy lenses!)

It is interesting to note that this is exactly the same thing that happens when one focal length is used with different sized film formats. For example, a 50mm lens is considered a mid-range focal length for 35mm, but it is a wide-angle lens for medium format cameras. The focal length of the lens doesn't really change, but the field of view that the camera captures changes. In other words, this isn't an artifact of digital photography, it's just physics!

NOTE: Unless stated otherwise, I refer to the actual focal length of a lens throughout the rest of the chapter, not its 35mm equivalent.

CHOOSING LENSES

The focal length and design of a lens have a huge effect on how you photograph. The correct lens makes photography a joy; the wrong one makes you leave the camera at home. One approach for choosing a lens is to determine if you are frustrated with your current lens. Do you constantly want to see more of the scene than the lens allows? If so, then consider a wider-angle lens. However, if it often seems to you that the subject is too small in your photos, then it might be a good idea to look into acquiring a zoom or telephoto lens with a longer focal length. Do you need more light-gathering ability? Maybe a fixed-focal-length (prime) lens is needed.

Certain subjects lend themselves to specific focal lengths. Wildlife and sports action are best photographed using focal lengths of 200mm or more, although nearby action can be managed with focal lengths as short as 125mm. Portraits look great when shot with focal lengths of 50–65mm. Interiors often demand wide-angle lenses, such as 12mm.

Many people also like wide-angles for landscapes, but telephotos can come in handy for distant scenes. Close-ups can be shot with nearly any focal length, though skittish subjects such as butterflies might need a rather long lens.

The inherent magnification factor is great news for the photographer who needs long focal lengths for wildlife or sports. A standard 300mm lens for 35mm film now seems like a 480mm lens on the 60D. It feels like you get a long focal length in a smaller lens, often with a wider maximum f/stop, and with a much lower price tag. But this news is tough for people who need wide angles, since the width of what the digital camera sees is significantly cropped in comparison to what a 35mm camera would see using the same lens. You need lenses with shorter focal lengths to see the same field of view you may have been used to with film.

ZOOM VS. PRIME LENSES

When zoom lenses first came on the market, they were not even close to a prime , or single-focal-length, lens in sharpness, color rendition, or contrast. Today, you can get superb image quality from either type. There are some important differences, though. The biggest is maximum f/stop.

Zoom lenses are rarely as fast (e.g., rarely have as big a maximum aperture) as single-focal-length (prime) lenses. A 28–200mm zoom lens, for example, might have a maximum aperture at 200mm of f/5.6, yet a prime lens might be f/4 or even f/2.8. When zoom lenses come close to a prime lens in f/stops, they are usually considerably bigger and more expensive than the prime lens. Of course, they also offer a whole range of focal lengths, which a prime lens cannot do. There is no question that zoom lenses are versatile.

Also, the aperture is not constant with many zoom lenses as you move through focal lengths. A lens that is rated f/3.5–5.6 means that its maximum aperture will be f/3.5 at its widest-angle focal length, compared to f/5.6 when at full telephoto range. This can affect autoexposure if you lock your exposure when the lens is fully wide and then zoom in—your image will be underexposed.

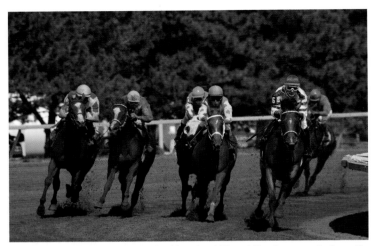
∧ A zoom lens allows you to change focal length quickly and therefore correctly frame the shot when the action is happening fast.

EF-SERIES LENSES

Canon EF lenses include some unique technologies. In order to focus swiftly, the focusing elements within the lens need to move with quick precision. Canon developed the lens-based ultrasonic motor for this purpose. This technology makes the lens motor spin with ultrasonic oscillations, instead of using the conventional drive-train system (which tends to be noisy). This allows lenses to autofocus almost instantly with hardly any noise, and it uses less battery power than traditional systems. Canon lenses that use this motor are labeled USM. (Lower-priced Canon lenses have small motors in the lenses too, but they don't use USM technology, and can be slower and noisier.)

Canon was also a pioneer in the use of image-stabilizing technologies. Image-stabilized (IS) lenses utilize sophisticated motors and sensors to adapt to slight movement during exposure. It's pretty amazing—the lens actually has vibration-detecting gyrostabilizers that move a special image-stabilizing lens group in response to lens movement. This dampens movement that occurs from handholding a camera and allows much slower shutter speeds to be used. IS also allows big telephoto lenses (such as the EF 500mm IS lens) to be used on tripods that are lighter than would normally be used with non-IS telephoto lenses.

NOTE: The key to understanding what the name of a lens means is to break it into parts. For Canon, a lens starts with EF or EF-S. This relates to the lens mount. Next is the focal length, which is a range for zooms (17–55mm) or a single number for primes (14mm). After that comes the maximum aperture of the lens. This is the widest f/stop you'll be able to set. It is also a measure of how fast (lets in a lot of light) or slow (lets in less light) a lens is. An f/2 lens is faster and able to shoot in lower light levels than an f/4 lens. Aperture can be a single value or a range on zoom lenses. If the lens has special coatings and high performance optical elements, it might carry the "L" designation, indicating a high performance lens. After that nomenclature, there may be additional letters indicating other technology: IS—image stabilization; DO—diffractive optics; II—generation; USM—ultrasonic motors, etc.

The IS technology is part of many zoom lenses, and does a great job overall. However, IS zoom lenses in the mid-focal length range have tended to be slower than single-focal-length lenses. For example, compare the EF 28–135mm f/3.5–5.6 IS lens to the EF 85mm f/1.8 lens. The former has a great zoom range, but allows less light at maximum aperture. At 85mm (a good focal length for people), the EF 28–135mm is an f/4 lens, more than two stops slower than the f/1.8 single-focal-length lens, when both are shot "wide-open" (typical of low-light situations). While you could make up the two stops in "hand-holdability" due to the IS technology, that also means you must shoot two full shutter speeds slower, which can be a real problem in stopping subject movement.

EF-S SERIES LENSES

EF lenses are the standard lenses for all Canon EOS cameras. EF-S lenses are small, compact lenses designed for use on digital SLRs with smaller-type sensors—such as the Digital Rebel series, the 60D, and the 7D. EF-S lenses were introduced with the EF-S 18-55mm lens packaged with the original EOS Digital Rebel. They cannot be used with film EOS cameras, nor with any of the EOS-1D cameras, nor with the 5D cameras, because the image circle projected by EF-S lenses is smaller than those cameras' full-frame sensors.

NOTE: While these EF-S lenses are designed specifically for EOS cameras with smaller image sensors, focal length is still focal length. It is incorrect to assume that the focal length labeled on the lens has been adjusted for smaller image sensors.

> The EF-S lens lineup offers a good range of focal length lenses to choose from.

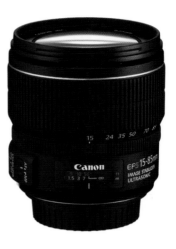

Currently Canon has nine EF-S lenses; all but one are zoom lenses. The EF-S 15–85mm f/3.5–5.6 IS USM is an image-stabilized zoom in a compact package with a fairly wide angle. The EF-S 17-55mm f/2.8 IS USM offers an image-stabilized zoom with a wide aperture. A little slower is the EF-S 17–85mm f/4–5.6 IS USM. The EF-S 18–55mm f/3.5–5.6 IS is the least expensive EF-S lens. If you are looking for a bit more range, there is the EF-S 18–135mm f/3.5–5.6 IS, the kit lens that is often sold with the 60D. The EF-S 18–200mm f3.5–5.6 IS lens offers even more telephoto range.

The EF-S 10–22mm f/3.5–4.5 USM zoom brings an excellent wide-angle range to the 60D. On the opposite end of the lens spectrum is the EF-S 55–250mm f/4–5.6 IS, which offers a very useful telephoto range. For macro shooting, Canon offers the EF-S 60mm f/2.8 Macro USM that focuses down to life-size magnification.

NOTE: The EF-S series offers good value and great performance. The lenses make a great match for the 60D. Remember though, that if you see yourself stepping up to a full-frame sensor EOS camera, you will have to replace an EF-S lens—it will not work on a full-frame camera.

L-SERIES LENSES

Canon's L-series lenses use special optical technologies for high-quality lens correction, including low-dispersion glass, fluorite elements, and aspherical designs. UD (ultra-low dispersion) glass is used in telephoto lenses to minimize chromatic aberration, which occurs when the lens cannot focus all colors equally at the same point on the sensor (or on the film in a traditional camera), resulting in less sharpness and contrast. Low-dispersion glass focuses colors more equally for sharper, crisper images.

Fluorite elements are even more effective (though more expensive) and have the corrective power of two UD lens elements. Aspherical designs are used with wide-angle and mid-focal length lenses to correct the challenges of spherical aberration in such focal lengths. Spherical aberration is a problem caused by lens elements with extreme curvature (usually found in wide-angle and wide-angle zoom lenses). Glass tends to focus light differently through different parts of such a lens, causing a slight, overall softening of the image even though the lens is focused sharply. Aspherical lenses use a special design that compensates for this optical defect.

DO-SERIES LENSES

Another Canon optical design is DO (diffractive optic). This technology significantly reduces the size and weight of a lens, and is therefore useful for big telephotos and zooms. Yet, the lens quality is unchanged. The lenses produced by Canon in this series are an EF 400mm f/4 DO IS USM pro lens that is only two-thirds the size and weight of the equivalent standard lens; and on the other end of the price range, an EF 70–300mm f/4.5–5.6 DO IS USM lens that offers a great focal length range. Both lenses include image stabilization.

MACRO LENSES

Canon also makes a wide variety of macro lenses for close-up photography. Macro lenses are prime lenses optimized for high sharpness throughout their focus range, from very close (1:1 or 1:2) magnifications to infinity. They also provide even resolution and contrast across the entire area of the image. While Canon already had a great quality 100mm macro in their lens lineup, the EF 100mm f/2.8L Macro IS USM lens is the first L-series macro lens, and also the first macro to offer image stabilization (IS).

> This new macro lens requires an adapter—the Macrolite Adapter 67—to use it with Canon's two macro Speedlites: the Macro Twin Lite MT-24EX and the Macro Ring Lite MR-14EX.

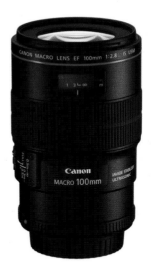

In addition to the lens mentioned above, the full line of macro lenses ranges from 50mm to 180mm. The macro lineup includes the EF 50mm f/2.5 Compact Macro, the EF-S 60mm f/2.8 Macro USM, the MP-E 65mm f/2.8 Macro 1–5x Macro Photo, and the EF 180mm f/3.5L Macro USM. You can tell from the model number that the MP-E 65mm f/2.8 is a little bit different from the other macro lenses in the lineup. It only offers manual focusing, but it does allow you to get close enough to your subjects to produce images that are 5 times life-size.

TILT-SHIFT LENSES

Tilt-shift lenses are unique lenses that shift up and down or tilt toward or away from the subject. In Canon nomenclature, the model number starts with TS (even though it still uses the EF lens mount). Tilt-shift lenses mimic the controls of a view camera. Shift lets the photographer keep the back of the camera parallel to the scene and move the lens to get a tall subject into the composition. This keeps vertical lines vertical and is extremely valuable for architectural photographers. Tilt changes the plane of focus so that sharpness can be changed without changing the f/stop. Focus can be extended from near to far by tilting the lens toward the subject, or sharpness can be limited by tilting the lens away from the subject (which has been a trendy advertising photographic technique lately).

Canon has recently updated their tilt-shift offerings. New to the lineup is their first wide-angle tilt-shift, the TS-E 17mm f/4L. They have also enhanced their TS-E 24mm f/3.5L II model by improving optical performance with updated coatings, a wider range of tilt and shift, and new optical elements. The TS-E 45mm f/2.8 and TS-E 90mm f/2.8 complete the tilt-shift line.

INDEPENDENT LENS BRANDS

Independent lens manufacturers also make some excellent lenses that fit the 60D. I've seen quite a range in capabilities from these lenses. Some include low-dispersion glass and are stunningly sharp. Others may not match the best Canon lenses, but offer features (such as focal length range or a great price) that make them worth considering. To a degree, you get what you pay for. A low-priced Canon lens probably won't be much different than a low-priced independent lens. On the other hand, the high level of engineering and construction found on a Canon L-series lens can be difficult to match.

On the fun side of independent lens brands is the Lensbaby (see lensbaby.com). These lenses offer selective focus and replaceable optics to give you a range of creative options when photographing. They also offer a host of accessories to change the look of your images.

CLOSE-UP PHOTOGRAPHY

Close-up photography is a striking and unique way to capture a scene. Most of the photographs we see on a day-to-day basis are not close-ups, making those that do make their way to our eyes all the more noticeable. But how do you create pictures with that special close-up look?

CLOSE-UP LENSES AND ACCESSORIES

It is surprising to me that many photographers think the only way to shoot close-ups is with a macro lens. There are, however, several options for close-up photography. The following are four of the most common:

Zoom Lenses with a Macro or Close-Focus Feature: Most zoom lenses allow you to focus up-close without accessories, although focal-length choices may become limited when using the close-focus feature. These lenses are an easy and effective way to start shooting close-ups. Keep in mind, however, that even though these may say they have a macro setting, it is really just a close-focus setting and not a true macro lens.

Close-up Accessory Lenses: You can buy lenses, sometimes called filters, which screw onto the front of your lens to allow it to focus even closer. The advantage is that you now have the whole range of zoom focal lengths available and there are no exposure corrections. Close-up filters can do this, but the image quality is not great. More expensive achromatic accessory lenses (highly-corrected, multi-element lenses) do a superb job with close-up work, but their quality is limited by the original lens.

Extension Tubes: Extension tubes fit in between the lens and the camera body of an SLR. This allows the lens to focus much closer than it normally could. While extension tubes are designed to work with many of the lenses for your camera, there may be some combinations that might not have the optical performance you would expect. Read any instructions that came with the extension tube, and experiment. Also, older extension tubes won't always match some of the new lenses made specifically for digital cameras. Be aware that extension tubes cause a loss of light.

Macro Lenses: Though relatively expensive, macro lenses are designed for superb sharpness at all distances, across the entire field of view, and focus from mere inches to infinity. In addition, they are typically very sharp at all f/stops.

CLOSE-UP SHARPNESS

Sharpness problems usually result from three factors: limited depth of field, incorrect focus placement, and camera movement. The closer you get to a subject, the shallower the depth of field becomes. While you can stop your lens down as far as it will go for more depth of field, it is critical that focus is placed correctly on the subject. If the back of an insect is sharp but its eyes aren't, the photo appears to have a focus problem. At these close distances, every detail counts. If only half of the flower petals are in focus, the overall photo does not look sharp. Using autofocus up close can also cause a real problem with critical focus placement because the camera often focuses on the wrong part of the photo.

Of course, you can review your photo on the LCD monitor to be sure the focus is correct before leaving your subject. You can also try manual focus. One technique is to focus the lens at a reasonable distance, then move the camera toward and away from the subject as you watch it go in and out of focus. This can really help, but still, you may find that taking multiple photos is the best way to guarantee proper focus at these close distances. Another good technique is to shoot using a continuous drive mode (⊒, ⊒H) and fire multiple photos. You may find at least one shot with the critical part of your subject in focus. This is a great technique when you are handholding and when you want to capture moving subjects.

When you are focusing close, even slight movement can shift the camera dramatically in relationship to the subject. The way to help correct this is to use a high shutter speed or put the camera on a tripod. Two advantages to using a digital camera during close-up work are the ability to check the image to see if you are having camera movement problems, and the ability to change ISO settings from picture to picture (enabling a faster shutter speed if you deem it necessary).

CLOSE-UP CONTRAST

The best looking close-up images are often ones that allow the subject to contrast with its background, making it stand out, and adding some drama to the photo. Although maximizing contrast is important in any photograph where you want to emphasize the subject, it is particularly critical for close-up subjects where a slight movement of the camera can totally change the background. There are three important contrast options to keep in mind:

Tonal or Brightness Contrasts: Look for a background that is darker or lighter than your close-up subject. This may mean a small adjustment in camera position. Backlight is excellent for this since it offers bright edges on your subject with lots of dark shadows behind it.

Color Contrasts: Color contrast is a great way to make your subject stand out from the background. Flowers are popular close-up subjects and, with their bright colors, they are perfect candidates for this type of contrast. Just look for a background that is either a completely different color (such as green grass behind red flowers) or a different saturation of color (such as a bright green bug against dark green grass).

Sharpness Contrast: One of the best close-up techniques is to work with the inherent limit in depth of field and deliberately set a sharp subject against an out-of-focus background or foreground. Look at the distance between your subject and its surroundings. How close are other objects to your subject? Move to a different angle so that distractions do not conflict with the edges of your subject. Try different f/stops to change the look of an out-of-focus background or foreground.

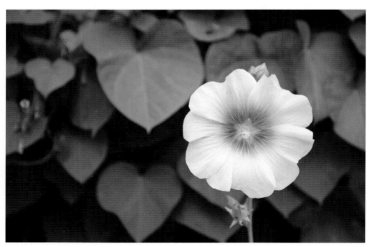

∧ Pay attention to backgrounds when composing for close-ups. Often they are the key to accentuating your main subject.

FILTERS

Many people assume that filters aren't needed for digital photography because adjustments for color and light can be made in the computer. But by no means are filters obsolete! They save a substantial amount of work in the digital darkroom by allowing you to capture the desired color and tonalities for your image right from the start. Even if you can do certain things in the computer, why take the time if you can do them more efficiently while shooting?

Of course, the LCD monitor comes in handy once again. By using it, you can assist yourself in getting the best from your filters. If you aren't sure how a filter works, simply try it and see the results immediately on the monitor. This is like using a Polaroid, only better, because you need no extra gear. Just take the shot, review it, and make adjustments to the exposure or white balance to help the filter do its job. If a picture doesn't come out the way you would like, discard it, and take another right away.

Attaching filters to the camera depends entirely on your lenses. Usually, a properly sized filter can either be screwed directly onto a lens or fitted into a holder that screws onto the front of the lens. There are adapters to make a given size filter fit several lenses, but the filter must cover the lens from edge to edge or it will cause dark corners in the photo (vignetting). A photographer may even hold a filter over the lens with his or her hand. There are a number of different types of filters that perform different tasks.

POLARIZING FILTERS

This important outdoor filter should be in every camera bag. Its effects cannot be duplicated with software because it actually affects the way light is perceived by the sensor.

The filter rotates in its mount, and as you move it, the strength of the effect changes. One primary use is to darken skies. This effect is greatest when used at an angle that is 90° to the sun. As you move off this angle, the effect diminishes. If your back is to the sun or you are shooting towards the direction of the sun, the polarizer will have no effect. A polarizer can also reduce glare (often making colors look more saturated), and remove reflections. While you can darken skies on the computer, the polarizer reduces the amount of work you have to perform in the digital darkroom.

There are two types of polarizing filters: linear and circular. While linear polarizers often have the strongest effect, they can cause problems with exposure, and often prevent the camera from autofocusing. Consequently, you are safer using a circular polarizer with the 60D.

NEUTRAL DENSITY (GRAY) FILTERS

Called ND filters, this type of filter is a helpful accessory. ND filters simply reduce the light coming through the lens. They are called neutral because they do not add any color tint to the scene. They come in different strengths, each reducing different quantities of light. They give additional exposure options under bright conditions, such as a beach or snow (where a filter with a strength of 4x is often appropriate). If you like the effect when slow shutter speeds are used with moving subjects like waterfalls, a strong neutral density filter (such as 8x) usually works well, allowing you to use long shutter speeds without overexposing the image. Of course, the great advantage of the digital camera, again, is that you can see the result immediately on the LCD monitor, and modify your exposure for the best possible effect.

GRADUATED NEUTRAL DENSITY FILTERS

Many photographers consider this filter an essential tool. It is half clear and half dark (gray). It is used to reduce bright areas (such as sky) in tone, while not affecting darker areas (such as the ground). The computer can mimic its effects, but you may not be able to recreate the scene you wanted. A digital camera's sensor can only respond to a certain range of brightness at any given exposure. If a part of the scene is too bright compared to the overall exposure, detail is washed out and no amount of work in the computer will bring it back. While you could try to capture two shots of the same scene at different exposure settings and then combine them on the computer, a graduated ND might be quicker.

UV AND SKYLIGHT FILTERS

Most people use UV or skylight filters as protection for the front of their lens. Whether or not to use a protective filter on your lens is a never-ending debate. A lens hood/shade usually offers more protection than a glass filter and should be used at all times, even when the sun isn't out. Still, UV or skylight filters can be useful when photographing under such conditions as strong wind, rain, blowing sand, or going through brush.

If you use a filter for lens protection, a high-quality filter is best, as a cheap filter can degrade the optical quality of the lens. Remember that the manufacturer made the lens/sensor combination with very strict tolerances. A protective filter needs to be invisible—literally—and only high-quality filters can guarantee that.

A successful approach to getting the most from a digital camera is to be aware that camera movement can affect sharpness and tonal brilliance in an image. Even slight movement during the exposure can cause the loss of fine details and the blurring of highlights. These effects are especially glaring when you compare an affected image to a photo that has no motion problems. In addition, affected images do not enlarge well.

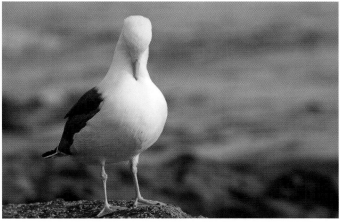

⌃ A tripod can help keep your images sharp, and allow for more exposure options.

You must minimize camera movement in order to maximize the capabilities of your lens and sensor. A steady hold on the camera is a start. Fast shutter speeds, as well as the use of flash, help to ensure sharp photos, although you can get away with slower shutter speeds when using wider-angle lenses. When shutter speeds go down, however, it is advisable to use a camera-stabilizing device. Tripods, beanbags, monopods, mini-tripods, shoulder stocks, clamps, and more, all help. Many photographers carry a small beanbag or a clamp pod with their camera equipment for those situations where the camera needs support but a tripod isn't available.

Check your local camera store for a variety of stabilizing equipment. A good tripod is an excellent investment and it will last through many different camera upgrades. When buying one, extend it all the way to see how easy it is to open, then lean on it to see how stiff it is. Both aluminum and carbon fiber tripods offer great rigidity. Carbon fiber is much lighter, but also more expensive. Another option that is in the middle in price/performance between aluminum and carbon fiber is basalt. Basalt tripods are stronger than aluminum but not quite as light as carbon fiber.

The tripod head is a very important part of the tripod and may be sold separately. There are two basic types for still photography: the ball head and the pan-and-tilt head. Both designs are capable of solid support and both have their passionate advocates. The biggest difference between them is how you loosen the controls and adjust the camera. Try both and see which seems to work better for you. Be sure to do this with a camera on the tripod because that added weight changes how the head works. Make sure that the tripod and head you choose can properly support the weight of the 60D and all the lenses you will be using.

When shooting video, it is often necessary to pan the camera left or right, or tilt the camera up and down to follow action. Some tripod heads allow panning, but many may not have a panning handle that allows you to operate the head while looking at the LCD monitor. If your tripod head does allow panning, it may not have the ability to tilt smoothly while recording video. Consider adding a video head to your tripod. Look for a fluid video head that offers smooth movement in all directions. Once again, make sure that the head is the right size for the 60D and the lenses and lens accessories that you plan to use.

LCD HOODS

When shooting video or trying to evaluate your image, it can be almost impossible to see the LCD monitor in broad daylight. Several manufacturers make accessory finders or loupes that can be held up to the LCD screen in order to evaluate still images. They can also be attached to the 60D for hands-free use when shooting video. These devices magnify the LCD display and have an eyecup that blocks out extraneous light. Two manufacturers are www.hoodmanusa.com and www.zacuto.com.

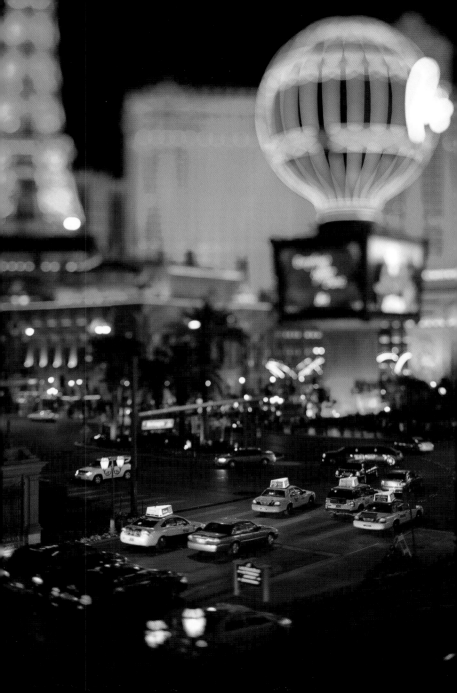

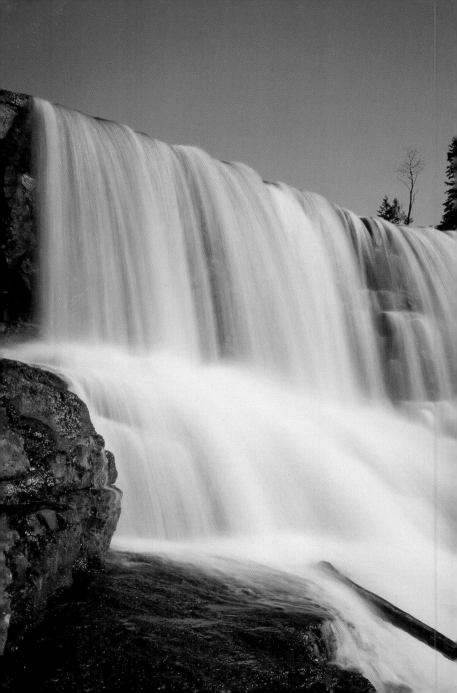

Output

FROM CAMERA TO COMPUTER

Clearly you will need to move photos and movies to your computer as they accumulate on your memory card or they will soon fill the card to capacity. There are three primary methods of transferring digital files—both still images and movies—from the memory card. One way is to download them directly from the 60D using a USB interface cable (included with the camera at the time of purchase). Another method is to use a media card reader. Many computers have a built-in card reader where you can insert the memory card for instant download. Card readers are also available as accessories that connect to your computer. They can remain plugged in and ready to download your images or videos. A third way uses a special type of SD card, called an Eye-Fi card, to transfer your photos wirelessly to your computer. Eye-fi cards are new but growing in popularity. Their clear advantage is their ability to transfer files from virtually any location wirelessly.

DIRECT FROM CAMERA

The primary benefit to downloading directly from the camera is that you don't need to buy a card reader. However, there are some distinct disadvantages. For one, cameras generally download much more slowly than card readers (given the same connections). Plus, a camera has to be unplugged from the computer after each use, while accessory card readers can be left attached. In addition to these drawbacks, downloading directly from a camera uses its battery power (and shortens battery life by using up charge cycles), or requires you to plug it into AC power.

If you do want to download directly from the 60D, you need to install all of the software that came with the camera. One piece of that software is EOS Utility. (On some computers you can see the camera mounted as a drive, but that varies among computer setups.) Once you connect the camera via the USB port to your computer, turn it on. EOS Utility may start up automatically, or you might have to start the application manually. Once it's running, you can download all the images on the card, or select just a few.

NOTE: When downloading from a camera or card reader, EOS Utility will copy the files into separate folders based on when the picture was taken, if you so choose. In this way, you can organize your images during the download process.

THE CARD READER

Accessory card readers can be purchased at most camera or electronics outlets. There are several different types, including single-card readers that read only one particular type of memory card, or multi-readers that are able to utilize several different kinds of cards. (The latter are important with the 60D only if you have several cameras using different memory card types.)

> It is best to use high capacity memory cards because the files generated by the 60D for both stills and movies are quite large.

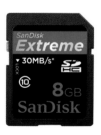

NOTE: If you are going to use SDHC or SDXC memory cards (as I recommend), you must use a card reader that supports SDHC or SDXC. Just because the card fits into an SD slot does not mean it will work. See page 26 to learn more about SDHC and SDXC.

You can connect your accessory card reader to your computer via a FireWire or USB port. FireWire (also called iLink or 1394) is faster than USB, but might not be standard on your computer. There are several types of USB: USB 1.0, 2.0, 2.0 Hi-Speed and, more recently, 3.0. Older computers and card readers will have the 1.0 version, but new devices are most likely 2.0 Hi-Speed. This version of USB is much faster than the old. However, if you have both versions of USB devices plugged into the same bus, the older devices will slow down the faster ones. USB 3.0 is appearing in some new computers, but at this point it certainly isn't ubiquitous.

After your card reader is connected to your computer, remove the memory card from your camera and put it into the appropriate slot in your card reader. The card usually appears as an additional drive on your computer (on Windows and Mac operating systems—for other versions you may have to install the drivers that come with the card reader). When the computer recognizes the card, it may also give instructions for downloading. Follow these instructions if you are unsure about opening and moving the files yourself, or simply select your files and drag them to the folder or drive where you want them (a much faster approach). Make sure you "eject" the card before removing it from the reader: If using Windows, you right click on the drive and select eject; on a Mac, you can do the same or drag the memory card icon to the trash.

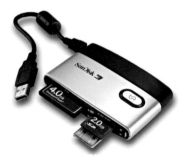

⟨ As a handy accessory, some readers can handle several different kinds of memory card formats. Make sure your card reader can accept SDHC or SDXC memory cards since you cannot use CompactFlash in the 60D.

Card readers can also be used with laptops, though PC card adapters may be more convenient when you're on the move. As long as your laptop has a PC card slot (not all do), all you need is a PC card adapter for SDHC or SDXC memory cards. Insert the memory card into the PC adapter, and then insert the PC adapter into your laptop's PC card slot. Once the computer recognizes this as a new drive, drag and drop images from the card to the hard drive. The latest PC card adapter models tend to be faster—but are also more expensive—than card readers.

A new way to transfer files on-the-go starts with a special memory card called an Eye-Fi card. The specially designed card acts like a regular memory card but also has a built-in wireless transmitter. You can have the Eye-Fi card automatically and wirelessly transfer your photos to your computer or a photo-sharing site each time you take a picture. The card can connect to your home wireless network and it, too, can automatically separate your images by date during the transfer process. It also connects to many public Wi-Fi hotspots so that you don't have to wait to return home to start uploading files.

NOTE: Before using this function, you must set up the Eye-Fi card with your computer. Follow the instructions that come with the card or consult the manufacturer's website: www.eye.fi.

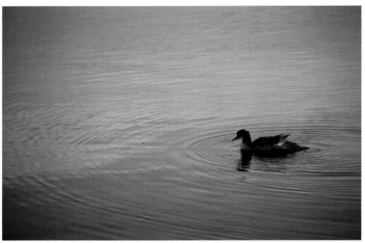

⌃ Eye-Fi can connect to various hotspot networks so that images can be uploaded while you are out and about photographing.

The Eye-Fi card is designed to work in most any camera that uses an SD memory card, but Canon has added features to the 60D in order to more fully support the technology. For example, in the Set-up 1 menu ⚙' there is an **[Eye-Fi settings]** option (if there is an Eye-Fi card installed in the camera). Use this to enable and disable file transmission. You can also see what network the card is connected to and view status messages about file transmission.

Fortunately you don't have to use this menu to see when files are being transferred. A special icon on the LCD indicates when a file is being transmitted: 📶. The icon flashes when the card is connecting to the network, and then animates when the file is being transferred. Any image that has been uploaded via the Eye-Fi card will display the 📶 icon near the bottom left of the image information screen.

In addition, the Auto power off function on the 60D is delayed until all images have been transmitted. You can also program the card—using the computer not the camera—to upload only those images that have been protected (see page 114). While not many people use the protect function in the normal operation of the 60D, using it for Eye-Fi allows you great control for uploading images.

ARCHIVING

Without proper care, your digital images and movies can be lost or destroyed. Many photographers back up their files with a second drive, either added to the inside of the computer or as an external USB or FireWire drive. This is a popular and somewhat cost-effective method of safeguarding your data.

Hard drives and memory cards do a great job of recording image files and movie clips for processing, transmitting, and sharing, but are not great for long-term storage. Hard drives are designed to spin; just sitting on a shelf can cause problems. This type of media has been known to lose data within ten years. And since drives and cards are getting progressively larger, the chance that a failure will wipe out thousands of images and movies rather than "just one roll of shots or tape" is always increasing. Computer viruses or power surges can also wipe out files from a hard drive. Even the best drives can crash, rendering them unusable. Plus, we are all capable of accidentally erasing or saving over an important photo or movie. Consider using redundant drives for critical data backup.

For more permanent backup, burn your files to optical discs: CD or DVD (recommended). A CD-writer (or "burner") used to be the standard for the digital photographer, but image files are getting too big and high-definition movie files are just about out of the question for CDs. DVDs can handle about seven times the data that can be saved on a CD, but even standard DVDs are becoming inconvenient for larger file sizes like movies. Blu-ray discs (see below) may be the solution.

There are two types of DVDs (and CDs) that can be used for recording data: R-designated (i.e., DVD-R) recordable discs; and RW-designated (i.e., DVD-RW) rewritable discs. DVD-R discs can only be recorded once—they cannot be erased. DVD-RWs, on the other hand, can be recorded on, erased, and then reused later. If you want long-term storage of your images, use R discs rather than RWs. (The latter is best used for temporary storage, such as transporting images to a new location.) The storage medium used for R discs is more stable than that of RWs (which makes sense since the DVD-RWs are designed to be erasable).

As mentioned above, a new format, Blu-ray, is starting to be an option. This system uses a different colored laser (blue-violet) to read data. The use of a higher frequency light source means more data can be written to the disc. A single-layer Blu-ray disc can hold about 25GB of data, which is more than five times as much data as a single-layer DVD. A dual-layer Blu-ray disc can hold 50GB. This technology is quite new, however, so be aware that there may be some growing pains. As with DVDs and CDs, there are write-once (BD-R) and erasable (BD-RE) discs. Stick to BD-R for archive reliability. Blu-ray discs require a Blu-ray writer.

Optical discs take the place of negatives in the digital world. Set up a DVD binder for your digital "negatives." You may want to keep your original and edited images on separate discs (or separate folders on the same disc).

As previously mentioned, stay away from optical media that is rewriteable like DVD-RW or, for Blu-ray, BD-RE. You want the most reliable archive. At this point rewritable discs, while convenient, are not as reliable for archiving. Also avoid any options that let you create multiple "sessions" on the disc. This feature allows you to add more data to the disc until it is full. For the highest reliability, write all of the data to the disc at once.

Buy quality media. Inexpensive discs may not preserve your image files as long as you would like them to. Read the box. Look for information about the life of the disc. Most long-lived discs are labeled as such and cost a little more. And once you have written to the disc, store and handle it properly according to the manufacturer's directions.

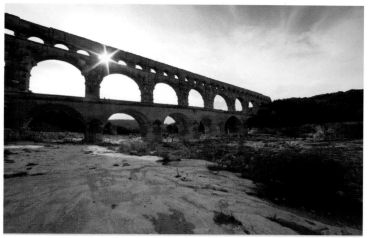

^ Proper archiving techniques can hopefully make sure this image lasts as long as possible.

WORKING WITH STILL IMAGES

How do you edit and file your digital photos so they are accessible and easy to use? You can organize your folders alphabetically or by date inside a "parent" folder. The organization and processing of images is called workflow. (If you want to start a heated conversation among digital photographers, ask them about workflow!)

> **NOTE:** Even though the 60D puts both image and movie files into the same folder on the memory card, it is a good idea to divide the files by type and put them in separate folders once you get them onto your computer. This will help when you use the separate image-editing and video-editing applications.

Be sure to edit your stills to remove extraneous shots. Unwanted files stored on your computer waste storage space on your hard drive. They also increase the time you must spend when you browse through your images, so store only the ones you intend to keep. Take a moment to review your files while the card is still in the camera. Erase the ones you don't want, and download the rest. You can also delete files once they are downloaded to the computer by using a browser program (described below).

Here's how I deal with digital still files. (Later in this chapter I cover movies.) First, I set up an image filing system. I use a folder called Digital Images. Inside Digital Images, I have folders by year, and within those, the individual shoots or folders created for specific groups of images (you could use locations, events, or categories like landscapes, sports, state fair, family, etc.; whatever works for you). This is really no different than setting up an office filing cabinet with hanging folders or envelopes to hold photos. Consider the Digital Images folder to be the file cabinet, and the individual folders inside to be the equivalent of the file cabinet's hanging folders.

Next, I use a memory card reader that shows up as a drive on my computer. Using the computer's file system, I open the memory card as a window or open folder (this is the same basic view on both Windows and Mac computers) showing the images in the appropriate folder. I then open another window or folder for the computer's hard drive and navigate to the Digital Images folder, then to the year folder. I create a new subfolder labeled to signify the photographs on the memory card, such as Place, Topic, Date.

Then, I select all the still images (no movies) in the memory card folder and drag them to the new folder on my hard drive. This copies all the images onto the hard drive and into my "filing cabinet." It is actually better than using a physical filing cabinet because, for example, I can use browser software to rename all the photos in the new folder, giving information about each photo; for example, using the title Chamonix_Sept10.

I also set up a group of folders in a separate "filing cabinet" (a different folder at the level of Digital Images) for edited photos. In this second filing cabinet, I include subfolders specific to types of photography, such as landscapes, close-ups, people, etc. Within these subfolders, I can break down categories even further when that helps to organize my photos. Inside the subfolders I place copies of original images that I have examined and decided are definite keepers, both unprocessed (direct from the camera) and processed images (keeping such files separate). Make sure these are copies (don't just move the files here), as it is important to keep all original photo files in the original folder that they went to when first downloaded.

Image browser programs allow you to quickly look at photos on your computer, rename them one at a time or all at once, read all major files, move photos from folder to folder, resize photos for e-mailing, create simple slideshows, and more. Some are good at image processing, and some are not.

One of the most popular names in image processing is Adobe, and their flagship application is Adobe Photoshop. While Photoshop is an image processing and enhancement program, it comes with Adobe Bridge, which can help organize photos. There are currently a number of other programs that help you view and organize your images.

NOTE: As manufacturers update their applications, they may add numbers to the application name, such as Photoshop CS5, Lightroom 3, or Final Cut Pro 7. For simplicity, in the rest of this chapter I refer to the basic name, without the version number.

ACDSee is a superb program with a customizable interface and an easy-to-use keyboard method of rating images. It also has some unique characteristics, such as a calendar feature that lets you find photos by date (though the non-pro version is Windows-only). Another program, Apple's Aperture (only available for the Mac), uses a digital loupe to magnify your images while browsing. Aperture is more than just a browser—it offers full image editing too.

Adobe's Lightroom is also an option. Like Aperture, Lightroom is more than just a browser. It has full image processing tools, as well as tools for printing pictures, making slide shows, and building web pages. The concept behind Lightroom (and Aperture) is to build an application that is specifically designed for photographers, rather than a program that has a lot of tools for other uses. There is also a somewhat scaled back version of Adobe Photoshop, called Adobe Photoshop Elements that contains most of the important tools and functionality of Photoshop, but is less intimidating and much less expensive.

All of these programs include some database functions (such as keyword searches) and many operate on both Windows and Mac platforms. Most of them have full-featured trial versions that are useful for checking to see if they will do the job for you.

An important function of browser programs is their ability to print customized index prints. You can then give a title to each of the index prints and list additional information about the photographer, as well as the photos' file locations. The index print is a hard copy that allows easy reference (and visual searches). If you include an index print with every DVD you burn, you can quickly see what is on the DVD and find the file you need. A combination of uniquely labeled file folders on your hard drive, a browser program, and index prints, helps you maintain a fast and easy way to find and sort images.

CANON'S IMAGE PROCESSING

Once the files—JPEG or RAW—are organized on your computer, you must consider image processing. Of course, you can process the 60D's JPEG files in any image-processing program. One important characteristic of JPEGs is that they are universally recognized: Any program on any computer that reads image files will identify JPEGs. They are often used directly from your camera, but don't overlook the fact that JPEG files can be processed to get more out of them.

On the other hand, RAW—CR2 is the Canon version—cannot be read by just any imaging software, but requires a particular type of program in order to be opened. This format is significant in large part because it does increase the options for adjustment of your images. In fact, when you shoot RAW, you basically have to process every image; otherwise it will look dull and lifeless. This changes your workflow. You might want to take advantage of the 60D's ability to shoot RAW and JPEG simultaneously; that way you can save time and work with RAW only as needed.

A big advantage to the 60D RAW file is that it captures more directly what the sensor sees. It holds more information (14 bits vs. the standard eight bits, per color) and stronger correction can be applied to it (compared to JPEG images) before artifacts appear. This can be particularly helpful when there are difficulties with exposure or color balance. (Keep in mind that the image file from the camera holds 14 bits of data even though it is contained in a 16-bit file. So while you can get a 16-bit TIFF file from the RAW file, it is based on 14 bits of data.)

NOTE: EOS 60D RAW files may fill your memory card quite quickly because each can be over 20MB. Large file sizes lead to an increase in processing and workflow times.

Canon offers two ways to convert CR2 files to standard files that can be optimized in an image-processing program like Photoshop: a file viewer utility (ZoomBrowser EX for Windows or ImageBrowser for Mac), and the Digital Photo Professional software. In addition, Photoshop, Lightroom, and Aperture, have built-in RAW processing. There are also dedicated RAW processing applications like Phase One's Capture One. Each application has its own RAW processing "engine" that interprets the images, so there is a slight difference between programs in the final result.

NOTE: If you have an older version of any of these programs, you probably need to update your software in order to open the latest version of the RAW CR2 files. Even though all Canon RAW files have the CR2 file extension, they may not all be the same. Each new camera model changes the CR2 file format a bit. Unfortunately, the older versions of some image-processing applications are no longer updated to handle the 60D's new RAW files. Also, you may have to update drivers for your operating system in order to view files (or thumbnails of your files) at the folder level of your computer.

The File Viewer Utility: Canon's ZoomBrowser EX (Windows)/ ImageBrowser (Mac) supplied with the camera is easy to use. It is a good browser program that lets you view and organize RAW and JPEG files. It will convert RAW files, though it is a pretty basic program and doesn't offer some of the features available in other RAW processing software. Even so, it does a very good job of translating details from the RAW file into TIFF, PICT, BMP or JPEG form. Once converted, any image-processing program can read the new TIFF or JPEG. TIFF is the preferred file format because it is uncompressed; JPEG should only be used if you have file space limitations. You can also use the software to create an image suitable for email, to print images, and even to present a quick slide show of selected images.

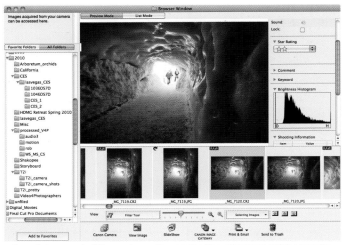

∧ Canon's browser, in this case Image Browser for Mac, allows you quick access to your RAW files and a way to keep them organized. You can even rate your photos and add comments if desirable.

Digital Photo Professional Software: This is Canon's advanced proprietary program for processing RAW and JPEG images. Included with the 60D, Digital Photo Professional (DPP) has a powerful processing engine. It can be used to process both CR2 files and JPEG files. The advantage to processing JPEG files is that DPP is quicker and easier to use than Photoshop, yet it is still quite powerful. For fast and simple JPEG processing, DPP works quite well.

I believe if you are going to shoot RAW, DPP is a program you must try. It is fast, full-featured, and gives excellent results. One big advantage that DPP offers over any other RAW-processing program is the ability to use Dust Delete Data that is embedded in the RAW file (see page 32). It can also read the aspect ratio information embedded in the image files, so it can crop images automatically.

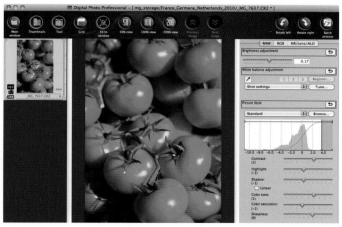

∧ Canon's own Digital Photo Professional is a great software option for processing and enhancing the photo files from your EOS 60D. It possesses a number of powerful tools, follows an efficient workflow, and can be used in conjunction with other processing programs.

EOS Utility: This application serves as a gateway for several operations with the 60D and accessories. First, it is used to download images (all images or just those selected) when the camera is connected via USB to the computer.

EOS Utility is also used for remote or "tethered" shooting. When you start up this feature, you can use the computer to fire the shutter, adjust shutter speed, aperture, ISO, white balance, metering mode, and file recording type (JPEG/RAW). There is limited access to menus: you can set Picture Style, white balance shift, and peripheral illumination correction in the Shooting menu displayed on the computer. You can use the peripheral illumination/lens aberration correction option to see which lenses have correction data available and are "registered" so that when those lenses are attached, the 60D will apply the correction.

NOTE: The 60D can store lens correction data for 40 lenses.

You can remotely pop up the built-in flash on the camera using the EOS Utility Flash menu. Although this is not a very useful feature, if you are using the 60D with multiple Speedlites you have access to the flash

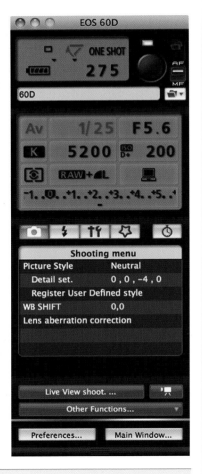

> The EOS Utility software is included with the 60D and offers some interesting options for controlling and customizing your camera.

function settings (see page 257). More importantly you can actually save different flash ratio setups.

In the EOS Utility Setup menu on the computer, you can set the camera owner's name, enter copyright information, change the date and time, enable Live View, and update the firmware.

NOTE: The 60D supports embedding copyright information in the metadata of your images. Your name, a year, and any other text can be added to this metadata field. The only way to enter this data is by using EOS Utility.

Access to My menu ★ while tethered is a fast way to set up your ★ choices (see page 153). Even if you never shoot tethered, consider hooking up the camera to set up My menu. Instead of scrolling through seemingly endless options on the 60D's small LCD monitor, use the remote camera control to point and click your way through selections using your computer's much larger display.

While tethered, you can turn on Live View or movie shooting for a powerful studio-style, image-preview shooting setup. An instant histogram and the ability to check focus are helpful during tethered Live View. You have the choice of capturing the images to the computer, or to the computer and the memory card in the camera. As you record each picture, it can open automatically in Digital Photo Professional or in the image processor of your choice. Movies are only recorded to the memory card, but after you finish recording they can be downloaded to the computer using the EOS Utility.

EOS Utility also offers the option of timed shooting. The computer acts as an intervalometer, taking a picture every few seconds (from five seconds to 99 hours and 59 seconds). You can also do a Bulb exposure from five seconds to 99 hours and 59 seconds. In most cases, Live View shooting—timed or Bulb—will require the computer and camera to operate off AC power.

Picture Style Editor: The Picture Style Editor is a program that lets you create your own styles. When you import a RAW image, it allows

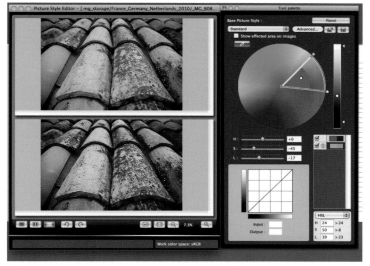

^ You can create your own Pictures Styles with the supplied software, but it is not intuitive.

you to adjust its overall tone curve, as well as the normal Picture Style parameters of sharpness, contrast, color saturation, and color tone. But the Picture Style Editor's most powerful feature is the ability to change individual colors in the image. Use an eyedropper tool to pick a color and then adjust the hue, saturation, and luminance values of the color. You can pick multiple colors and also choose how wide or how narrow a range of colors (around the selected color) is adjusted. These custom Picture Styles can then be uploaded to the 60D using the EOS Utility. You can also download new Picture Styles that have been created by Canon engineers at: www.usa.canon.com/content/picturestyle/file/index.html or www.canon.co.jp/imaging/picturestyle/file/index.html.

PRINTING

If you use certain compatible Canon printers, you can control printing directly from the 60D. Simply connect the camera to the printer using the dedicated USB cord that comes with the 60D. Compatible Canon printers provide access to many direct printing features, including:

- O Contact-sheet style index prints with 35 images
- O Print date and filename
- O Print shooting information
- O Face brightening
- O Red-eye reduction
- O Print sizes (printer dependent), including 4 x 6 inches, 5 x 7 inches, 8.5 x 11 inches (10.1 x 15.4 cm, 12.7 x 17.8 cm, and 21.6 x 27.9 cm, respectively)
- O Support for other paper types
- O Print effects and image optimization: Natural, Vivid, B/W, Cool Tone, Warm Tone
- O Noise reduction

NOTE: Because of the wide variety of printers, it is possible that not all the printing features mentioned in this chapter are on your printer. For a detailed list of options available when the 60D is connected to your Canon printer, consult your printer's manual.

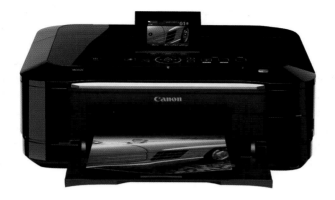

⌃ Most Canon printers and those manufactured by others support PictBridge connections for printing directly from the 60D.

The 60D is PictBridge-compatible, meaning that it can be connected directly to PictBridge printers from several manufacturers. Nearly all new photo printers are PictBridge-compatible. (More information on PictBridge can be found at: www.canon.com/pictbridge/.)

NOTE: Both RAW and JPEG files can be used for the direct printing options mentioned in this section, but movies cannot be printed.

To start the printing process, first make sure that both the camera and the printer are turned off. Connect the camera to the printer with the camera's USB cord (the connections are straightforward since the plugs only work one way). Turn on the printer first, then the camera—this lets the camera recognize the printer. Some printers may turn on automatically when the power cable is connected. Depending on the printer, the camera's direct printing features may vary.

NOTE: You might not have to power off your printer before hooking up your camera.

Press the Playback button ▶. Once it is successfully connected to the printer, the camera will display a print screen with the PictBridge icon ⬆ in the upper left of the LCD. Use ✳ to select an image on the LCD monitor that you want to print. Press **SET** to display the print setting screen, listing such printing choices as printing effects, whether to imprint the date, the number of copies, trimming area, and paper settings (size, type, borders, or borderless).

Trimming is a great choice because you can crop your photo right in the LCD monitor before printing, allowing you to tighten up the composition if needed. To trim, first use ✳ to select **[Trimming]** and press **SET**. Use the Magnify ⬭ and Reduce ⬛·⬭ buttons to adjust the size of the crop; use ✳ to adjust the position of the crop. Use the Info button INFO. to rotate the crop 90°, and the Main dial ⬭ to rotate the image within the crop in 0.5° increments. Press **SET** to accept the crop setting.

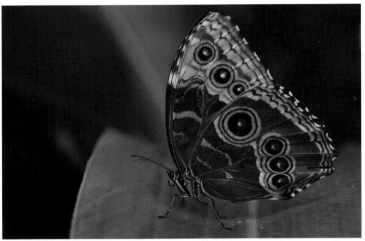

∧ The trimming function and the high-resolution image sensor in the 60D allow you to crop in on your subject.

Depending on your printer, you can also adjust print effects to print images in black and white—in a neutral tone, cool tone, or warm tone. Other effects include noise reduction, face brightening, and red-eye correction. You can also choose to use a natural or vivid color setting. Press **SET** to select printing effects ⬒, the top listing in the print setting screen, and then use ✳ to select the type of printing effect.

(Some printers may not support all effects.) Press INFO. to further refine your choices, then the Menu button MENU to back out.

Continue using ✦ and SET to select other settings. These choices may change, depending on the printer; refer to the printer's manual if necessary.

You can preview your trimming and print effect changes in the thumbnail image in the upper left section of the LCD monitor. Once you have selected the options you want, then use ✦ to select [Print] and press SET to start printing. The LCD monitor confirms that the image is being printed and reminds you not to disconnect the cable during the printing process. Wait for that message to disappear before disconnecting the camera from the printer. If you wish to use the same settings for additional prints, use ✦ to move to the next picture, then simply press the Direct print button 凸 (which is also the UNLOCK button located immediately below ✦) to print it.

NOTE: The amount of control you have over the image when you print directly from the camera is limited solely by the printer. If you need more image control, print from the computer.

If you shoot a lot of images for direct printing, do some test shots and set up the 60D's Picture Styles (see pages 66-72) to optimize the prints before shooting the final pictures. You may even want to create a custom setting that increases sharpness and saturation just for this purpose.

OUTPUT

303

DIGITAL PRINT ORDER FORMAT (DPOF)

Another of the 60D's printing features is DPOF (Digital Print Order Format) ꓥ. This allows you to decide which images to print before you actually do any printing. Then, if you use a printer that recognizes DPOF, the printer automatically prints just the images you have chosen. DPOF is also a way to select images on a memory card for printing at a photo lab. After the images on your SD card are selected using DPOF, drop it off at the photo lab—assuming their equipment recognizes DPOF (ask before you leave your card)—and they will know which prints you want.

> Tell your printer (or photofinisher) which images to print from your memory card by selecting the DPOF feature in the Playback 1 menu. The Standard selection will print one image per page, while the Index selection will print a number of thumbnails on a page.

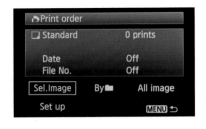

DPOF is accessible through the Playback 1 menu ▣ under **[Print order]**. You can choose several options: Select **[Set Up]** to choose **[Print type]** (**[Standard]**, **[Index]**, or **[Both]**), **[Date]** (**[On]** or **[Off]**), and **[File No.]** (**[On]** or **[Off]**). Once you set your print options, press MENU to return to **[Print order]**. From there you have several ways to select images to print: Select **[All image]**, **[By ▬]** or select images manually. To select images manually, highlight **[Sel.Image]**, press SET and then use ✷ or the Quick Control dial ◯ to scroll through your images. Press SET to "order" a print of the image. Use ✷ to increase the number of copies to print for the current image, and press SET to accept the quantity. If you are printing an index print, use SET to select an image to include on the index print. You can also press ▦·◎ to bring up a three-image display to select images. Use ✷ and SET to go through and mark all of the images to be printed. Press MENU to return to the **[Print order]** screen. The total number of prints ordered appears on the screen.

NOTE: RAW and movie files cannot be selected for DPOF printing. If you shoot RAW+JPEG, then you can use DPOF. The JPEG versions of the files will be printed.

If you are printing the images yourself, you may now connect the camera to the printer. Press SET to start printing. Or go to the **[Print order]** screen in ▣ and you will see a **[Print]** button. Use ✷ to highlight it, and then press SET. Set up image optimization and paper settings, then

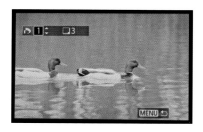

< When marking images for printing via DPOF, a running total of how many prints will be created is listed on the screen.

select **[OK]** and press **SET** to start the printing process. If you are using a photofinisher for DPOF, make sure that you back up your memory card and that the photofinisher supports DPOF.

WORKING WITH MOVIES

Workflow for movies is different from that used for still images. File sizes can be extremely large—often gigabytes instead of megabytes— and some editing programs work best if the files are in a certain place. Generally, movie clips need to be edited together, as opposed to an image that may stand alone as a single photograph. In other words, video clips are often "program" based; a single clip won't have the impact that a single photograph does. In addition, video may be scripted or storyboarded.

My workflow for video is very much project-based. It also requires a concerted effort to think about archiving even before I start editing the project. Once I have finished recording, I create a project folder on a high-speed external drive. Depending on the size of the drive, that folder might be within another folder that includes the year or the month, so I can keep projects separate. For example, I might have a structure of 2010/September/Annecy/. Once the file structure is in place, I copy my footage into the new folder.

Depending on the software application I choose for video editing, I may then view each file and rename the files. If I were doing interviews, I would rename the file with the person's last name and then a take number, such as Kelly01, Kelly02, etc. If I use an editing application like Final Cut Pro, I might leave the file name alone and do all of the descriptive data entry in the editing program.

The nice part about changing the name at the file level is that it is more descriptive. You can search within the file system, rather than opening up an editing application. On the other hand, the advantage of changing the name in the editing program is that you can use longer names and you can include information like take number, comments, camera angle, script notes, whether a clip is good or bad, etc., in columns next to the file name (depending on your editing software).

> **NOTE:** Once you bring the files into your editor and you start to edit, don't change the file names of the movies using the file system. The files may become unlinked from your project. Also, don't move them from the folders that they are in, as this could break the link too. Although there are ways to relink files, they don't always work.

Once I have the file names set, I copy the folder to my archive drive, or—if the folder is small enough—to an optical disc (Blu-ray). This way I have a working copy on the high-speed drive and an untouched copy for archive. When you edit video, you don't change pixels on the original files; to revise a project, all you need is the project file and the original movies the project is linked to.

VIEWING MOVIES

Canon's ZoomBrowser EX (Windows)/ImageBrowser (Mac), supplied with the 60D, can play back individual movie clips, trim them, and even save a still frame, but it can't edit the clips into a sequence. If you merely want to view your files, QuickTime player is a good (and free!) application. The Pro version of QuickTime lets you trim clips and even build a rough sequence, but it is not very intuitive and does not foster much creativity. For that, you need a real editing application for use with your computer.

> **NOTE:** If you are on the Windows platform, you may need to install QuickTime in order to view your movie clips. Download the Windows version at www.apple.com/quicktime/. For simple playback of movies, it is not necessary to buy the QuickTime Pro version or download iTunes with QuickTime. Download just the "plain" version of QuickTime.

There is quite an assortment of video-editing applications for both Windows and Mac computer platforms, and for all budgets. On the Windows side, there are Adobe Premiere and Premiere Elements, Sony Vegas, Pinnacle Studio, and Corel VideoStudio Pro X3. For Mac users, there are Adobe Premiere, Avid's Media Composer, Media 100, and Apple's iMovie, Final Cut Express, and Final Cut Pro.

Costs for the software alone range from "included with your computer" to thousands of dollars. The less expensive options can work if you do simple cuts and dissolves, but not much in the way of effects, layering, or complicated projects. The more expensive applications give you more options for the output of your finished project—compression for the web or authoring Blu-ray discs.

Manipulating HD video is very taxing on a computer. These are essentially large image files that are flying by at 30 or 60 frames per second, so you need a computer that can handle it. Bulk up on RAM and processor speed—as much as you can afford.

Several of the editing applications—Premiere and Vegas, for example—can edit natively (without having to convert to another file format) in the h.264 codec. The h.264 is a highly efficient algorithm. It reduces both file size and the data rate needed to record the movie. Unfortunately, it takes a great deal of computing power to make this happen. You may find that your computer, which worked fine running Photoshop and editing RAW files, can struggle just to play back a single movie file without stuttering frames. Generally this is caused either by a slow disc drive or by a slow processor (CPU).

Will editing natively in the h.264 codec work for you? It all depends on the application you are using, your computer's horsepower, and your tolerance for the process. Since h.264 is not really optimized as an editing format, there are several workarounds to overcome the need for the fastest computer and the most RAM. One method is to "transcode" the file to another codec. Transcoding a file means making a copy and recompressing it. If your computer is slowing down, try a codec that is uncompressed or one that is more suitable for editing (like XDCAM-HD or Apple's ProRes). Some problems with transcoding are that the color space, or dynamic range, might change; some highlights might change; detail may disappear; and/or colors might shift. Make sure you compare the transcoded file to the original. Another issue may be rendering times if you need to output back to an h.264 file. If this is the case, you should perform some test renders so you know how long it will take. You don't want to be surprised if your final project takes three hours to render, especially if it was supposed to be completed an hour ago.

Another option to reduce processor load is to edit in a low-resolution proxy mode. Proxies are to movies what thumbnails are to photos. They are low-resolution video clips. This is the technique that Corel VideoStudio Pro X3 uses. It converts the high-definition movies to smaller movies that are easier to use during the editing process. Once the edit is complete, the software links up to the original high-definition files for output.

MOVIE OUTPUT

When you have finished editing, you'll have to output the movie. It is important to consider this process before you begin editing. When you work with still images, you have fewer output options: prints or digital files for computer display? (Of course there are others, but these two are the usual ones.) When you work with movies, it may appear there are only a few options, but they can quickly multiply.

For example, say you are asked to deliver to a web site. Once you start asking questions, you'll be surprised at the complexity. First, there is window size: most places can't take the full 1920 x 1080, or 1280 x 720, or even 640 x 480 file, and may ask for 1/2 size or 1/4 size. Then there is the file type: Do they want h.264, Windows Media (.wmv), Flash, Quicktime? How about the file size? This is not the same as the window size. Internet delivery is highly dependent on connection bandwidth. The amount of compression you apply to a movie directly affects how much bandwidth is needed. Finally, there is frame rate. Some sites can play back a 30 fps movie; others require half that rate.

NOTE: There isn't one "best" solution. Each website or host has its own requirements that, unfortunately, may constantly change. It is important that you do your research before you start shooting, so you know what you need to deliver. In fact, you may need to deliver multiple versions of the file.

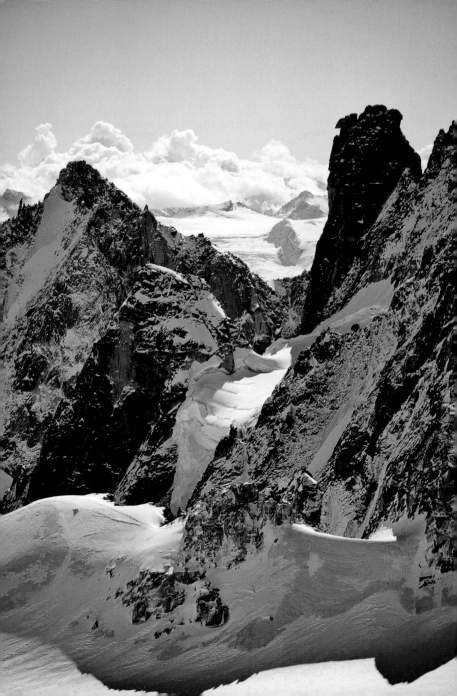

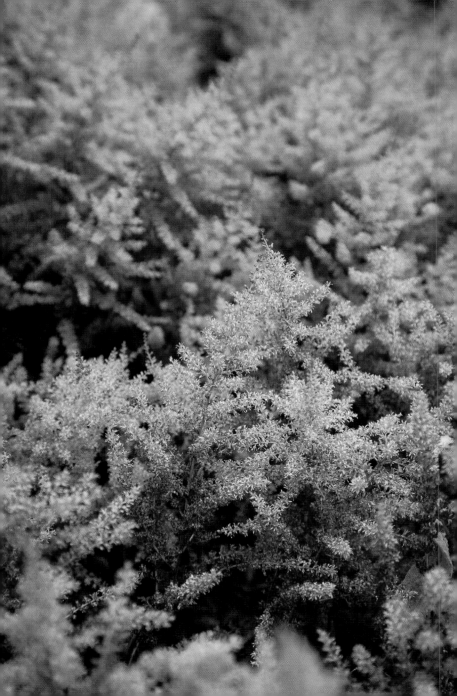

If you want to deliver high definition on optical disc, there are two options. First, you can compress your finished program into a codec that is supported on Blu-ray. You then author a Blu-ray disc that can play on a set-top Blu-ray player. Many of the applications above can do this, or can tie into disc-authoring programs from the same manufacturer. Of course this requires your computer to have a Blu-ray drive that can write discs.

A second option is to create a high-definition file that you burn onto a regular DVD. You then play the DVD in an advanced DVD player that is capable of playing HD files. Although this is not a common feature on DVD players, there are some are out there that can do it. Before Blu-ray burners were available, this was one of the few ways to play back HD content in the field.

Whatever you have to deliver, the more you can control the compression, the better looking the final result will be. It is not uncommon for a file to be compressed more than one time, but you should avoid multiple steps of compression, just like when you work with image files. And remember, the large file sizes for movies mean longer times to upload, download, archive, and transfer from one location to another.

Glossary

aberration
An optical flaw in a lens that causes the image to be distorted, or unclear.

angle of view
The area seen by a lens, usually measured in degrees across the diagonal of the film frame.

aperture
The opening in the lens that allows light to enter the camera. Apertures are usually described as f/numbers. The higher the f/number, the smaller the aperture. The lower the f/number, the larger the aperture.

aperture priority
A type of automatic exposure in which you manually select the aperture and the camera automatically selects the shutter speed.

automatic exposure
When the camera calculates and adjusts the amount of light necessary to properly form an image on the sensor.

automatic flash
An electronic flash unit that reads the light reflected from a subject, fires, then shuts itself off as soon as ample light has reached the sensor.

automatic focus
When the camera automatically adjusts the focusing ring on the lens to sharply render the subject.

available light
The amount of illumination at a given location. Applies to natural and environmental light sources but not those supplied specifically for photography. Also called existing light or ambient light.

backlight
Light that projects toward the camera from behind the subject.

barrel distortion
A defect in the lens that makes straight lines curve outward away from the middle of the image.

bit
Stands for binary digit. The basic unit of binary computation.

bit depth
The number of bits per pixel. Determines the number of colors the image can display. Eight bits per pixel are necessary for a quality photographic image.

bounce light
Light that reflects off another surface, before illuminating the subject.

brightness
A subjective measure of illumination. See luminance.

bulb
The shutter speed setting that comes after 30". Allows the shutter to stay open as long as the shutter release is depressed.

chrominance
A form of noise that appears as a random scattering of densely packed colored "grain." See also, luminance and noise.

color balance
The sensor's interpretation of the actual colors of the subject.

color cast
A colored hue over the image often caused by improper lighting or incorrect white balance settings. Can be produced intentionally for creative effect.

color space
A template for determining appropriate hue, brightness, and color saturation.

compression
Method of reducing file size through removal of superfluous data, as with the JPEG file format.

contrast
The difference in luminance, density, or darkness, between two tones.

critical focus
The most sharply focused point of an image.

dedicated flash
An electronic flash unit that automatically sets the shutter to the proper

synchronization speed and usually also activates a signal in the viewfinder that indicates that the flash is fully charged.

depth of field
The image space in front of and behind the plane of focus which appears acceptably sharp in the photograph.

diaphragm
A mechanism that determines the size of the opening that allows light to pass into the camera when taking a photo.

diopter
A measurement of the refractive power of a lens, or a supplementary lens, which is defined by its focal length and power of magnification.

dpi
Stands for dots per inch. Refers to printing resolution.

electronic flash
A device with a glass or plastic tube filled with gas that, when electrified, creates an intense flash of light. Also called a strobe. Unlike a flash bulb, it is reusable.

extension tube
A hollow metal ring that can be fitted between the camera and lens. Increases the distance between the optical center of the lens and the sensor. Decreases the minimum focus distance of the lens.

filter
Usually a piece of plastic or glass. Used to control how certain wavelengths

of light are recorded. Absorbs selected wavelengths, preventing them from reaching the sensor. Also, software available in image editing programs that can produce filter effects for your image on the computer.

flare
Unwanted light streaks or rings that appear in the viewfinder, on the recorded image, or both. Caused by unwanted light entering the camera during shooting. Use of a lens hood can often prevent this undesirable effect.

focal length (f)
When the lens is focused on infinity, it is the distance from the optical center of the lens to the focal plane.

focal plane
The plane on which a lens forms a sharp image. Also, the film plane or sensor plane.

f/stop
The size of the aperture or diaphragm opening of a lens. Also referred to as f/number or stop. Stands for the ratio of the focal length (f) of the lens to the width of its aperture opening. (Ex. f/1.4mm = wide opening and f/22mm = narrow opening.) Each stop up (lower f/number) doubles the amount of light reaching the sensor. Each stop down (higher f/number) halves the amount of light reaching the sensor.

gray card
A card used to take accurate exposure readings. Typically has a white side that reflects 90% of the light and a gray side that reflects 18%.

grayscale
A successive series of tones ranging between black and white.

guide number (GN)
A number used to quantify the output of a flash unit. Derived by using this formula: GN = aperture x distance. Guide numbers are expressed in either feet or meters.

histogram
A graphic representation of image tones.

hot shoe
An electronically connected flash mount on the camera body. Enables direct connection between the camera and an external flash. Syncs the shutter release with the firing of the flash.

hyperfocal distance
When focused at infinity, there is an area in front of the infinite focus that also appears sharp. The point closest to you that is still in sharp focus marks the hyperfocal distance. If you then focus the lens on this point, your depth of field increases to include sharp focus of any objects within the range of half the hyperfocal distance and infinity.

ISO

Traditionally applied to film, this number indicates the relative light sensitivity of the recording medium—the sensor, in this case. Can be adjusted for each shot on the EOS 60D.

LCD

Stands for liquid crystal display. A flat screen with two clear polarizing sheets on either side of a liquid crystal solution. When activated by an electric current, it causes the crystals to either pass through or block light.

lens hood

A short tube that can be attached to the front of a lens to prevent flare. Keeps undesirable light from reaching the front of the lens. Also called a lens shade.

light meter

Also called an exposure meter, it is a device that measures light levels and calculates the correct aperture and shutter speed.

luminance

A term used to describe directional brightness. Also, a form of noise that appears as a sprinkling of black "grain." See also, chrominance and noise.

macro lens

Used for close-up photography subjects, such as flowers.

manual exposure

A camera operating mode that allows you to determine and set both the aperture and shutter speed yourself. The opposite of automatic exposure—the mode in which the camera makes these decisions for you.

middle gray

An average gray tone with 18% reflectance. See also, gray card.

midtone

Appears as medium brightness, or medium gray tone, in a print.

noise

The digital equivalent of grain. Often caused by sensor or other internal electronic heat. Usually undesirable, but may be added for creative effect using an image-editing program. See also, chrominance and luminance.

perspective

The perceived size and depth of objects in an image.

polarization

Achieved either by using a polarizing filter or software filter effect. Minimizes reflections from non-metallic surfaces like water and glass. Often makes skies appear bluer and less hazy.

RAW

An image file format that has little or no internal processing applied by the camera. Contains 12-bit color information, more complete data than other file formats offer.

resolution

Refers to image quality and clarity, measured in pixels or megapixels. Also, lines per inch on a monitor, or dots per inch on a printed image.

saturation

Refers to dominant, pure color lacking muddied tones.

short lens

A lens with a short focal length. It produces a greater angle of view than you would see with your eyes.

shutter priority

An exposure mode in which you manually select the shutter speed and the camera automatically selects an aperture to match.

single-lens reflex (SLR)

A camera with a mirror that reflects the image entering the lens through a pentaprism onto the viewfinder screen. When you take the picture, the mirror reflexes out of the way, the shutter opens, and the image is recorded.

standard lens

A fixed-focal-length lens usually in the range of 45 to 55mm. Gives a realistically proportionate perspective of the scene, in contrast to wide-angle or telephoto lenses. Also known as a normal lens.

stop down

To reduce the size of the diaphragm opening. Use a higher f/number.

stop up

To increase the size of the diaphragm opening. Use a lower f/number.

strobe

Abbreviation for stroboscopic. An electronic light source that produces a series of evenly spaced bursts of light.

telephoto effect

When objects in an image appear closer than they really are through the use of a telephoto lens.

telephoto lens

A lens with a long focal length that enlarges the subject and produces a narrower angle of view than you would see with your eyes.

vignetting

A reduction in light at the edge of an image due to use of a filter or an inappropriate lens hood for the particular lens.

wide-angle lens

Produces a greater angle of view than you would see with your eyes, often causing the image to appear stretched. See also, short lens.

zoom lens

A lens that can be adjusted to cover a wide range of focal lengths.

Index

LCD PANEL

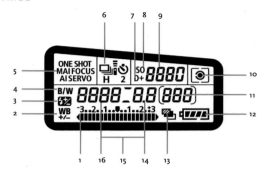

1. Exposure level/Exposure compensation indicator
2. White balance correction
3. Flash exposure compensation
4. Monochrome mode
5. Focus mode
6. Drive mode
7. Highlight tone priority
8. ISO indicator

9. ISO setting
10. Metering mode
11. Shots remaining/Self-timer countdown
12. Battery level indicator
13. Autoexposure bracketing (AEB)
14. Aperture
15. Warning messages
16. Shutter speed

QUICK CONTROL SCREEN

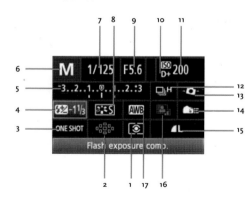

1. Metering mode
2. AF point selection
3. Focus mode
4. Flash exposure compensation
5. Exposure compensation/Autoexposure bracketing (AEB)
6. Shooting mode indicator (cannot be set from Quick control screen)
7. Shutter speed
8. Picture style

9. Aperture
10. Highlight tone priority (cannot be set from Quick control screen)
11. ISO setting
12. Drive mode
13. Electronic level
14. Custom controls
15. Image recording quality
16. Auto lighting optimizer
17. White balance